Translation and Wo

Translation and World Literature offers a variety of international perspectives on the complex role of translation in the dissemination of literatures around the world. Eleven chapters written by multilingual scholars explore issues and themes as diverse as the geopolitics of translation, cosmopolitanism, changing media environments and transdisciplinarity. This book locates translation firmly within current debates about the transcultural movements of texts and challenges the hegemony of English in world literature. *Translation and World Literature* is an indispensable resource for students and scholars working in the fields of translation studies, comparative literature and world literature.

Susan Bassnett is Professor of Comparative Literature at the University of Glasgow and Professor Emerita at the University of Warwick. She is a Fellow of the Royal Society of Literature, a Fellow of the Institute of Linguists and President of the British Comparative Literature Association. She is author of *Translation Studies 4th Edition* (2014), *Translation* (2014) and *Translation in Global News* (2009), all with Routledge.

New Perspectives in Translation and Interpreting Studies

Series Editors:

Michael Cronin holds a Personal Chair in the Faculty of Humanities and Social Sciences at Dublin City University.

Moira Inghilleri is Associate Professor and Director of Translation Studies in the Comparative Literature Program at the University of Massachusetts Amherst.

The New Perspectives in Translation and Interpreting Studies series aims to address changing needs in the fields of translation studies and interpreting studies. The series features works by leading scholars in both disciplines, on emerging and up to date topics. Key features of the titles in this series are accessibility, relevance and innovation.

These lively and highly readable texts provide an exploration into various areas of translation and interpreting studies for undergraduate and postgraduate students of translation studies, interpreting studies and cultural studies.

Translation and Rewriting in the Age of Post-Translation Studies
Edwin Gentzler

Eco-Translation
Michael Cronin

Translation and Migration
Moira Inghilleri

Fictional Translators
Rosemary Arrojo

Translation and World Literature
Susan Bassnett

For more information on any of these and other titles, or to order, please go to https://www.routledge.com/New-Perspectives-in-Translation-and-Interpreting-Studies/book-series/NPTS

Additional resources for Translation and Interpreting Studies are available on the Routledge Translation Studies Portal: http://cw.routledge.com/textbooks/translationstudies

Translation and World Literature

Edited by
Susan Bassnett

 Routledge
Taylor & Francis Group

LONDON AND NEW YORK

First published 2019
by Routledge
2 Park Square, Milton Park, Abingdon, Oxon OX14 4RN

and by Routledge
711 Third Avenue, New York, NY 10017

Routledge is an imprint of the Taylor & Francis Group, an informa business

British Library Cataloguing-in-Publication Data
A catalogue record for this book is available from the British Library

Library of Congress Cataloging-in-Publication Data
Names: Bassnett, Susan editor.
Title: Translation and world literature / Susan Bassnett [editor].
Description: London ; New York, NY : Routledge, 2018. | Series: New perspectives in translation and interpreting studies | Includes bibliographical references and index.
Identifiers: LCCN 2018003025 (print) | LCCN 2018012059 (ebook) | ISBN 9781315630298 (Master) | ISBN 9781138641730 (hardback : alk. paper) | ISBN 9781138641754 (pbk. : alk. paper)
Subjects: LCSH: Literature--Translations--History and criticism. | Translating and interpreting.
Classification: LCC PN241 (ebook) | LCC PN241 .T733 2018 (print) | DDC 418/.04--dc23
LC record available at https://lccn.loc.gov/2018003025

ISBN: 978-1-138-64173-0 (hbk)
ISBN: 978-1-138-64175-4 (pbk)
ISBN: 978-1-3156-3029-8 (ebk)

Typeset in Sabon
by Taylor & Francis Books

This book is dedicated to all my students, past and present, from whom I have learned so much.

Contents

Contributors

Cecilia Alvstad is Professor of Spanish at the University of Oslo and Professor of Translation Studies at Stockholm University. At the University of Oslo she is the project manager of *Traveling Texts: Translation and Transnational Reception*. She has recently closed the project: *Voices of Translation: Rewriting Literary Texts in a Scandinavian Context*, which had funding from the Norwegian Research Council 2012–2017. Alvstad participates in several advisory boards of Translation Studies journals and book series (*Benjamins Translation Library, Perspectives: Studies in Translation Theory and Practice, Linguistica Antverpiensia, TRANS*). In 2011 to 2013 she was the Vice-President of the European Society for Translation Studies and in 2010 to 2014 the review editor of *Perspectives*.

Azucena G. Blanco is Ramón y Cajal Associate Professor at the University of Granada. Her current research focuses on the relationship between literature, politics and philosophy, and on world literature, independent publishers and literary translation. She has published, among others, "Towards a politics of literature in late Foucault: mimesis and parrhesia" (2018); and "Littérature mondiale et conflits dialectaux: Marché glocal pour la poésie en traduction espagnol" (forthcoming). She is editor of *Theory Now. Journal of Literature, Critique and Thought* and principal researcher of *Processes of Subjectivation* (https://procesosdesubjetivacion.com).

César Domínguez (cesar.dominguez@usc.es) is Senior Lecturer in comparative literature at the University of Santiago de Compostela and Honorary Chair Professor at Sichuan University. His teaching and research focus upon theory of comparative literature, European literature, translation, cosmopolitanism and world literature.

Charles Forsdick is James Barrow Professor of French at the University of Liverpool. He is currently Arts and Humanities Research Council theme leadership fellow for 'Translating Cultures'. He has published on travel writing, colonial history, postcolonial and world literature, and the memorialization of slavery. Recent publications include *The Black Jacobins Reader* (co-edited with Christian Høgsbjerg) with Duke University Press, and *Toussaint*

Louverture: Black Jacobin in an Age of Revolution (co-authored with Christian Høgsbjerg) with Pluto. Among his current research, he is co-editing a volume on *Transnational French Studies* for Liverpool University Press, and also leads a project with colleagues in France and Australia on dark tourism and penal heritage. He is Chair of the Editorial Advisory Board at Liverpool University Press and a member of the Academy of Europe.

Martín Gaspar is Assistant Professor at Bryn Mawr College. He is the author of *La condición traductora* [Translation as Temperament] (2014), on the rise of translator-heroes and narrators in contemporary Latin American fiction. His research engages translation, Latin American intellectual history since the 19th century, and visibility in literature, film, arts and media. His articles on "The Tradition of Anonymity in the Andes" and "La liturgia del duelo y la voz popular en tres relatos de cuchilleros de Borges" are part of an ongoing project on representations of anonymous subjects in Latin American arts and letters.

Karin Littau is Professor of English and Comparative Literature at the University of Essex, UK. She has published on book and film history, adaptation, translation and reception studies. Her articles on translation have appeared in journals such as Forum for Modern Language Studies, MLN, Translation Studies TTR and most recently in IJoC and SubStance. Her next book is a history of the relations between literature and film for Routledge; others include *Theories of Reading: Books, Bodies and Bibliomania* (2006; translated by Manantial into Spanish in 2008), *A Companion to Translation Studies* (2007, with Piotr Kuhiwczak) and *Cinematicity in Media History* (2013, with Jeffrey Geiger).

Paulo de Medeiros is Professor of English and Comparative Literary Studies at the University of Warwick, where he holds a Chair in Modern and Contemporary World Literatures. He was Associate Professor at Bryant College (USA) and Professor at Utrecht University before moving to Warwick. In 2011–2012 he was Keeley Fellow at Wadham College Oxford and in 2013–2014 President of the American Portuguese Studies Association. Most recently he published *Pessoa's Geometry of the Abyss: Modernity and the Book of Disquiet* (Oxford: Legenda, 2013). His O *silencio das Sereias: Ensaio sobre o Livro do Desassossego* (Lisbon: Tinta da China, 2015) was awarded the PEN Portugal Proze for best book of essays in 2016. Current projects include a study on post-imperial Europe.

Svetlana Page (neé Skomorokhova) teaches Translation Studies and English for Academic Purposes at the University of Birmingham, UK. Her research interests cover world literature and postcolonial theories in application to Eastern European literary processes, minority literatures and Russian translation studies. Her latest publications include 'Plating "Russian Gold" with "French Copper": Aleksandr Sumarokov and Eighteenth-Century Franco-Russian Translation' (In *French and Russian in Imperial Russia*. EUP, 2015) *and Self-Translation and Power: Negotiating Identities in European Multi-lingual Contexts* (co-edited with Olga Castro and Sergi Mainer, Palgrave Macmillan, 2017)

Sherry Simon is a professor in the French Department at Concordia University. She has published widely in the areas of literary, intercultural and translation studies, most recently exploring the cultural history of linguistically divided cities and the multilingual cities of the former Habsburg empire. ⊠Among her publications are *Translating Montreal. Episodes in the Life of a Divided City* (2006) and *Cities in Translation: Intersections of Language and Memory.* (2012), both of which have appeared in French translation, *Translation Effects: The Shaping of Modern Canadian* Culture (edited with K. Mezei and L. von Flotow, 2014) and the edited volume *Speaking Memory. How Translation Shapes City Life* (2016). She is a Fellow of the Royal Society of Canada and a member of the Académie des lettres du Québec.

Stephanos Stephanides is a Cypriot-born author, poet, translator, critic, ethnographer and documentary filmmaker. Representative publications include *Translating Kali's Feast: The Goddess in Indo-Caribbean Ritual and Fiction* (2000), *Blue Moon in Rajasthan and Other Poems* (2005). In 1992, he was appointed as part of the founding faculty of the University of Cyprus from where he retired as Professor of English and Comparative Literature in 2017. https://stephanosstephanides.com

Harish Trivedi, former Professor of English at the University of Delhi, was visiting professor at the universities of Chicago and London. He is the author of *Colonial Transactions: English Literature and India* (1995) and has co-edited *Interdisciplinary Alter-natives in Comparative Literature* (2013); *The Nation across the World: Postcolonial Literary Representations* (2007); *Literature and Nation: Britain and India 1800–1990* (2000); *Post-colonial Translation: Theory and Practice* (1999); and *Interrogating Post-colonialism: Theory, Text and Context* (1996; rpt. 2000, 2006). He also guest-edited a special issue on "Comparative Literature in India" (1997) of the British journal *New Comparison*. He has edited with an introduction and notes Thomas Hardy's *Tess* (1988; several reprints) and Rudyard Kipling's *Kim* (Penguin Classics, 2011), and contributed to the *Cambridge Companion* volumes on Gandhi as well as Kipling (both 2011). He is currently one of the contributing editors of an international project based in Stockholm for writing a history of World Literature.

Acknowledgements

Many thanks to Hannah Rowe for her patience and understanding throughout the whole editing process. I am especially grateful to Caroline Parker, with whom I have worked for many years and whose secretarial skills are second to none. Thanks to Louisa Semylen for all her assistance, also to Michael Cronin and Moira Inghilleri, series editors.

Introduction

The rocky relationship between translation studies and world literature

Susan Bassnett

The idea for this book arose from a series of discussions in various parts of the world about the current relationship between translation studies and world literature. Obviously translation plays a key role in the movement of texts across linguistic and cultural boundaries, and this is widely recognised, but until recently, there seems to have been relatively little awareness on the part of literary scholarship of the research undertaken under the aegis of translation studies. Back in 2014, during the World Literature Institute Summer School programme at Harvard, where Lawrence Venuti and I had been invited to weave a translation studies strand into the programme, we found ourselves reflecting on what seemed like an abyss between the study of world literature and the study of translation, despite the multilingual, multinational community of scholars gathered together. How could this be, we wondered, given the global development and diffusion of the field of study known as Translation Studies over several decades? Yet few of the colleagues who said they were working in world literature had come across translation studies research, and those who had seemed to think that it was a branch of Applied Linguistics and so irrelevant to literary studies.

To some extent, translation studies can also share the blame for the lack of communication with other disciplines, for despite its global success over the last few years there has not been as much engagement with literary studies as was promised back in the 1990s in the wake of the 'cultural turn' in the discipline. Today, there is a sizeable body of research in translation technology, rather than in literary translation, while many of the programmes in universities calling themselves translation studies have a strong vocational element and might be better described as translator training, often linked to interpreting. This was by no means the case when the subject was founded and started to evolve through the 1980s and 1990s. Translation Studies came into being in the late 1970s, alongside other fields that were challenging traditional, canonical approaches to literature, such as women and gender studies, postcolonial studies, media and cultural studies, to name but three. A main objective of the new field was to raise awareness of the role played by translation in literary history by engaging with a series of key questions, including why some cultures translate more than others at different moments in time, what are the criteria that determine ages of greater or lesser translation activity, what is the relationship of translations to dominant aesthetic norms at particular times, whether translations can be a force for literary innovation and if so, how. Above all, scholars such as Itamar Even-Zohar, Gideon Toury, André Lefevere and José Lambert posed the fundamental question of why so little attention had been paid to the impact of translations on literary systems. Lefevere wrote what can, with hindsight, be seen as a kind of manifesto for translation studies, *Translation, Rewriting and the Manipulation of Literary Fame*, in which he argued that translation should be seen as one of many forms of 'rewriting', all of which are manipulative and subject to ideological constraints:

> Whether they produce translations, literary histories or their more compact spin-offs, reference works, anthologies, criticism, or editions, rewriters adapt, manipulate the originals they work with to some extent, usually to make them fit in with the dominant, or one of the dominant ideological and poetological currents of their time.
>
> (Lefevere, 1992/2017: 6)

Translation is here viewed as one type of rewriting, along with a range of texts that all, in different ways, can be seen as derivative. The difference, of course, is that translators are moving texts across linguistic boundaries, whereas editors, literary theorists or critics may be working within one language. Nevertheless, all in some way are engaged in an exercise that involves the manipulation of a text produced by someone else, somewhere else, in another moment in time. What sets translation apart is the fact that it is an activity which involves reading a text written in one language and then endeavouring to recreate it in another language. Translators, unlike literary critics or other rewriters, have to be able to work in more than one language and herein lies the fundamental problem that bedevils discourse about translation, the old question about faithfulness: how can readers of a translation be sure that the text they have before them is a 'faithful' rendering of a text they cannot read because it was written in a language they do not know? Arguments about what constitutes faithfulness have raged for centuries, accompanied by debates about whether there can be 'exact equivalence' between languages. Definitions of faithfulness and equivalence have changed over time too, and the endless debates have proved pointless. James Holmes, the man who coined the term 'translation studies', dismissed the idea that there could ever be exact equivalence across languages as 'perverse', pointing out that each translator will produce his or her own version of a text and no two will be identical (Holmes, 1988: 53). Even a beginner attempting to learn another language can see that languages are structured differently, have different grammars and vocabularies, and different modes of expression, so any attempt to translate something written in one language into another will necessarily involve transforming that text into something else. The process of change will, of course, involve both loss and gain, though the discourse around translation has tended to focus on what is lost. Yet, as Karen Emmerich points out, the rhetoric of loss depends on the erroneous assumption that translation is simply a matter of transferring invariant content from language to language. 'But' she adds, 'translation does no such thing. Particularly with regard to works of literature, a translation is an embodied interpretation of what an extant work of literature means, and of how that meaning is manifested' (Emmerich, 2017: 362). In other words, a translation is the manifestation of one reader's reading, and that reader is a product of his or her own culture and age.

In his book about translation, *Is That a Fish in Your Ear?* David Bellos opens his chapter on 'Things people say about translation' with the following:

> It's a well-known fact that a translation is no substitute for the original. It's also perfectly obvious that this is wrong. Translations *are* substitutes for original texts. You use them in the place of a work written in a language you cannot read with ease.
>
> (Bellos, 2011: 34)

Translations are indeed substitutes for original texts, they are the means through which we can access works which would otherwise be beyond our reach.

In *How to Read World Literature*, David Damrosch states the seemingly obvious: that most literature circulates around the world in translation. He points to the power of global English in ensuring the diffusion of popular writers such as Stephen King and J.K. Rowling, and notes the importance of translation into English for writers of less widely spoken languages. But he then goes on to add that 'translation has long had a bad reputation', and qualifies this by referring to myths of the inadequacy of translation, which hold that translations are inevitably inferior to their originals (Damrosch, 2009: 65). Damrosch is right to cite this mythology of course, for it is deeply rooted in Western literary tradition, where translation has long been seen as a second-class activity, with translators often poorly paid and unrecognised. Acknowledging this also helps with understanding the marginalisation of translations in the production of literary histories.

Doubts about the authenticity and status of translations abound in literary studies, exacerbated today by the rise of global English, for in the English-speaking world there has long been a divide between the study of literature and the study of language. In the years when English Literature programmes were being set up in universities, the problem then was the integration of philology. My generation studied Anglo-Saxon as a compulsory subject, but by the end of the 1970s philology was being phased out, replaced in a few cases by linguistics. However, linguistics was also seeking to establish itself as a discipline in its own right, with the result that today there are institutional distinctions between programmes in literature and in linguistics, with very little dialogue taking place between them. There is also a tacit belief that literary studies occupies a higher position than language studies and linguistics, a belief unfortunately also enshrined in Modern Language studies, where language assistants are seen as far lower down the food chain than professors who write about literature. Nor has the communicative approach to language teaching helped, because the shift away from rote learning of verb tables and declensions in favour of more conversation in the classroom has only reinforced the myth of the superior status of literature in contrast with the mere mechanics of language learning.

Translation, which is an activity that necessarily involves languages, suffers the same opprobrium. Ezra Pound's comment that 'literature is language charged with meaning' carries little weight in the language versus literature debates that continue to the present day (Pound, 1951: 28).

There is also another reason for the low status in which translation is held by scholars of literature. Early translation studies was also critical of what was perceived as the post-Romantic monolingualisation of literary history, a tendency we can see growing with the desire to establish national literatures in the nineteenth century, for in devising a narrative of a literature based on national identity, the issue then becomes one of claiming native origins, hence the process of importation through translation was played down or erased altogether. A good example of this is the traditional English literature curriculum that highlighted Chaucer as 'the father of English poetry', as Dryden called him, then ignored the next two centuries until the arrival of Marlowe and Shakespeare. Yet in that intervening period, the years of both the European Renaissance and the Reformation, there was immense translation activity, which would lay the ground for the poetry and drama of the sixteenth century, and for the Authorised Version of the Bible that appeared in 1611 and which has been such an influential work for later writers, whether religious or secular. As Ezra Pound notes, 'a great age of literature is perhaps always a great age of translations: or follows it' (Pound, 1968: 232), though in constructing the literary history of a nation, the role played by translations has too often been ignored. But the great foundation texts of so many cultures, both secular and sacred, have come down to us through translations: only a small number of people today are able to read texts written in Aramaic, Sanskrit, Ancient Greek, Classical Chinese, Old Tibetan, Anglo-Saxon or even Latin. Without translations, works including the Bible, Buddhist scriptures and ancient epics would be inaccessible to most of us.

Translation Studies at the outset was closely linked to comparative literature, a field which has so often been described as being in a state of crisis that Haun Saussy, a leading comparatist and an expert in both Western and Asian languages and cultures, warns ironically that the crisis is not going to go away, because comparative literature 'is always in crisis', adding that 'nothing has ever defined comp. lit. so well as the search for its own definition' (Saussy, 2017: 24). Saussy makes this statement in the ACLA State of the Discipline Report, *Futures of Comparative Literature* edited by Ursula Heise in 2017. This is not dissimilar to Franco Moretti's view that world literature is a problem asking for a new critical method, which he then develops into his notion of 'distant reading' (Moretti, 2000). However, theorising about the problematics of defining comparative and world literature (including whether there is any methodological distinction to be made between these terms) has never prioritised the role of translation in the local or global circulation of texts. Indeed, there has been some anxiety expressed about the danger of a concept of world or comparative literature becoming monolingual. Writing back in 2001, in her book *Writing Outside the Nation*, Azade Seyhan warned of the dangers of ignoring linguistic difference diversity. Although literary and cultural studies has become more sensitive to issues of race, ethnicity, gender and class, there is still inadequate acknowledgement of the significance of language, raising the possibility that 'our newly developed transnational, postcolonial literature courses will not be very different from the traditional World Literature in English Translation courses' (Seyhan, 2001: 157).

Eliot Weinberger similarly is critical of what he sees as a failure to engage with language and consequently with translation by advocates of multiculturalism. The original critique of the Eurocentrist canon, though obviously of great importance, did not lead, in his opinion, to a new internationalism, 'where Wordsworth would be read alongside Wang Wei, the Greek anthology next to Vidyakara's *Treasury*, Ono no Komachi with H.D. Instead it led to a new form of nationalism ...' (Weinberger, 2002: 107). He suggests that most US freshman literature courses teach Chinese-American writers, but do not teach Chinese, Latino writers but not Latin American writers, and students all too often do not learn any Spanish. The expansion of the canon has resulted in the inclusion of a great many writers, but all who write in a variety of English. Without any understanding of interlingual translation, everything becomes absorbed into the dominant system. Translation, Weinberger argues, 'is change and motion', adding that 'literature dies when it stays the same, when it has no place to go' (Weinberger, 2002: 118). As he points out, critiques of the Eurocentric canon have not resulted in greater recognition of non-English literature. In some respects, therefore, multiculturalism and postcolonialism have continued the old nationalist agenda, still asserting the supremacy of the English language, albeit recognising that there are many variants of English.

We can see this same concern emerging in Emily Apter's polemical *Against World Literature* (Apter, 2013). Subtitled *On the Politics of Untranslatability*, Apter seeks to make a case for the importance of the Untranslatable, defined as that which resists easy comprehension and, in consequence, easy consumption. Her argument is that understanding Untranslatability depends on knowing more than one language, so to this extent she is making a case against monolingualism and against the domestication of the foreign for a target audience. On the surface, this looks like an important point, but as anyone who has ever engaged in translating anything knows, the primary task for any translator is to engage with untranslatability which is an inevitable aspect of all translating. Linguistic and cultural differences have to be negotiated, so that any translation, from the simplest phrase to the most complex text, involves a process of decoding in the first language and re-encoding in the second language. There is always going to be engagement with that which can be seen on one level as untranslatable, be it a culture-bound term such as *ennui* or *saudade* or a word in daily use such as *doch* or *ciao*. Taking issue with Apter, Lawrence Venuti points out that untranslatability should not be seen solely as an aesthetic or philosophical category. He sees the current fashionable focus on untranslatability as a purely abstract idea, which he argues discourages anyone who wishes to investigate the politics of translation 'by smearing translatability as dubious' (Venuti, 2016: 202). He accuses comparative and world literature as having latched on to ideas of 'untranslatability' as a way of side-stepping investigation into the actual processes of translation and the ideological frames within which translations happen. Once again, we are confronted with the divide between literature and language, and with the relegation of translation to an inferior position.

Haun Saussy suggests that three things need to be done to ensure the vital connection between literature and language: so-called national language departments, without which comparative literature cannot survive, have to be maintained and supported, the intellectual value of putting together complex and discrepant material that was never intended to be drawn together needs to be highlighted and 'new ways of making sense exactly where existing canons and methods fail us' have to be sought (Saussy, 2017: 28). It is the contention of the contributors to this volume that the most obvious way of making sense is to emphasise the importance of translation, since the study of translating and of translations necessarily involves both close and distant reading.

Lucas Klein, whose essay 'Reading and speaking for translation' is subtitled 'De-institutionalizing the institutions of literary study', also stresses the importance of translation, reminding us again that 'translation has long proven embarrassing for ideas of comparative literature perhaps even more so for ideas of national literature' (Klein, 2017: 216). He, like many others, sees the emphasis on studying literatures under national headings as problematic, because this can lead to isolationist thinking. His view is that the rise of importance of literary theory can be linked to the ways in which comparatists have had to search for new grounds upon which to base their comparisons, since they could no longer rely on the common assumptions of 'national' literature departments. This is an interesting idea, and he goes further, suggesting that the future of comparative literature should evolve into an increased emphasis on the importance of translation in national literary histories, using the study of translation to 'dismantle the lock nations have had on our study of literature' (Klein, 2017: 218).

While stressing the central significance of translation, it is also important to emphasise that what is being suggested is not that everything should be read in the original language, nor only in translation, but rather that there is a need for greater understanding of how translations are produced, how they circulate and how they are read. This requires an understanding not only of the role which translations have played in the development of individual literatures and in their dissemination, but also an understanding of the actual processes of translation itself, processes which necessarily involve language. The contributors to this book all share that view: the time has come for literary and cultural studies to acknowledge the significance of translation, to recognise that, as Bella Brodzki so eloquently argues, translations are embedded in the extensive social and political networks of language relations and the shifting perspectives that result from intercultural exchange of all kinds. Brodzki goes so far as to propose that just as it has become impossible today to ignore the impact of gender, 'so it should be inconceivable to overlook translation's integral role in every discursive field' (Brodzki, 2007: 2). Brodzki holds a Chair in Comparative Literature, but her views are echoed by translation scholars too. Edwin Gentzler's provocatively titled *Translation and Rewriting in the Age of Post-Translation Studies* (2017) argues that translation is of such fundamental importance that it needs to be rethought as 'an always-ongoing process of *every* communication' and asks:

> What if translation becomes viewed less as a temporal act carried out between languages and cultures and instead as a *precondition* underlying the languages and cultures upon which communication is based? What if we consider the political, social and economic structures as built upon translation?
>
> (Genztler, 2017: 5)

With Brodzki and Gentzler we can see hopes of a fusion between translation studies and literary studies, or at the very least, hopes that the importance of translation in literary and cultural history can finally be acknowledged. The authors of the chapters included in this volume share these hopes, regardless of their starting point. Originating from very diverse contexts, some have published principally within translation studies, others are known as comparative or world literature scholars, but none claim to be specialists in any particular discipline, preferring to work across and in between different fields, drawing upon different theoretical positions but committed to the belief that translation matters.

In the first chapter, Harish Trivedi considers the question of translation and world literature from an Indian perspective. He begins with an optimistic point – there cannot be such a thing as world literature without translation. But then Trivedi suggests that there is a contradiction at the heart of current thinking about world literature, particularly through the identification of world literature in terms of consumption. He is concerned that the global dominance of English carries with it colonial and neocolonial overtones, and sees the very term 'world literature' as 'somewhat contaminated'. His contention is that the history of translation from and into Indian languages is unique and does not necessarily fit any of the patterns expounded by Western theorists of world literature. He suggests that there has been a considerable amount of English translation of Indian writing, but that these translations cover only a tiny percentage of canonical works composed in the 24 major literary languages of India over three thousand years and remain little known outside India. He also notes that until the latter half of the nineteenth century there were very few translations of any foreign literature into Indian languages, a point which raises the interesting question of when and why literatures feel the need to translate.

Trivedi reminds us that writers attain a much larger circulation if they write in a major Western language, noting that literature is now produced mainly, if not exclusively, in the languages of the colonisers in many former colonies. However, he also points out that English is only one of the 24 languages, noting that the foremost literary prize in India, established in 1965, only very recently began to consider books published in English as eligible.

The chapter concludes with reference to a different, specifically Indian form of globalisation – best-selling books produced in English but for local consumption. Trivedi writes that bookshops in Indian airports now have two different categories of best-sellers, those written in English by Indian authors for Indian readers, and those written in or translated into English. Quite what this may mean for the future is questionable, and the chapter leaves us with a question: if world literature to date has been inconceivable without translation, might it be that localised English will be the language of the future and can this too be seen as a form of translation?

With Charles Forsdick's chapter we move from the Anglophone to the Francophone world. He investigates the phenomenon of the 2007 manifesto advocating a *littérature-monde en français* (world-literature in French), arguing that this idea has taken little account of other related concepts such as 'world literature' or *Weltliteratur* and can be seen as a monolingually French concept. The chapter traces the origins and development of this idea, stressing the contradictions inherent in positing a world literature in only one language. The juxtaposition of 'world-literature' and 'in French' can be seen as oxymoronic, as the manifesto failed to acknowledge the Gallocentrism of the French-language literary marketplace. However, Forsdick sees signs of a shift through increasing sensitivity to issues of translation, arguing that terms such as 'Francopolyphone' are gradually replacing the older 'Francophone' with its ethnolinguistic nationalist connotations. The way forward, he proposes, is to challenge the idea that literary production begins in one unique language, and to acknowledge the mixing of languages, the 'translanguaging' of pluralistic, polyphonic literary production. He quotes the Moroccan writer Abdelfattah Kilito's 2013 book, entitled *Je parle toutes les langues, mais en arabe* (I can speak all languages, but in Arabic) and concludes with a call to acknowledge the cohabitation and interaction of multiple languages in literary history.

Azucena Blanco's chapter also stresses the importance of pluralistic and collaborative models in any study of world literature. She argues that a concept of community is fundamentally important, and looks at the ways in which translation has been significant in the transformation of the Romantic idea of *Weltliteratur* into contemporary notions of world literature as pluriversal. She sees *Weltliteratur* as a totalising concept, based on what she calls 'the myth of the Absolute', and then explores how translation might be instrumental in disrupting that myth. She cites Borges' famous story 'The Library of Babel' to show the impossibility of an unlimited, total community of knowledge, then considers Borges' essay on the translators of the *Thousand and One Nights*. Borges' argument is that all translations are alike in their infidelities, for translation acts to disrupt the myth of the total communion of any linguistic community by making visible the unfinished nature of a literary text. Translation involves a reorganisation of modes of making visible, and as an example Blanco cites the debates around the title of Franz Kafka's *Die Verwandlungen* (Metamorphosis) in Spanish.

The 1999 translator, Jordi Llovet, proposed to change the established title *La metamorfosis* to *La transformación,* following Borges, but also so as to link Kafka more directly with other socially critical writers. Llovet's title therefore opens up the possibility of a reading that sees Kafka's work as linked to other critiques of Western capitalism. Blanco uses this example to argue that the translator's choices are effectively verbal moves that vary the source text, thereby demolishing the ideal of a unique, stable identity. Literary translations expose the continuous processes of transformation and the plurivocality of all texts.

In his chapter on translation and cosmopolitanism, Paulo de Medeiros considers the case of Portuguese, a language which is considered 'minor', despite it being spoken by millions around the world and having played a major role in imperial and colonial history. De Medeiros cites Kwame Anthony Appiah on the ethical implications of cosmopolitanism, in which he warns against a notion of a (mythical) cosmopolitan Europe in contrast with the rest of the world. He also discusses Esperanca Bielsa's proposition that a new global idea of cosmopolitanism will need to be based on translation, but he is concerned that what he calls the double invisibility of Portuguese needs to be understood as directly related to the market forces and capital flows that have shaped the world today. He uses two examples to demonstrate the relative invisibility of Portuguese writing in the world literature canon, the case of the modernist poet Fernando Pessoa and the contemporary Mozambican writer Mia Couto. Both writers embody cosmopolitan views, both have come to be known outside their own contexts, but the paths through which they have come to a wider readership are labyrinthine and reflect the complex power structures that underlie the commissioning, distribution and marketing of texts in translation. Pessoa's international reputation began through French and German, with his success in English coming later. In considering Mia Couto, De Medeiros posits that African literatures in Portuguese can be seen as suffering from what he calls a triple form of invisibility. The point de Medeiros stresses is that the highly complex work of these two writers, both of whom can be seen as truly cosmopolitan since both use language in unexpected and innovative ways, demands a different kind of translation. They can never be domesticated, as the task of the translator involves attempting to render the radical difference of the original. The chapter concludes with a quote from Mia Couto about the 'magic' of cultural exchange and the production of hybritidies. This, de Medeiros suggests, sums up the important relationship between translation and cosmopolitanism.

César Domínguez explores new ground with his chapter on the extraordinary success of Walter Scott in nineteenth-century Latin America. He focuses on what the historian Robert Darnton termed 'the communication circuit' of book history, which runs from author to publisher, to distributor and finally to bookseller. Domínguez, like de Medeiros, sees the need to examine these physical processes, along with translation itself of course, in order to understand how texts circulate and enter into world literature. Translation, he argues, is instrumental both within a single language world-literature, and in world literature as a global interlingual phenomenon.

Domínguez has assembled a corpus of 109 works from the period 1823–1850 by Walter Scott, referred to in the chapter by his more familiar Spanish name, Gualtiero Escoto. These include translations, reprints, a couple of forgeries and a wrongly attributed work. He has examined the circulation of these texts and comes to the unexpected conclusion that the global capitals of postcolonial Spanish-speaking communities were London and Paris. Rudolph Ackermann in London and Frederic Rosa in Paris are described as 'transcontinental entrepreneurs'. Gualtiero Escoto's writing circulated across Latin America through various forms of translation – from English directly, from English through French and from a variety of what can be loosely termed adaptations. Domínguez concludes that his research shows the need to move beyond the dichotomy of national versus world literature, since the success of Gualtiero Escoto was made possible by the global role of non-Spanish-speaking centres, London and Paris, with Madrid and Barcelona playing only a minimal role.

Sherry Simon is also concerned with the mechanics and politics of text circulation, only in this chapter we move from consideration of the fortunes of a writer across a continent to a library in the city of Czernowitz. She begins with an account of a return to the city that the writer Marianne Hirsch's parents had to leave at the end of the Second World War. Hirsch provides a detailed account of the bookshelves of her cousin Rosa, books mainly in German but comprising classical authors, local authors, translations of non-German authors, books on wartime concentration camps – a library that can be seen as both local and worldly. Simon, who has written extensively on the idea of the multilingual city, here focuses on the relationship between German, translation and the world from the perspective of former Mitteleuropa.

Simon argues that Czernowitz, like other multilingual cities, was a translational space. She also proposes that the multilingual city complicates the definition of world literature as 'non-national', since there is a web of inter-relatedness between what might be termed local and foreign forms. She considers the relative absence of discussion of German by world literature scholars, and suggests that inadequate attention has been paid to the linguistic amalgams – Germano-Jewish, Germano-Slavic, Germano-Hungarian, Germano-Romanian – which characterised pre-war Central Europe. In the latter part of the chapter Simon looks briefly at four Czernowitz writers, all creating what she identifies as different modes of translational writing, and concludes that for these writers that multilingual milieu in which they lived and worked involved continued interaction with other languages, on both a conscious and unconscious level.

Martín Gaspar's chapter also challenges some of the assumptions within both world literature and translation studies, arguing that too much attention has been given to texts that are either aesthetically innovative or politically subversive. His conclusion is that by focussing on newness and/or disruption, some of the best-selling conventional literature has been ignored by researchers in both fields. Yet, as he points out, it is conventional literature that has tended to be widely circulated in translation. Jack London's *The Call of the Wild* has been more extensively translated than any other twentieth century American or

English novelist. Gaspar's point is that by tracing the fortunes of works such as this, we can discover aspects of translation and text circulation that diverge from what we know from examining what he calls the world-literature-as-innovation and the-translation-as-agent-of change paradigms.

The chapter looks at the demand for translated fiction in the early twentieth century Latin America, linking it with rising literacy, increased urbanisation and mass migration. The figures he cites are extraordinarily high, and through cheap editions and reworkings of popular texts generations of readers were introduced to a whole range of novels, including those by Jack London. Gaspar goes on to analyse 13 translations of *The Call of the Wild* published between 1958 and 2012. He focuses on four textual elements – translations of the word 'wild', the opening lines, the treatment of euthanasia in the novel and the treatment of the character Manuel. His close reading exposes an absence of consistency both in terms of lexis and ideology and shows how diverse the strategies employed by different translators actually are. He then goes on to consider the impact of popular, populist translations of this kind produced in a hurry, on readers who encountered these books in their formative years. He quotes Che Guevara's *La sierra y el llano* (1961) in which he remembers 'an old Jack London story', a reference picked up in 1973 by Julio Cortázar. Gaspar's chapter reminds us that the emphasis placed on innovation and aesthetically significant writing by world literature and translation studies may be misplaced if we start to think about the impact of other kinds of writing aimed at a mass audience and, in particular, at a mass audience in their formative years.

Svetlana Page takes issue with world literature scholarship from a different perspective. Her chapter looks at the way in which Western world literature has constructed a narrative that is at odds with the history of Russian literature in the twentieth century. The case she considers is Maxim Gorky's World Literature Project, which has received little attention outside Russia, and she poses a series of questions about whether the project was, as has been suggested, a Soviet experiment closely aligned with the dominant ideology and hence relatively short-lived. Page's fundamental question is whether Gorky's World Literature Project can be seen as evolutionary within Russian publishing of its time. Was Gorky trying to do something genuinely innovative, or was he caught up in the machinations of the Soviet power hierarchy? Her view is that the project was an educational large-scale translation project for mass audiences, which grew out of the dominant enlightenment tradition within Russian literary publishing and so can be linked to educational projects of pre-revolutionary Russia. Gorky's approach was twofold – there was to be a Popular Series of books aimed at general readers, and a Main Series that would involve translating classical writing. Page is interested in the legacy of the World Literature project, which she argues has been extremely important in that it pioneered the establishment of professional translator training and research into translation theory. Her argument is that Gorky's project should not be limited by Soviet time frames, but should be seen as an enterprise within a continuum, since it grew out of pre-Revolutionary attitudes to imported literature and its influence can be seen today in post-Soviet Russia.

Page's chapter reminds us of the emphasis placed by Translation Studies on understanding the diachronics of literary systems. In her chapter on Borges in Swedish and English translation, Cecilia Alvstad takes up another important strand of translation studies research, that is, the way in which different translations create different images of the same author and even of the same text. Alvstad takes Borges' story 'El jardín de senteros que se bifurcan' (The Garden of Forking Paths) to show the extent to which readings differ with each translation. She shows how the choices made by different translators affect the way in which the text is interpreted, and then goes on in the section on Borges in Swedish to show how the reception context also has an impact on ways of reading. Her argument is that when an author begins to be translated, a new 'logic of growth' is set in motion, since translation rarely if ever repeats the chronology of the author's original production. In the case of Borges, different stories were selected for translation at different times. She reinforces this argument by contrasting the Norwegian, Swedish and English volumes all entitled *Labyrinths*, but all very different, noting in passing that Borges never published a book in Spanish with that title. What she points out is that if we consider the various translations and often irreconcilable interpretations of 'The Garden of Forking Paths', we end up with what she terms a Borgesian universe reminiscent of the forking paths of the story. Alvstad draws attention not only to the context in which Borges' work is read, but also to the specific lexical and syntactical choices of each translator.

Karin Littau explores the role of media in the worlding of literature, and argues that the concept of world literature in Goethe's time was equally media-dependent, albeit of course in different ways. Reflecting on the rise of world literature since the mid-1990s, Littau notes the move away from reading texts in the original language but sees this as reinforcing the need to think in terms of the significance of translation, but translation as more than the interlingual. She makes the case for transliteracy, which is defined as the ability to read across a range of media platforms. Her argument is that in Goethe's day, the world literature paradigm emerged when there was an abundance of print media, whereas today it is emerging in an age with an abundance of non-print media. Littau is intrigued by online digital works, and gives the example of the YHCHI which presents translations on a split screen in such a way as to make it impossible for anyone to read the texts simultaneously. This experiment with translations in motion means that although we can see that a translation is happening, we cannot apperceive the translation as translation. Littau reflects on what is actually going on here; she returns to David Damrosch's proposition that world literature is a mode of circulation and of reading, but asks a question about what if world literature were no longer read or seen. How might we read and respond to some of the multimedia, plurilingual, interconnective art works of the kind that Littau describes, which articulate their own material conditions of production while resisting incorporation into globalised communication infrastructures?

If Littau's chapter leaves us with a question about the future of how we approach world literature and translation, the final chapter by the Greek Cypriot poet and translator Stephanos Stephanides takes up the complex question of identity in a multilingual world. Stephanides's chapter is both theoretical and autobiographical, and starts out with his belief that the idea of world is the performative outcome of our own interventions. Translation, he suggests, is one such performative intervention, as fundamental to an understanding of world literature as ethnographic practice is to anthropology. He calls for both close and distant reading as essential for what he terms 'a new poetics of the imaginary and the imagined', which will involve political and ethical forms of negotiation. The island of Cyprus with its long, complex and deeply fraught history enables Stephanides to focus on what he perceives as the gateways to creative moments that come about through the fractures of geological, social and political upheaval. In this chapter, he ranges across the Mediterranean, discussing Ovid, Orhan Pamuk, Cavafy, Dante, Ibn Arabi, Seferis, Ivi Meleagrou, then, following his autobiographical thread, crosses the Atlantic to the Caribbean, before returning to the island. In his conclusion, he notes that the central mountain range of Cyprus is a rare geological phenomenon, because as the tectonic plate of Africa and Europe collided millions of years ago, the oldest rocks with fragments of ocean crust were flung upwards and so the higher one climbs, the deeper one goes into time. He uses this image to draw attention to the endless shifting of horizons of expectation, reinforcing the importance of the role of the translator in what he terms 'the ruptures of dislocation in a layered cosmopolitanism'.

All the contributors to this book, in different ways, share similar concerns – how to examine the role of translations in world literature, how to map interlingual movement over time, to what extent do translations shape our understanding of other literatures, what are the political, social, economic and ethical factors that underpin the way in which texts move, how do writers become canonised and decanonised in different contexts, how can we engage in both close and distant reading, how do we wrestle with both the local and the global, and, perhaps most significantly of all, how do we deal with our conscious and unconscious bias when studying literary texts. Complex though these issues are, the key seems to be the prioritisation of translation as both the instrument and the precondition for the spatial and temporal movement of texts.

Select bibliography

Apter, Emily (2013) *Against World Literature*. London: Verso.

Bellos, David (2011) *Is That a Fish in Your Ear? Translation and the Meaning of Everything*. London: Penguin.

Brodzki, Bella (2007) *Can These Bones Live? Translation, Survival and Cultural Memory*. Stanford: Stanford University Press.

Damrosch, David (2009) *How to Read World Literature*. London: Wiley-Blackwell.

Emmerich, Karen (2017). Translation, in Mads Rosendahl Thomsen*et al*. eds. *Literature. An Introduction to Theory and Analysis*. London: Bloomsbury, pp. 361–372

Even-Zohar, Itamar (2000/1978) The Position of Translated Literature in the Literary Polysystem, in Lawrence Venuti ed. *The Translation Studies Reader*. London and New York: Routledge, pp. 192–197.

Gentzler, Edwin (2017) *Translation and Rewriting in the Age of Post-Translation Studies*. London and New York: Routledge.

Helgesson, Stefan and Pieter Vermeulen, eds (2016) *Institutions of World Literature. Writing, Translation, Markets*. London and New York: Routledge.

Holmes, James (1988) *Translated! Papers on Literary Translation and Translation Studies*. Amsterdam: Rodopi.

Klein, Lucas (2017) Reading and Speaking for Translation: De-institutionalizing the Institutions of Literary Study, in Ursula K. Heise et al. eds. *Futures of Comparative Literature*. London and New York: Routledge, pp. 215–220.

Lefevere, Andre (2017/1992) *Translation, Rewriting and the Manipulation of Literary Fame*. London and New York: Routledge.

Moretti, Franco (2000) Conjectures on World Literature, *New Left Review* 1(Jan–Feb), 54–68.

Pound, Ezra (1951) *An ABC of Reading*. London: Faber and Faber.

Pound, Ezra (1968) Notes on Elizabethan Classicists, in T. S. Eliot ed. *Literary Essays*. New York: New Directions.

Saussy, Haun (2017) Comparative Literature: The Next Ten Years, in Ursula K. Heise et al. eds. *Futures of Comparative Literature*. London and New York: Routledge, pp. 24–30.

Seyhan, Azde (2001) *Writing Outside the Nation*. Princeton and Oxford: Princeton University Press.

Venuti, Lawrence (2016) Hijacking Translation: How Comp Lit Continues to Suppress Translated Texts, *boundary 2* 43(2), 179–204.

Weinberger, Eliot (2002) A Talk on Translators and Translation, in Daniel Balderston and Marcy E. Schwartz eds. *Voice-Overs. Translation and Latin American Literature*. Albany: State University of New York Press, pp. 104–118.

1 Translation and world literature

The Indian context

Harish Trivedi

Literature, translation and the world

Can there be World Literature without translation? The answer would seem to be an obvious and resounding 'No'. But this answer would also serve to betray a contradiction and defect at the heart of the current formulations of World Literature, which require Word Literature not simply to exist but also to be available and accessible through translation into a designated language, English. The question, therefore, may be thought to be analogous to the hoary philosophical issue being discussed by some Cambridge undergraduates at the beginning of E. M. Forster's novel, *The Longest Journey* (1907): is there a cow in the quad when there is no one to see it? In this long-running philosophical debate between Idealism and Realism, the cow is the symbol 'for the reality that exists whether we acknowledge it or not' (Rosenbaum 1979: 49–50). The literatures of the wide world exist whether the First World acknowledges their existence or not, but there is a fair chance that in the self-assured fervour of a Cambridge college quad or its intellectual equivalent, they may well be argued out of existence by some of the interlocutors.

Going by the definitions offered so far, World Literature is identified as such not in terms of production but in terms of consumption, which is, of course, entirely in conformity with our super-consumerist age. All over the world, literature has for centuries and millennia been produced, and continues to be produced, in several thousand languages. The number of living languages in the world is currently estimated to be about 6,000 and it may be a fair surmise to say that regular and substantial literary production in the written form takes place in at least half of them, to say nothing of the corollary corpus of orality. These literatures are constantly being translated from their original versions into many other languages, both neighbouring and distant, but it is not until they appear in an English translation that they begin to be deemed as a part of World Literature, at least in Anglophone discourse.

These literatures have to be, so to say, born again, or at least conducted through a vital rite of passage through translation into English, before they can be seen by the world to begin to exist. Brahmins in India have traditionally been called *dvija*, the twice-born, for they qualified to be Brahmins in a meaningful sense not by biological birth but only after they had gone through the *upanayana* ceremony at the age of 9 or 11, when a sacred and exclusive Sanskrit *mantra* was whispered into their ears, and they set off at the end of the ceremony for Kashi (also called Varanasi), the classic seat of Sanskrit learning, to learn Vedic and secular knowledge there. In an ironic reference to this ceremony (still observed tokenistically even in Brahmin households located thousands of miles away from Varanasi), an early critical study of Indian novels written in English was titled *The Twice-Born Fiction* (Mukherjee 1971). We may similarly call World Litera-ture the Twice-Born Literature, with the parallel proviso that, in this case, a work of literature in any language except English must leave its native home and travel far away to be re-issued (pardon the pun) by a set of new parents, a translator and a publisher, in the UK or the USA, and thus acquire a new and more visible life.

However, a vital difference between a young Brahmin as described above and a work of literature travelling out to gain admittance to World Literature is that at the end of his studies in Kashi, the young Brahmin returned to his local community to enrich it by serving it for the rest of his life as a scholar, priest and doctor. On the other hand, a work of literature translated into English migrates forever to another cultural world, and exploits it to its own deraci-nated individual advantage. Such a work is thus not so much like a traditional Brahmin but rather more like a modern 'techie', who leaves his Third-World home on an H1-B work visa to contribute to the wealth and prosperity of the USA and correspondingly to the impoverishment of his home country through brain-drain. In the case of a literary work, this would be through relative devaluation and neglect of works not so translated.

The implicit insistence on translation into English as a primary requirement for a literary work to gain entry into the corpus of World Literature inevitably carries colonial and neocolonial overtones. The 'world' in 'World Literature' is defined and shaped by just those powers which until recently ruled the world and continue to exercise global hegemony in both cultural and commercial terms. Throughout the history of colonialism, countries that were militarily and economically subjugated, such as India, refused to concede that they were cul-turally inferior to the West and it was precisely such a surge of cultural nationalism that lent ballast to the struggle for decolonization and eventually led to freedom. The emergence and spread of World Literature over the last couple of decades may seem to some of us to be another wave of the Western will to dominate the world in areas not hitherto conquered.

For these and some other reasons, the term 'World Literature' is already somewhat contaminated. A projected multi-volume history of World Literature organized by the Stockholm Collegium at Stockholm University, for example, has decided to distance itself from the term by calling itself 'Literature: A World History'. The nomenclature sounds awkward and may raise other issues but at least it is not 'World Literature' – that sweeping, airy-fairy, user-friendly con-coction, the main proof of whose worth lies apparently in how widely it can circulate. For as we may recall, in influential early formulations, World Literature was projected as a kind of literature made easy for all comers. Franco Moretti (2000) advocated the mode of 'distant reading', especially of the novel, which is seen as a typically Western genre which spread from the West to the rest of the world – as distinct, one may note, from poetry which needs to be close-read and is endemic to all parts of the word without any Western intervention. David Damrosch defined World Literature as encompassing 'all literary works that circulate beyond their culture of origin, either in translation or in their original language' (Damrosch 2003: 4) which again accords priority to that which gets translated, for whatever random reason, or to works in a few Western languages, predominantly English, which alone in effect can expect to circulate widely without translation (for a fuller discussion, see Trivedi 2013). In subsequent formulations, both Moretti and Damrosch have refined their initial positions, Moretti for example by admitting of instances of novels which combine '*a plot from the core* [the West] and *style from the periphery* [the non-West]' (Moretti 2006: 118; his emphasis), and Damrosch by acknowledging that works of World Literature need to be paid 'close attention' with regard to the 'particular national and regional systems' from which they originate. (Damrosch 2006: 213)

In his essay cited above, Moretti began by saying, 'We do not know what world literature is', and in his conclusion seven pages later he confessed: 'we still do not know what world literature is' (Moretti 2006: 113, 120). In the decade and more that has elapsed, World Literature has advanced to be a buzzword and has become increasingly more acceptable and respectable as an idea and as a desideratum. We may still not understand quite what it is, but many more of us seem to want more of it. This development may be ascribable to two broad reasons. The first is that due to ever multiplying migration and virtual connectivity, we impinge on each other more and more on a global scale, and one way of coping with this is through the many shades of translation. As some of us have always maintained, even the worst of translations (and even machine translations are palpably improving) is better than no translation, for translation opens a door to wider knowledge and better understanding as nothing else could have.

Secondly, there is a wide post-socialist acceptance of the fact, after the collapse of the Second World, that we have only one world, however uneven it may be, and that the only way to reduce inequality in it is, paradoxically, to participate in it on its own terms. 'The world is what it is,' wrote V. S. Naipaul in the opening sentence of one of his finest and bleakest novels (in a formulation so simple, profound and characteristic that it was adopted as the title of his authorized biography by Patrick French) and all of us have to make our terms and our peace with it. World Literature may not be what anyone seems to want in particular but it is what it is, and we are going to have more of it if we can read effectively in only one language. The term that World Literature has supplanted is not national literature, as is sometimes mistakenly thought, but rather, Comparative Literature, which is now perhaps too dead for anyone even to try and flog it back to life. And the reason it died was because, contrary to its original impulse, it began to be done more and more not in the original languages but in translation. Susan Bassnett prophetically pronounced it dead in 1993 for she said its methodological *raison d'être* had been appropriated by translation, and Gayatri Spivak in 2003 declared that it was bound to die unless it aligned itself with Area Studies as instituted in the USA, which still insisted on language learning (which may be, as she did not add, for partly nefarious reasons to do with the national security of the USA) (Bassnett 1993; Spivak 2003) Perhaps the best that can be said for World Literature is that even as it encourages monolingualism, it also acknowledges and promotes the essential role of translation in our present world order, and that it seeks to bring together under the same covers literature not only originating from the West but also as outsourced from the rest of the world.

In what follows in this chapter, I shall discuss World Literature as currently constituted in relation to a particularly fertile and various literary field, India. I shall look firstly at what is available in English translation of Indian literature of the last 3,500 years and what is not, and at what precisely and how much of it has been thought suitable to be regarded as and included in a canonical anthology of World Literature. I shall look next at some Indian endeavours to access, in translation, literatures of the world, with their own quite distinct preferences and considerations. These less than systematic configurations of World Literature have been constituted from what has been translated of foreign literatures into the Indian languages. They also offer indications of what the Indian literary 'world' comprised before the West 'discovered' India, especially in the first millennium of the Common Era when a Sanskrit Cosmopolis was the norm in South Asia and South-East Asia, as well as a presence in Tibet and China in the East, and Afghanistan and the Arab world in the West. In conclusion, I shall revisit the debate on untranslatability as revived in some recent formulations, to attempt to surmise how World Literature may develop in the future and what may become of it.

India in translation and World Literature

Contemporary anthologists of Indian literature often complain that not enough translations, or enough good translations (as judged by some unstated criteria), are available for them to make a fair and representative selection. This may well be so, and in a basic sense will always remain so, but it is not as if Indian literature were not as well served by translation into English as perhaps any non-European literature. Translations from Sanskrit began in the last quarter of the 18th century, in the first excited flush of what later came to be acclaimed as Orientalism – and still later to be denounced as such. It may be remembered that the first few works from Sanskrit to be translated into English were not random finds by Englishmen but among the most canonical works in all of Sanskrit, apparently recommended by Indian pundits to their British pupils. These included the foremost religious text, the *Bhagavad-Gita*, first translated by Charles Wilkins in 1785 (and estimated to have been re-translated into English about 300 times since then) and probably the best Sanskrit play ever written, the *Abhijnana-Shakauntalam* (for short called Shakuntala), translated by Sir William Jones in 1789.

There is, of course, much that is palpably oriental and orientalist in the translations that followed, in the sense of them being selected and projected as arcane, exotic or just different. Many of the classic Sanskrit texts were, and still are, translated through grand collective enterprises that were founded in the Victorian era and published with the academic authority of the best of the university presses. Max Mueller, a German Sanskritist (after whom a road was named in central Delhi after Indian independence), edited a 50-volume series of *The Sacred Books of the East* which was published between 1879 and 1910 by the Oxford University Press. In this eclectic assemblage, 21 of the texts were Hindu, 10 Buddhist, 8 Zoroastrian, 6 Chinese, 2 Islamic and 2 Jain (with the 50th volume being the Index). The ongoing Harvard Oriental Series under successive editors has published from 1891 up to January 2018 a total of 86 titles, of which nearly every one relates to Indian religions and literature, including some recent ones about oral literature, though some of the volumes are not translations, but rather editions or concordances.

The latest and the most ambitious of such series of volumes is the Murty Classical Library of India, also published by the Harvard University Press and named after a young Indian alumnus, Rohan Narayana Murty. While doing a PhD at Harvard in computer science, Murty realized that he knew very little about India's literary and cultural heritage and, as the scion of the family that owns the Indian software company Infosys, he decided to make a gift of $5.2 million to found this library of Indian classics in translation in 2010 (see www.murtylibrary.com; also Kuruvilla 2015). The Library began publication in 2015, had brought out 18 volumes by January 2018, and proposes to issue, on the pattern of the Loeb Classical Library, five volumes per year until the number 500 is reached in due course. In a significant advance on the previous two series, the Murty Library publishes translations of classics not only from Sanskrit but also from the 'vernaculars', i.e., the modern Indian languages, though it stipulates that it will not consider translations of texts composed after the year 1800. However, this limitation is more than compensated for by many commercial presses, such as Penguin India, Orient Blackswan or HarperCollins India, as well as the Oxford University Press India, preferring to publish newer works. The OUP India alone has a list of over 40 Indian novels in translation by contemporary writers.

Indian literature, then, would seem to be quite as well served by translations into English as say Chinese literature or Arabic-Persian literature. It perhaps has no works which proved to be such spectacular successes in translation as *The Thousand and One Nights*, or *The Rubaiyat of Omar Khayyam* (the latter having been in fact substantially reconceptualised and rearranged in translation by Edward Fitzgerald). The Indian title with a comparable worldwide recognition would probably be the *Kama-Sutra*, with the difference that this gnomic taxonomical text is often translated with its standard commentary merged with the short text, and it is hardly ever printed or bought without a whole array of erotic illustrations often taken from sculptures in Indian temples which were, of course, no part of the original text. Altogether, it may be correct to say that so far as classical Indian literature in concerned, i.e. literature written between

1200 BCE and 1500 CE, there is hardly any canonical work which has not been translated into English at least once, even though many of the translations may have been by and for erudite Orientalist scholars.

In contrast, a substantial proportion of the translations of Indian works published in the twentieth century have been rendered into English not by Western translators but by Indians themselves. This has come about due to two main reasons. Firstly, there was the unique example of the Bengali writer Rabindranath Tagore who translated into English some of his own mystical-devotional lyrics in a slim volume under the untranslated title *Gitanjali: Song Offerings* in 1912, and promptly went on to win the Nobel prize the following year. The lightning of the Nobel, which of course is a hallowed short cut to instant entry into World Literature, has not struck an Indian self-translator again in the one hundred years and more that have elapsed since then (nor any other Indian writer for that matter), but that has not deterred Indian self-translators from persisting and hoping against hope. Sujit Mukherjee in his book *Translation as Discovery* devoted two chapters to this complex phenomenon, each pointing out the paradoxical nature of self-translation. In 'Translation as Perjury', he took Tagore to task for catering to Western taste by exoticizing his own work in his self-translations, a process that Tagore admitted later was like 'falsifying my own coins' (cited in Mukherjee 1981: 123). In another essay titled 'Translation as Patriotism', he examined a related phenomenon of works by writers from Indian languages translated into English by fellow Indians and then brought out by Indian publishers with no international reach – which too may be called a form of self-translation, by extension. India is after all the third largest publisher of books in English, and the industry is sustained by the fact that books published in the country are bought and read largely within the country.

Thus, a fair amount of Indian literature, both classical and modern, is available in English translation of varying quality. At the same time, it may be seriously doubted whether it constitutes even 5% of the corpus of works composed in the 24 major languages of India over the last one or two or three millennia (as may be the case for each of the languages.). Indian literature is perhaps like an elephant, and all of us who speak about it in the original or in translation are like the six blind men in the old story, each of whom gets hold of some random part of the beast and thinks it to be the whole.

To change metaphors again, the proof of the pudding of any national literature in English translation is just what and how much of it finds wider circulation and is picked up to be part of the canon of World Literature. Here, only a sample of such a canon will be examined, by looking at the *Longman Anthology of World Literature* in six volumes amounting to approximately 6,508 pages (Damrosch 2004), and the space Indian literature occupies in it. In Volume A (3500 BCE–500 CE, but the chronology spans are often overlapping as will be seen below), out of a total of 1390 pages, Indian literature fills 240 pages, which is next only to Greek (approximately 600 pages). In Volume B (200–1492), however, as if to atone for the rather generous recognition accorded it in Volume A, Indian literature is not granted even a single page out of 1354 pages (if one does not count a Chinese monk briefly describing travels to India by earlier monks from that country, or a short extract from the *Tibetan Book of the Dead*). Thus, after Kalidasa (4th–5th century) in Volume A, the next Indian author we come across is Basavanna (1106–*c*.1167) in Volume C. It is as if Indian literature went into a deep coma for about seven hundred years – which of course is not the case at all, for the epic poets Bharavi (6th century) and Magha (7th century), the novelist Banabhatta (7th century), the playwright Bhavabhuti (8th century), and the lyric poet Jayadeva (12th century), all belong to the front rank of Sanskrit authors. In Volume C (1300–1670), Indian literature gets 28 pages out of 902, and in Volume D (1600–1798), it is 33 out of 670. In Volume E (the 19th century), Indian literature has 29 pages out of 917, and in Volume F (20th century), 41 out of 1158. This makes it altogether 371 pages out of 6,508, i.e. 5.7% of the total – which perhaps is not bad. For it's not as if Chinese (6.3%), Japanese (5.01%) or Arabic-Persian (5.73%) literatures do significantly better. In contrast, in volumes A to E, the literatures of Europe fill approximately two-thirds to three-quarters of the space. In the final volume, more parts of the world are admitted, but the dominant proportion of literature not translated but originally produced in English does not diminish. Of the 41 pages given to India, for example, 10 go to Salman Rushdie.

It could be argued that this is not only to be expected but is also understandable. This is an anthology compiled in English by a team of scholars located in the West, and published in New York for a largely Western readership. In fact, many aspects of the anthology are notably innovative and imaginative, such as detailed head-notes to each author which contain information as well as insights, and cross-cutting sections interspersed throughout to break up the linear chronological march. Each volume begins with a section titled 'Cross-Currents', followed now and then by sections titled 'Perspectives' and 'Resonances'. Even a chronological ordering in volumes such as these can throw up startling discoveries for readers everywhere. For example, in Volume F we get, in the following order, selections from Premchand, Lu Xun, James Joyce, Virginia Woolf and Akutagawa Ryunosuke, so that authors in translation from India, China and Japan flank on either side two fiction writers in English (Damrosch 2004: F, 121–222). They are brought together by the fact that they were all born within a few years of each other, between 1880 and 1892, but to read them one after the other will certainly broaden the horizons of readers from whichever part of the world. Similarly, in Volume E, Byron and Pushkin are separated by the Indian poet Ghalib (1795–1869) to produce a major defamiliarizing effect, and in the same volume, Chekhov (1860–1904) is immediately followed by Rabindranath Tagore (1861–1941). If this is not World Literature in a theorizable sense, it certainly feels like World Literature empirically, for it reminds the reader, wherever located, that there are worlds elsewhere besides the world in which he or she has grown up.

Indian formulations of World Literature

It would be instructive to compare this New York anthology with an anthology of World Literature produced and published beyond the West, but there is no such thing in India, for example, at least not yet, in either English or in an

Indian language. It is perhaps easier to speak of 'the world', and on behalf of the world, in a globalizing language such as English with a worldwide reach, even though the largest Indian language, Hindi, with over 400 million native-speakers and at least 100 million second-language speakers, is not far behind in raw numbers. But the Hindi-speakers are nearly all of them resident in India and the world does not impinge on them or they on the world in the same way as English-speakers.

In fact, an overview of the Indian awareness of and interaction with the rest of the world throws up the curious fact that, ever since antiquity and up to and some time after the arrival of the colonizing British, there are hardly any translations into India from any part of the world. In the whole millennium during which the Chinese were assiduously translating a whole canon of Buddhist texts from Sanskrit, there is not any translation of a Chinese text into Sanskrit to be found (see Trivedi (2013); and see Feeney (2016: 18) for a hypothetical parallel in the Greek-Latin situation). Later, the Arabs and the Persians translated many literary and scientific texts from India, which were then further transmitted into various European languages, but hardly any texts from Arabic or Persian were translated into the Indian languages, not even when Persian became the language of the Mughal rulers of India from the 16th century onwards and when major Indian works such as the two epics the *Ramayana* and the *Mahabharata*, and the philosophical Upanishads, were translated from Sanskrit into Persian at the initiative of Emperor Akbar and Prince Dara Shukoh, respectively, in the 16th and 17th centuries; it remained a one-way street. Again, when the British came, they began translating Indian texts into English in large numbers from about 1780 onwards, but translation of English or other Western literary texts into the Indian languages gained mass and momentum only about a century later.

Such indifference and apathy towards the rest of the world is difficult to account for, except perhaps in transcendent metaphysical terms in which traditionally in India, one is encouraged to explore and understand one's inner self rather than the outside material world which is an illusion, or *maya*, anyhow! This may seem to be not much of an explanation in our day and age, or perhaps even worse than no explanation, but that does not alter the fact that there was virtually no translation of any foreign literature into India until the latter half of the 19th century. This may alternatively be thought to be related to the phenomenon that traditionally, India showed no inclination either to conquer or to convert, and that the cultural hegemony of the vast Sanskrit cosmopolis, referred to above, was apparently achieved in a non-violent manner without battle or conquest.

Anyhow, some traces of such a non-material attitude towards the (rest of the) world may still be found in modern India. In 1897, some sixteen years before he self-translated his way to the Nobel prize, Tagore was invited to speak in Calcutta on the subject of Comparative Literature, and he began by saying that he would rather speak on what he in Bengali called '*vishva-sahitya*', i.e. World Literature. He then proceeded to talk at length about the self,

'Himself' (i.e. God), the soul, the heart, the truth and 'the innermost spirit' and 'the outside world'. It was only on the eleventh page of his 13-page lecture that he finally named some authors and works including, fleetingly, two Western writers, Tennyson and Kipling (Tagore 148; cited and discussed in Trivedi 2013: 18) In his youth, especially after his sojourn in England in his teens, he was taken up with the English Romantics and translated some extracts from authors such as Robert Burns, Thomas Moore and Byron, but these were more in the nature of youthful literary exercises.

In contrast, the greatest modern writer in Hindi, Premchand (1880–1936), showed a broader awareness of writers from several countries, whose works he went to the trouble of translating. He had begun writing in Urdu before he moved to Hindi, and had grown up devouring magical-fantastical Perso-Arabic narratives in their Urdu versions; later, he translated a selection (of 670 pages) of a vast comic episodic Urdu narrative written in a pre-novelistic mode titled *Fasana-e-Azad* into Hindi (1925). He also translated or adapted Maurice Maeterlinck's play *The Sightless* (into Urdu, 1919), a novel by George Eliot (*Silas Marner*, into Hindi, 1920–1921), a selection of twenty-three short stories by Tolstoy (into Hindi, 1923), Anatole France's novel *Thais* (into Hindi, 1925–1926), and had a supervisory hand in the translation of three plays by John Galsworthy (into Hindi, 1932–1933) (see Rai 1982: 270, 412). He found the time to bring these foreign works home while he wrote thirteen novels and over 300 short stories of his own before passing away at the age of 56. He may have been prompted to choose these authors for a variety of reasons, such as the award of the Nobel prize to Maeterlinck in 1911 and to Galsworthy in 1932 though the translation of his plays had already been in progress by then. But that does not detract from the affinity he apparently felt with them and his creative effort in translating them.

To look at the literary universe of just one more Indian writer, who like Tagore and Premchand is regarded as arguably the foremost modern writer in his language, Kannada, but who unlike them does not find a place in the *Longman Anthology*, Kuvempu (1904–1994) in his epic *Sri-Ramayana-Darshanam* (The Vision of the Ramayana), produces a litany of great writers from all over the world to whom he bows in reverence:

> To Homer, to Virgil, to Dante and Milton
> To Naranappa, to Pampa, to sage Vyasa
> To elders like Bhasa, Bhavabhuti and Kalidasa,
> To Narahari, Tulasidasa and Krittivasa,
> To Naranayya, Firdausi, Kamban and Aurobindo
> To the old, to the new, to elders and to young,
> Without considering the differences in time, space, speech and caste
> To all the art-masters of the world,
> Seeing divine greatness wherever the light is
> I bow down with folded hands.
>
> (trans. by and cited in Satyanath 2013: 71)

This is not as eclectic or random a list as it may at first appear. All the writers named here are Kuvempu's significant predecessors in being either epic poets of world stature, or writers who have narrated the Rama story before him, or both. Besides the four Western epic poets who are accorded the courtesy of being named first (or, alternatively, got out of the way before the richer resonances begin), we have four writers from Sanskrit, one from Persian, three from the author's own Kannada, four who each re-wrote the Ramayana in their own respective Indian languages, and one modern Indian epic poet, named last, who was the spiritual guru of Kuvempu. This could be said to be the poet's personal canon of World Literature, and it may not prove easy to think of another poet anywhere in the world who displays such a wide and cosmopolitan range in what is virtually the Acknowledgements page of his *magnum opus*.

Untranslatability and the need to translate

In some recent debates, the validity and the viability of World Literature has been questioned in the name of what is claimed to be untranslatable and therefore must forever remain outside and beyond reach. A major intervention here is by Emily Apter in her book *Against World Literature: On the Politics of Untranslatability*, in which the opening chapter is titled 'Untranslatables: A World System' (Apter 2013, 31–56), as if this system stood as a full-scale alternative to and repudiation of the translatables gathered under the rubric of World Literature. But this turns out to be more bark than bite for already in her Introduction, Apter had stated: 'Certainly, as this book will make clear, I endorse World Literature's deprovincialization of the canon and the way in which, at its best, it draws on translation to deliver surprising cognitive landscapes hailing from inaccessible linguistic folds ...' (Apter 2013, 2). But she is 'left uneasy', she adds, 'in the face of the entrepreneurial, bulimic drive to anthologize and curricularize the world's cultural resources' and therefore offers 'untranslatability as a deflationary gesture towards the expansionism ... of world-literary endeavours' (Apter 2013: 3). It is, apparently, not World Literature that she objects to but its rapid institutional success; what she wants to throw out really is not the baby but only the bath-water. Soon enough, a broad aggregation of similar and not so similar factors, including 'non-translation, mistranslation, incomparability and untranslatability' (Apter 2013: 4) emerges to form a common front against not World Literature but its current circulation and trending popularity.

There has, of course, been a more substantial older argument in favour of untranslatability which relates firstly to what used to be called 'culture-specific' words (until the cultural turn, when all words in any language were granted to be culture-specific more or less), and secondly, to scriptures. The first category comprises only a few words in any language, such as *avatar* or *pizza*, and because they are untranslatable, they are soon enough assimilated as such in other languages, thus obviating the need for translation. As for scriptures, the situation is again not universal but religion-specific, so to say. For example, while there was for centuries a stern prohibition against translating the Koran, which led to people from many parts of the world learning by rote parts of that text or even all of it in the original Arabic, the Bible has always been aggressively translated into thousands of languages as a main tool of conversion by spreading the word of the Lord in a user-friendly manner. Between these extremes of the 'holy untranslatable' and the fervently translatable lie shades of relative untranslatability, some of which are highlighted for example by Kate Crosby in her essay 'What Does Not Get Translated in Buddhist Studies'. The main varieties of untranslated religious texts according to Crosby are texts in remote source languages, texts for which suitable terminology does not exist in the target language, texts which are thought to be obscene in the target language, texts meant only for the initiated and therefore suitably abstruse, texts that are even longer than the Bible, or 'unliterary' ritualistic texts which may for example 'repeat the same few words a thousand times in slightly differing order' (Crosby 2005: 44–47). It would seem then that as distinct from what is deliberately left translated for various reasons, there is nothing that is untranslatable. This would not be news to Apter who in an earlier book, *The Translation Zone* (2006, where she was not arguing against World Literature) had formulated twenty theses on translation, of which the first was that 'nothing is translatable' and the last that 'everything is translatable' – which playful paradox may help us conclude, as it did Zhang Longxi, that '[u]ntranslatabilty is a misnomer' (Apter cited and discussed in Zhang Longxi, 2013: 56).

There is quite another kind of correlation between translation and wider circulation postulated by Pascale Casanova in her book *The World Republic of Letters,* a title that could be read as a characteristically French rendering of the term World Literature. In a chapter titled 'The Tragedy of Translated Men', she discusses the case of a writer such as Kafka, a Jew who lived in Prague but wrote not in Yiddish or Czech, but in German, and felt that he 'did not love [his] mother as she deserved … only because the German language prevented it' (cited in Casanova 2004: 273). Naming Mario de Andrade, Salman Rushdie, Nuruddin Farah and several others as sharing the same predicament, she characterizes such authors as 'translated' authors and speaks of the 'pathos of their situation' (Casanova 2004: 260, 262). Even when these authors willingly opted to write in the language they did, some of them characterize their act as not one of assimilationist submission but as one of rebellion. As Kateb Yacine put it, 'I write in French in order to say to the French that I am not French' (cited in Casanova 2004: 260).

It could be argued that such bravado is often no more than bluster and in any case self-serving. When all is said and done, and written and published, writers using a big metropolitan language have given themselves a chance to attain a considerably larger circulation and to be regarded potentially as part of World Literature. There has in fact been a surge all over the postcolonial world for writers to leave behind their own native languages and to begin writing in the language of the erstwhile colonial masters – with only the Kenyan novelist Ngugi wa Thiong'o providing a solitary example of a writer beginning to write in English and in mid-career reverting to writing in his native language, though Ngugi has latterly felt obliged to act as his own translator from Gikuyu into English. It is not easy to get away from the hegemony of master languages; it often turns out to be a double bind.

Ngugi's singular exception notwithstanding, literature is now produced mainly if not exclusively in the language of the colonizer in a large number of former colonies. Though mutually antipathetic in cultural and political terms, the Caribbean writers V. S. Naipaul and Derek Walcott, both Nobel winners, had in common that they both wrote in English. So have Chinua Achebe and Wole Soyinka, also a Nobel winner, from Nigeria. In his book *Translation and Globalization*, Michael Cronin reminds us of 'the Irish mass self-translation of the nineteenth century (from Irish speakers into English speakers)' (Cronin 2003: 154). In India, however, the prospect of English becoming the primary language of literary creation is yet so distant as to be even doubtful. English in India is still only one of the twenty-four major literary languages, and writers and readers in the other twenty-three languages do not feel particularly oppressed or eclipsed by English. The foremost literary prize in India, the Jnanpith, awarded annually since 1965, did not even consider books published in English until two years ago (Jnanpith n.d.)

Over the last decade or so, however, a new phenomenon has emerged in Indian publishing. About half a dozen young writers in English have come up who, unlike Salman Rushdie, Vikram Seth or Arundhati Roy, are published only in India and not in the West, do not look for Western critical endorsement or prizes, and are bought and read almost exclusively within India. To name the most prominent and best-selling of them, Chetan Bhagat and Anuja Chauhan write boy-meets-girl romances while ostensibly addressing some contemporary social issue in each book, Durjoy Datta writes Mills-and-Boon kind of romances plain and simple, while probably the biggest-seller of them all, Amish (sometimes by-lined as Amish Tripathi), has completed a mythological trilogy on the life of the god Shiva and is now into another series of novels on the god Rama, all employing not a sublime high register but instead the demotic colloquial English idiom of our day. Each of these writers sells more than any writer in any of the Indian languages, probably because though each of those languages may have many more speakers, it is the Anglophone middle class in India which has the money and the leisure to spend on books to read for pleasure. On the Amazon India website, the top 20 sellers in the category 'Literature and Fiction' comprise 15 books by Indian authors and 5 by foreign authors, including 7 titles by Amish alone (Amazon India n.d.) So far, what is variously called popular fiction, airport fiction or pulp fiction in English (or in English translation, such as books by Paulo Coelho), was the same globally, at each and every airport. But the bookshops in Indian airports now display two different series of bestsellers in two separate shelves, of which one has books by

Indian authors, all written originally in English, and the other by all others, whether written in or translated into English.

This is a form of globalization too but with a difference, for the Indian shelf represents literature produced in the global language for local consumption. It therefore complicates the spread of English as the preferred language of literary creation in more and more areas of the world. The world will probably become increasingly monolingual with English putting more and more distance between itself and the remaining 6,000 languages of the world, in the process also reducing proportionately the need to translate much from any of them and thus further facilitating the flattening of the world. World Literature so far has been inconceivable without translation but, just conceivably, in the world to come, the brave new word may belong to English alone.

Works cited

Amazon India. www.amazon.in/gp/bestsellers/books/1318157031/ref=pd_zg_hrsr_b_1_2 (accessed 31 May 2017).

Apter, Emily 2006. *The Translation Zone: A New Comparative Literature*. Princeton: Princeton University Press.

Apter, Emily 2013. *Against World Literature: On the Politics of Untranslatability*. London: Verso.

Bassnett, Susan 1993. *Comparative Literature: A Critical Introduction*. Oxford: Blackwell.

Casanaova, Pascal 2004. *The World Republic of Letters*, tr. from the French by M.B. DeBoise. Cambridge MA: Harvard University Press.

Cronin, Michael 2003. *Translation and Globalization*. London: Routledge.

Crosby, Kate 2005. 'What Does Not Get Translated in Buddhist Studies and the Impact on Teaching', in *Translation and Religion: Holy Untranslatable?*, ed. Lynne Long. Clevedon: Multilingual Matters, pp. 41–53.

Damrosch, David 2003. *What Is World Literature?* Princeton: Princeton University Press.

Damrosch, David (ed.) 2004. *The Longman Anthology of World Literature*, vols. A to F. New York: Pearson/Longman.

Damrosch, David 2006. 'Where is World Literature?' in *Studying Transcultural Literary History*, ed. Gunilla Lindberg-Wada. Berlin: Walter de Gruyter, pp. 211–220.

Feeney, Denis 2016. *Beyond Greek: The Beginnings of Latin Literature*. Cambridge: Harvard University Press.

Jnanpith. https://en.wikipedia.org/wiki/Jnanpith_Award (accessed 21 May 2017).

Kuruvilla, Elizabeth 2015. 'The Modern Revivalists', *livemint* [newspaper], 24 January. www.livemint.com/Leisure/lFimgXZsUzD2jccaCD4VhI/The-modern-revivalists.html (accessed 1 May 2017).

Moretti, Franco 2000. 'Conjectures on World Literature', *New Left Review* 1:55–67

Moretti, Franco 2006. 'Evolution, World Systems, Weltliteratur', in *Studying Transcultural Literary History*, ed. Gunila Lindberg-Wada. Berlin: Walter de Gruyter, 2006, pp. 113–121.

Mukherjee, Meenakshi 1971. *The Twice Born Fiction*. Heinemann: New Delhi and London.

Mukherjee, Sujit 1981. *Translation as Discovery and Other Essays on Indian Literature in English Translation*. New Delhi: Allied Publishers.

Murty Classical Library of India. www.murtylibrary.com/people.php (accessed 1 May 2017).

Rai, Amrit 1982. *Premchand: A Life* trans. Harish Trivedi. New Delhi: People's Publishing House.

Rosenbaum, S. P. 1979. 'The Longest Journey: E. M. Forster's Refutation of Idealism', in *E. M. Forster: A Human Exploration: Centenary Essays*, eds G. K. Das and John Beer. London: Macmillan, pp. 32–54.

Satyanath, T. S. 2013. 'World Literature in the Context of Indian Literatures', in *Interdisciplinary Alter-natives in Comparative Literature*, eds. E. V. Ramakrishnan, Harish Trivedi and Chandra Mohan. New Delhi: Sage Publications, pp. 63–74.

Spivak, Gayatri Chakravorty 2003. *A Death of Discipline*. New York: Columbia University Press.

Stockholm Collegium of World Literary History. www.orient.su.se/polopoly_fs/1.146090.1378801800!/menu/standard/file/SCWHL2013.pdf (accessed 5 May 2017).

Trivedi, Harish. 2006. 'In Our Own Time, On Our Own Terms', in *Translating Others* Vol. I, ed. Theo Hermans. Manchester: St Jerome, pp. 102–119.

Trivedi, Harish 2013. 'Comparative Literature, World Literature and Indian Literature: Concepts and Models', in *Interdisciplinary Alter-natives in Comparative Literature*, eds. E. V. Ramakrishnan, Harish Trivedi and Chandra Mohan. New Delhi: Sage Publications, pp. 17–34.

Zhang, Longxi 2013. 'Crossroads, Distant Killing and Translation: On the Ethics and Politics of Comparison', in *Comparison: Theories, Approaches, Uses*, eds Rita Felski and Susan Friedman. Stanford: Stanford University Press, pp. 46–63.

2 *World-literature in French*

Monolingualism, Francopolyphonie and the dynamics of translation

Charles Forsdick

[Language] sweeps. It's like a tide. But that's why people are so aggressive and so angry about language. It's that thing that you can't control which makes you the most uncomfortable. That's why nations are always legislating languages. The French have an academy for it, the Japanese don't allow foreign words into their newspapers. They have a special vocabulary, a special language to show foreign words because they don't want the contamination. I think that speaks to the mongoose-like power of language, how difficult it is to contain.

(Celayo and Shook 2008, 17)

In the global languagescape, new forms of linguistic distribution are in play. […] As today's diasporic citizenries know, satellite television, email, internet telephone have transformed the linguistic face of migrant experience, and altered the relationship of migrancy to home. This is another reason why even the experts have no idea what the world will look like linguistically a hundred years from now. For many of the same reasons, we have no idea what literature will look like either.

(Pratt 2011, 279)

In the period of almost a decade since its publication, much critical attention has been paid to the manifesto—published in *Le Monde* in March 2007—advocating a *littérature-monde en français* [world-literature in French]. Jacqueline Dutton (2016, 413) has recently calculated that over 300 articles and chapters have subsequently been devoted to the phenomenon, but little of this commentary has explored the complex questions of translation implicit in, but never fully elucidated by, this polemical intervention. It is indeed striking that much discussion of *littérature-monde* often seems to be locked into the monolingual, Francocentric agenda created by the manifesto itself, despite the fact that one of the earliest critics of the document, Jean-Pierre Cavaillé (2007), signaled from the outset these limitations: 'What is unbearable is that the world, the wide world, is once again perceived, viewed exclusively via the small end of the telescope of the French language, and from its undisputed and indisputable centre.' The chapter responds to this critical echo chamber by seeking to explore the (un)translatability of *littérature-monde*. The phenomenon is understood initially as one that emerged in a specifically French and Francophone niche, taking little account of related and competing concepts—such as 'World Literature' or *Weltliteratur*—that have emerged in other linguistic traditions. *Littérature-monde en français* has been allowed to emerge and evolve, as a result, as a strangely oxymoronic category, monolingually French yet still aspiring towards the global reach that the hyphenation of 'literature' and 'world' implies. Following Mary Louise Pratt's speculative comments on the futures of multilingual, translingual literary forms, the final section of the chapter addresses the question of what a post-monolingual *world-literature in French* might resemble—and whether such a designation can remain in any way meaningful in the twenty-first century.

To understand the emergence and evolution of *world-literature in French*, there is a need to distinguish this phenomenon from an earlier and related literary movement from which it in part emerged, *littérature voyageuse* [travelling literature], the definition of which was first suggested in another manifesto fifteen years earlier (Le Bris et al. 1992). The *littérature voyageuse* and *littérature-monde* manifestos have a number of signatories in common (not least their initiator, Michel Le Bris), and both are linked closely to the 'Etonnants voyageurs' festival, held annually since its launch in 1990 in Saint Malo, where many of the authors associated with them periodically gather.[1] A mode of writing committed to travel and to various forms of engagement with the world understood as a physically lived reality, *littérature voyageuse* was a late twentieth-century movement actively formed in—and defined by—translation (into French). Its signatories were primarily French (with exceptions including the Francophone Swiss travel writer Nicolas Bouvier and the translingual author of Scottish origin, Kenneth White), but this collective was actively and openly inspired, both transnationally and translingually, by contemporary English-language travel writing, as well as by postcolonial works of Anglophone 'world fiction' from the late 1980s and early 1990s. A particular focal point for such activity, *Granta* served as a major influence: the short-lived *littérature voyageuse* periodical *Gulliver* was, in many ways, a French-language equivalent of the British publication, often including translations of articles that had already appeared in the English-language publication (on *Gulliver*, see Forsdick and Hindson 2013).

This earlier French movement proposed a reinvigoration of *fin-de-siècle* French literature through engagement with a range of texts from a number of different language traditions, of which a representative and illustrative range was set out in a bibliographical appendix to the collection of essays that served as its 1992 manifesto. The principal criterion for inclusion under the label *littérature voyageuse* was—beyond a commitment to acting as 'une littérature qui dise le monde' [a literature that expresses the world]—availability in French, with the result that *littérature voyageuse* operated according to a dual movement, defined both expansively (in terms of texts' varied cultural and linguistic origins), but also restrictedly (in relation to their circulation in French translation). Whereas *littérature voyageuse* was associated more with an 'asphyxiated' *fin-de-siècle* French national literature that claimed to be open at last to influences translated from elsewhere, *littérature-monde en français* emerged in 2007, as its name suggests, as a more actively and knowingly transnational phenomenon, but one nevertheless circumscribed linguistically—as the supplementary *en français* makes abundantly clear—by the linguistic parameters of the Francosphere.

The principal aim of the 2007 manifesto was to challenge the relationship between 'French' and 'Francophone' literature (i.e., texts written in France, and those produced in the wider French-speaking world), and to suggest (although not necessarily to demonstrate, given the persistently Gallocentric nature of publishing in French) that alternative configurations of creation, circulation, reception and recognition were possible. Unlike the polycentric practices of the global English-language literature industry, the dynamics of publishing in the French-speaking world have long been regulated according to a logic that, on the one hand, perpetuates a binary relationship between 'French' and 'Francophone' authors, and, on the other, imposes a dynamics that ensures a center-periphery approach based around the centrality of Paris in the production and circulation of texts (Collins 2015). It is true that alternative publishing hubs have emerged, not least in Quebec, and innovations in digital dissemination now provide publishing possibilities previously unimaginable. These developments remain eclipsed, however, largely as a result of the relative lack of influence (and related inability to distribute throughout the French-speaking world) of publishers outside France. There is no denying that these initial intra-francophone concerns, seen as central to debates regarding *littérature-monde*, remain fundamental to efforts to decolonize the persistent French-Francophone divide, but they nevertheless deflect attention away from the complex translation dynamics that might characterize a genuinely transnational world literature identified with a range of multilingual practices.

In this context, the adoption of the hyphenated term *littérature-monde* is to be understood as one of a set of other recent French terms relating to networks and systems including *histoire-monde, cinéma-monde, identité-monde, culture-monde*, and perhaps most significantly the Martiniquan intellectual Edouard Glissant's concept of the *Tout-Monde*. Rejecting unhyphenated alternatives such as *littérature mondiale* (a direct translation of the English 'world literature'), these designations appear to insist on the category of a closed system, an 'autonomous, self-sufficient, imagined community,' access to which is possible 'through both a common medium (literature) *and*'—despite the resonance with Glissant—'a common language (French)' (Kippur 2015, 8; emphasis in the original). The emphases of the *littérature-monde* manifesto on production in a single language continue to raise questions about the credibility and sustainability of an exclusively French-language *world-literature* in any transnational context, increasingly itself characterized by what Yasemin Yildiz (2012) has dubbed—in a German context, but one extendable to other spheres—a 'post-monolingual' condition.

The launch at the Etonnants Voyageurs festival in 2014 of two *world-literature* prizes in France—one for a work in French; the other for a text originally written in another language, but available in French translation—suggests an emerging recognition of multilingual questions and the importance of translation in their resolution. The two track approach continues to resonate, however, with issues central to this chapter: i.e., does this development reflect a new inclusivity, moving beyond initial French-language emphases to encompass work in different language traditions? Or does it instead perpetuate exclusivity by ensuring a distinction (and creating an implicit hierarchy) between texts written directly in French and those translated from languages other than French? In the absence of any clear statement or demonstration beyond the original 2007 manifesto, it remains unclear whether the 'world' in *littérature-monde* manifests itself, in this way, as fundamentally divided along linguistic lines, or whether an active inclusion of the concept of translation within its purview might open up new possibilities, currently unimagined. The reflections that follow deploy the apparent limitations of *littérature-monde en français* not as means of perpetuating the already substantial critique of the movement, but as a way of suggesting a new approach to this statement of literary aspiration by exploring contemporary approaches in both France and the wider Francosphere to literature and linguistic diversity. The chapter seeks to situate questions of language choice in relation to those of translation—with translation seen not only as a mode of circulation of texts between different linguistic spheres (as was the ultimately rather limited case with the *littérature voyageuse* movement, for which the vector of that circulation was exclusively *from* other languages *into* French), but instead as a site of creativity in its own right. Rather than seeing writing as variously monolingual, translingual or multilingual, the chapter outlines the possibilities afforded by understanding the world literary text itself as an increasingly dynamic interlingual 'translation zone' (a term suggested by Emily Apter—in a 2006 text translated into French in 2015 as *Zones de traduction*—to designate 'sites that are "in-translation", that is to say, belonging to no single, discrete language or single medium of communication'). Apter's designation is a useful one in the current context, for it makes explicit the literary and linguistic dimensions of a cognate concept, dubbed by Mary Louise Pratt a 'contact zone,' which describes 'an attempt to invoke the spatial and temporal co-presence of subjects previously separated by geographic and historical disjunctures, and whose trajectories now intersect' (Pratt 1992, 7). These contrasting ideas of 'co-presence' and 'disjuncture' encapsulate the phenomena of multilingualism and translation that underpin the reflections that follow, with the readability (or otherwise) of various multilingual practices and other literary manifestations of linguistic plurality linked to an understanding of translation as one of the emerging paradigms for exploring cultural production in the twenty-first century.

As this opening discussion has underlined, the limitations of the movement seeking a *littérature-monde en français* were apparent from the outset, most notably in the monolingual description of the very object—at once inclusive and exclusive—that the term designated, and to the production of which the authors associated with it aspired. This was not surprising, for the concept of world literature—and the long search, under that frustratingly vague title, for a form of post-national or transnational literature—has often tended to privilege a focus on the thematic, or an interest in the dynamics of production and circulation. This tendency in definition has often been to the detriment of any consideration of a specific poetics attentive to different forms of language use that may transcend rootedness in particular linguistic zones and foreground the actively translingual or translational elements that the association with 'world' may be seen to imply. These tendencies are already apparent in some of the earliest articulations of an emerging world literature project: these include Goethe's call in January 1827, almost two centuries before the 2007 publication of the *littérature-monde* manifesto, in an exchange with his young interlocutor Johann Peter Eckermann; or two decades later, in a very different text (*The Communist Manifesto*), the adoption by Marx and Engels themselves of the notion of *Weltliteratur*, and its harnessing to world revolutionary aspirations. Despite the cosmopolitanism of his range of reference, Goethe's principal concern was arguably the reinvigoration of German-language literature; and far from celebrating a literature that transcended national boundaries, Marx and Engels were in fact more concerned about the domestication of any such a development by the *bourgeoisie*. Despite apparent continuities in the types of literary production they appear to describe, from Goethe and the *Communist Manifesto* (1848) to the *littérature-monde* manifesto (2007), there is considerable historical, geographical and political distance (as well as clear shifts in what these terms designate). It is surprising nevertheless that in formulating their understanding of *littérature-monde*, Le Bris and his co-signatories failed to acknowledge the existence of an already extensive body of thinking, stretching back into the nineteenth century but also highly visible in the contemporary Anglophone academy and publishing world, on the subject of literature in post-national frames—surprising not least because this failure to acknowledge is in many ways further symptomatic evidence of the monolingualism with which the French movement is associated.[2]

Although the contexts of production of these interventions has changed so radically over time, there are inevitably continuities between the differing concepts of world literature with which they engage, not least in terms of the extent to which these seek to disrupt the relationship between literature and the conventional frames within which it is produced and consumed—a disruption summed up by Edward W. Said in his introduction to a 2001 collection of articles on 'Globalizing Literary Study': 'An increasing number of us feel that there is something basically unworkable or at least drastically changed about the traditional frameworks in which we study literature' (Said 2001, 64). Said alludes primarily here to the nation-state and its afterlives, and suggests that postcolonial approaches to literary production have implications that are genuinely global, and are not restricted to former colonized cultures and their diasporas. By factoring into such observations an additional and active awareness of translation, questions of language become central to these concerns, in terms not only of the cross-national and cross-lingual circulation of texts, but also of the possibility of forms of post-monolingual creativity.

It is striking—as has been noted above—that the publication of the French manifesto has attracted more attention among Anglophone scholars than it did in France itself, a development perhaps unsurprising given the increasing interest in the English-speaking world in 'world literature' as an object of study and a category of production, circulation and reception. A series of publications have explored the content and context of the French intervention, and sought to draw it into wider debates in the English-speaking academy.[3] One reason for this interest in the manifesto was that, despite its lapses of logic and critical blind spots, the text served as a fresh focus for a range of issues situated loosely in the overlapping fields of: comparatism, postcolonialism, translation, the framing of national literatures, and associated questions of language choice (or more specifically the ways in which writing does or does not capture – to borrow again from Yildiz – the 'post-monolingual' nature of the contemporary world).[4] The manifesto invited recognition and closer scrutiny of the emergence and existence of literatures in French that have long refused to respect national and even linguistic boundaries. Its apparently constitutive emphasis on a persistent French monolingualism triggered, however, additional questions as to whether such a genuinely multilingual literature remains possible, or whether there is a tendency for discussions of the subject of 'world literature,' whatever their linguistic context, to revert to exclusively monolingual sets of assumptions.

As has been suggested above, in failing to acknowledge the flaws in the globalized systems of literary production, dissemination and validation (evident not least in the continued Gallocentrism of the French-language literary marketplace explored above), the manifesto risked perpetuation of the very asymmetries it purported to expose. Far from being a reflection of a new openness, it might even be argued that the prize system it celebrated—and the publishing practices this system supports—in fact reproduces a conservatism and centralization in French-language literary production as well as its domination by specifically French national publishers. As Graham Huggan (2001) has demonstrated, the validation by a former colonial culture of literature from the Global South can reveal a 'marketing of the margins' that conceals a specifically postcolonial exoticism that tolerates limited and ultimately controlled literary and linguistic experimentation. There is accordingly resonance between the questions raised by *world-literature in French* and those that have for some time characterized postcolonial literatures more generally. The major blind spot in the manifesto relating to language, evident in the oxymoronic juxtaposition in its title of 'world-literature' and 'in French,' has long been apparent also in studies of Francophone postcolonial literary production, where a near exclusive emphasis on the postcolonial writer's often antagonistic relationship to French has eclipsed any wider evidence in their work of a translational dynamics encapsulating tensions between languages. In studying the poetics of *littérature-monde* and Francophone postcolonial literature, there is a need to address the implications for literary creation of functional multilingualism as well as everyday repertoires of multiple languages.

The shift in *littérature-monde* towards such monolingual emphases is striking. As has been suggested above, the imaginary library of the 1990s movement from which it emerged, *littérature voyageuse*, was contained in a bibliography included in its 1992 'manifesto,' and admitted works translated into French. It included, as a result, a range of authors, Anglophone and Hispanophone as well as writers in other prominent world languages, from Europe and the Americas (from Herta Müller to Wilfred Thesiger, from Werner Herzog to V.S. Naipaul). *World-literature in French*, by its very designation, does not entertain inclusion of such works in translation, and maintains language (i.e., creation in French) as one of the key criteria for inclusion. This does not necessarily restrict its corpus to texts written in the French-speaking world, and its signatories include prominent translingual writers such as the Chinese-born Dai Sijie, whose migration towards French-language culture has been accompanied by the choices inherent in parallel processes of linguistic switching, and is part of the creation of what has been called (in Dai's case) 'overseas Chinese literature' (Laifong 2006). It also encompasses authors such as Nancy Huston, who practices self-translation, and who regularly writes a single literary text for two different linguistic communities, Anglophone and Francophone. By acknowledging only part of such production, however (i.e., that published in French), even an apparently expansive category such as self-translation is reduced according to an 'interpretive methodology that still appears to depend on the rootedness of texts in particular linguistic and cultural contexts' (Kippur 2015, 12). The signatories also include Ananda Devi, an author who regularly deploys self-translation as a form of literary creativity, and who also adopts the translational dynamics of her Indian Ocean heritage to challenge any attempts to reduce her to a monolingually Francophone writer. Devi is also a translator in her own right, whose *Terre Maudite*—for example—is much more than a interlingual translation of David Dabydeen's *The Counting House*, but an exploration of the axes linking Indian Ocean and Indo-Guyanese cultures, as well as a transposition of Dabydeen's concerns to the context of French colonial histories (Devi and Waters 2013).

Despite the multiple practices, as well as diverse cultural and linguistic affiliations of its signatories, the manifesto continues, therefore, to highlight the *in French* (a tag that is significantly missing from the collection of essays published by the manifesto signatories in May 2007; see Le Bris and Rouaud 2007), and generates a partiality and selectivity that shapes in very specific ways the understanding of the 'world' in *littérature-monde*. There is an implicit (and even neo-colonial) reassertion of the dominance of French in the multilingual zones of the Francosphere, with production in French privileged over that other languages with which it has long coexisted in local repertoires (e.g., Wolof in Senegal, or Tahitian in Polynesia), or over that in post-contact languages (such as the francophone Creoles of the Caribbean and Indian Oceans). In addition, significant bi-cultural works such as those of the Haitian-American Edwidge Danticat—written in English, yet belonging firmly through their subject matter and intertextual resonances to the French-speaking world—are themselves denied access to the category. The risk remains that, despite increasing sensitivity to questions of translation, understandings of transnational or postcolonial literary production—in various contexts, perhaps notably Anglophone—remain monolingual, falling into the trap identified by Harish Trivedi (1999, 272) who also saw postcolonialism itself as having 'ears only for English,' privileging not only a single language but also a dominant language.

As Vijay Kumar has noted: 'We live in a society where heteroglossia is commonplace. It's a society where, if you seek to represent that society in a single language, no matter what that language is, you are in some profound way distorting the reality' (Kumar 2007, 104). This observation is linked to what Alison Phipps (2013) has called a more general 'unmooring' of languages in the twenty-first century, a situation generated in part because one of the key shifts inherent in the challenge of diversity is a recognition that the mono-lingualizing tendencies of historically centralized states such as France and the USA (tendencies often shored up by their cultural and literary institutions) are yielding increasingly to the contemporary condition of post-monolingualism. On the one hand, as a first possible step in this direction, *world-literature in French* seeks positively and inclusively to encompass multiple sites in which French is used to varying degrees as a shared language, and may as result be seen to acknowledge the semiodiversity that scholars such as Claire Kramsch consider essential to the study of languages and cultures. In Kramsch's terms:

> Monolingualism is a handicap, but so is the assumption that one language = one culture = adherence to one cultural community. Monolingualism is the name not only for a linguistic handicap but for a dangerously mono-lithic traffic in meaning. The problem [...] is not a lack of glossodiversity but of semiodiversity.
>
> (Kramsch 2006, 102)

World-literature in French can thus encompass works written in the same language but produced across multiple countries and continents, and may also acknowledge what Bakhtin called (almost a century ago) the 'heterology' of the apparently monolingual text—or what Derrida tellingly dubbed the 'monolingualism of the other' (see Candler Hayes 2012). This semiodiversity can also include the creation of a poetics, evident in modernist literature as well as—with different emphases—in postcolonial writing, that embeds various forms of orality within the literary text. On the other hand, however, by downplaying or even denying the place of what Kramsch dubs a complementary 'glossodiversity,' *world-literature in French* steers away from any recognition that French, English, Spanish and the world languages often seen as the media of world literature are not only languages variegated in their usage in this way, requiring, as a result, approaches that are more 'global and het-erodox' (Dubois and Mbembe 2014, 42); they are also a means of communication that exists in persistently and increasingly diglossic and polyglossic situations, not least in single countries such as France or Britain or Australia or the USA (see Rosenwalt 2008), where they are systematically subject to processes of translation, but also drawn into new linguistic and cultural phenomena such as creolization and translanguaging. Literature can, as a result, be seen as an increasingly multilingual formation, leading—as Simon Gikandi (2014) has suggested in a recent issue of PMLA—to the 'provincialization' of English (and indeed of French and other majority languages). Openness to a wider range of languages, or at least to a variety of linguistic interconnections, is integral to a reconfiguration of the frames in which literature emerges, meaning that a concept of literary belonging that allies a single language and to a unified geography (whether national or transnational) is increasingly redundant.

Studies of contemporary literature have recently responded to these linguistic, cultural and ideological concerns by actively foregrounding questions of translation, not only as a key phenomenon that enables reading interlingually across traditions, but as a source of resistance to and even incomprehension of the status quo. Translation has progressively embedded itself in understandings of the actual production of the translingual and transnational literary text, as if it is not only a mode of circulation and critical consumption, but also a site of creativity in its own right. A recent proliferation of studies on exophonic writing—whose authors opt to operate in languages other than their mother tongue—has underlined the contemporary visibility of the phenomenon in a variety of contexts, whilst excavating its historical precedents and their cross-cultural reach. Steven Kellman (2000) provided one of the first overviews, presenting translingualism as the active disruption of linguistic and national boundaries, and as the defiance of any attempt to create clear hierarchies between them. Importantly, however, his work suggests that there cannot be a universal understanding of translingualism. Translingual writing in English has, for instance, a dynamic of its own, associated with the dominant role (as well as the dominant scale) of the Anglosphere, but also attenuated by its polycentric nature, as a result of which there are clear tensions between Anglophone translingualism and that in other languages. The French case remains very different, not least because the linguistic strangeness generated by authors who migrate from other languages into French is more often associated not with (what Evelyn Nien-Ming Ch'ien dubs) the disruptive 'weirding' evident in the work of exophonic Anglophone authors such as Junot Diaz (Ch'ien 2004), but with a knowing intimacy with, proximity to and often deep respect for the French language—something the appointment of a number of translingual authors to the linguistically conservative *Académie française*, most recently François Cheng, Michael Edwards and Andrei Makine, makes abundantly clear.

Moving beyond the translingual towards the actively translational, recent studies such as Rebecca Walkowitz's (2015) *Born Translated* and Fiona Doloughan's (2016) *English as a Literature in Translation* have begun to suggest how, in English-language literature, translation is not secondary to much contemporary literature, but exists instead as an element integral to its production, linked closely to the poetics underpinning its creation. '[T]ranslation,' writes Walkowitz,

> functions as a thematic, structural, conceptual, and sometimes even typographical device. These works are *written for translation*, in the hope of being translated, but they are also often written as translations, pretending to take place in a language other than the one in which they have, in fact, been composed.
>
> (Walkowitz 2015, 4; emphasis in the original)

Much of Walkowitz's analysis overlaps with arguments around translingual writing, exploring texts that circulate in multiple languages so that the distinction between original and translation collapses. Underpinning this reflection is the idea that English is itself a language marked by increasing semiodiversity, and is what Alastair Pennycook calls 'a language in translation, a language of translingual use' (Pennycook 2008, 34).

The emphasis in this work is on writing in English, and for those interested in elaborating links between these patterns and other linguistic traditions, there are real risks of Anglocentrism—and of universalizing a dominant case. As Pascale Casanova's recent work *La Langue mondiale: traduction et domination* suggests: 'Translation and collective bilingualism are phenomena to be understood not "against" but "from the starting point of" linguistic domination and its effects: instead of avoiding the relationship of power between languages, these phenomena reproduce it' (Casanova 2015, 10). What is, as a result, currently unclear is the extent to which these reflections on literature as a 'translation zone' can be translated to other contexts, most notably—in the light of the debates regarding *littérature-monde en français*—that of French-language production. Alastair Pennycook describes nevertheless a more general process of 'language fortification,' a reassertion of monolingualism as a key characteristic of literature, whether this be conceived in national, regional or even global frames (Pennycook 2008, 36–40). Although his focus is again on English, it is striking that his analysis draws on the work of the Martinican *créolistes*, and is informed by the contrast between a *diversité*, which tends to essentialize competing differences, and a notion of *diversalité*, that encourages the recognition of new linguistic configurations and transformations (Pennycook 2008, 37–38). Such a distinction resonates with Walter Benjamin's identification of the 'basic error of the translator,' i.e., that 'he preserves the state in which his own language happens to be instead of allowing his language to be powerfully affected by the foreign tongue.' Understanding contemporary literature as a multilingual, translational space transmits this idea of 'productive interlingual interference,' shifting from the dynamics of transfer between source text and a translated equivalent, into qualities intrinsic in the poetics of literary creativity.

Such an understanding of literary potential echoes the observation of Reine Maylaerts on the ways in which multilingualism poses both challenges and opportunities for translation studies:

> Traditional definitions considered translation, implicitly or explicitly, as the *full* transposition of *one* source language message by *one* target language message for the benefit of a *monolingual* target public. Accordingly, the translation process would transfer the source language message from the source culture into the target culture, translations thus taking place between linguistically and geographically separated cultures. [...] At the heart of multilingualism, we find translation. Translation is not taking

place *in between monolingual* realities but rather *within multilingual* realities. In multilingual cultures (assuming there are such things as monolingual cultures), translation contributes to creating culture, in mutual exchange, resistance, interpenetration.

(Maylaerts 2012, 519)

Contemporary manifestations of these phenomena in literature need, of course, to be historicized in relation to a long tradition of multilingual writing and the production of 'translation effects' in the creative text. These are evident in early modern writing, before the clear codification of literary language, and can also be seen in the *hétérolinguisme* of the nineteenth-century Quebec novel or in the estrangement strategies adopted by European writers in the late nineteenth and early twentieth century, including poets such as Mallarmé, seeking clearer understanding of their own medium of expression (Taylor-Batty 2013). Contemporary examples of the literary text as 'translation zone' seem to indicate new directions, however, as translation exists 'firmly *in* the text, not *inbetween* texts,' and as there is a shift away from its traditional definition as the replacement of one language by another, of one literary text by another.

Such practices are far from normalized, despite increasing evidence in innovative phenomena in literary production such as self-translation, multilingual composition and the forms of translanguaging that undermine notions of literature's residual monolingualism. Although such work is no longer necessarily seen as experimental or *avant-garde*, with popular authors such as the Dominican-American Junot Diaz adopting an actively disruptive cross-lingual poetics, the question remains as to whether publishers and readers will support such experimentation. At the same time, these innovations are informed by the Glissantian notion of writing 'in the presence of all the languages of the world' (Glissant 1996, 40), and explores the extent to which actively heterolingual approaches might also imply an underlying 'henolingualism,' a term coined by David Gramling (2016) to describe the deployment of a specific linguistic repertoire whilst always already attuned to the existence of other languages beyond its immediate reach. Within literary production in the Francosphere, these tendencies are particularly manifest in recent developments in postcolonial writing, to which the chapter turns in conclusion.

Francophone postcolonial texts were from the outset central to the *littérature-monde* manifesto (among whose signatories were key figures such as Alain Mabanckou, Anna Moï et Abdourahman Waberi), and it is in work belonging to this category that translational writing is becoming apparent—work dependent on the co-presence of languages and cultures, challenging ideas of linguistic and cultural stability and actively testing the limits of expression. There have been striking recent developments in the area of translation: Éditions Zulma has, for instance, in collaboration with the Quebecois publisher Mémoire d'encrier, recently launched a new imprint called Céytu, in which major Francophone postcolonial texts (by authors such as Bâ, Césaire and Le Clézio) will be translated into Wolof and made available in a different linguistic context (for further details, see http://www.ceytu.fr/). Such shifts occur in parallel to the emergence of the types of innovative, translational poetics to which I have referred above. Kavita Ashana Singh has recently, for instance, analyzed in these terms the work of the Martinican poet and translator Monchoachi (pseudonym of André Pierre-Louis). Monchoachi's work engages with the linguistic contact zones in which the writer operates by adopting what Singh calls 'complicated curations between Creoles and standardized European languages' (Singh 2014, 91). Literature that emerges from such a poetics of intratextual translation depends at the same time on the introduction of translational skills in the act of reading: 'Frequently written between tongues, then, this linguistic and literary form of creoleness calls on readers to, consciously or otherwise, engage in continuous translation as they navigate these bilingual and multilingual texts' (Singh 2014, 91), suggesting that understandings of world literature are as much about reception as they are about production. Writing by authors such as Monchoachi is not so much a challenge to the translator as a questioning of the usefulness or necessity or even possibility of translation itself, as the text achieves a form of expression that Lise Gauvin, drawing on the work of Edouard Glissant, has called a 'Tout-langue.' This is not the search for a universal language, but the development of a linguistic consciousness in which translation and solidarity with wider networks of multiples languages become apparent (Gauvin n.d.). Paul Bandia has identified the more general implications for French-language poetics of such a shift, i.e., the emergence in postcolonial contexts—in the wake of pioneering earlier writers such as Ahmadou Kourouma—of a 'heterolingual literature, where several languages or language varieties are at play, defying traditional monolingual translation principles and calling into question the status of the original versus the translated text' (Bandia 2014, 421; on Kourouma, see Corcoran 2016). Complementary tendencies are also evident in contemporary North African literature, in which understandings of the novel can be seen as increasingly 'pluralistic, polyphonic and polysemic,' developing Abdelkebir Khatibi's earlier reflections on literary bilingualisms and the status of North African literature in French as a 'permanent translation' (El-Shakry 2016, 13; on Khatibi, see Candler Hayes 2012, 203–204). The contemporary Moroccan author Abdelfattah Kilito claims, in the title of a recent collection, *Je parle toutes les langues, mais en arabe* (Kilito 2013), a playful reflection not only on the politics of languages, but also on the practical impact of a historically multilingual context on literary practice, i.e., the possibility of writing 'French,' but not 'in French.'

A focus on the politics and practices of language use is central to understanding those processes shaping and determining the production and reception of emerging forms of contemporary literature in the Francosphere, where the problematic term of the 'Francophone' is slowly but increasingly yielding to alternatives such as the 'Francopolyphone' or the 'Francopolygraphe' (see, e.g., Saint-Loubert 2016).[5] Such an approach necessitates active reflection on questions of language—and specifically issues of monolingualism, and the risks of viewing contemporary literary production within a series of cross-cultural yet linguistically singularized frames. A growing number of contemporary texts—operating as 'translation zones,' characterized by new interlingual and intralingual configurations—challenge the traditional ethnolinguistic nationalism of which literature has long been an essential vehicle, and which interventions such as the *world-literature in French* manifesto risk unwittingly perpetuating. Understanding the literary text as a 'translation zone' means acknowledging a range of literary practices: from an awareness of the shuttling between languages inherent in much translingual production (and in the self-translation with which this is often associated), to the mixing of different languages—or translanguaging—on which the author who actively adopts a multilingual poetics depends. At the same time, the translational can illuminate two types of multilingualism embedded in the literary text: internal to a language deployed, identifying an inherent variegation of expression; but also external to it, reliant on the dynamic movement between languages. The implication of both is a challenge to the idea that literary production begins in a unique language—and this leads to the potential provincialization of the dominant languages in which much 'world' literature has been produced, or in which it tends to circulate. The solution to the challenges identified in this chapter lies, in part, in the pursuit of genuinely transcultural, transnational and translingual approaches to literary history. It also lies in the associated development of critical reading practices, willing to identify emerging poetics and to engage with a persistently multilingual world in which different languages have always cohabited and interacted, but where that cohabitation and interaction is increasingly apparent.

Notes

1 For a more detailed discussion of links between the two movements, see Forsdick 2010.
2 The translation of Pascale Casanova's *World Republic of Letters* has nevertheless been influential in Anglophone discussions of world literature. On links between different conception of 'world literature', see Forsdick 2011.
3 See, for example, Salhi 2009, Hargreaves and Cloonan 2010, and Hargreaves, Forsdick and Murphy 2010.
4 There is a need nevertheless to acknowledge discussions of the ethnocentrism of a term such as 'post-monolingualism' in a world where everyday multilingualism through the deployment of linguistic repertoires has always already been in evidence; nevertheless it allows us to understand what Ingrid Piller (2016) has recently and helpfully called 'monolingual ways of seeing' the multilingual.
5 These terms, whilst highly evocative of the forms of cultural, literary and linguistic diversification discussed in this chapter, are only slowly gaining traction. Pierre Laurette and Hans-George Ruprecht published *Poétiques et imaginaires: francopolyphonie litteraire des Ameriques* in 1995; 'Francopolyphonies' is a well-established book series edited for Brill by Kathleen Gyssels and Christa Stevens; and *La Francopolyphonie* is the title of a journal produced by the Universitatea Liberă Internaţională din Moldova (ULIM).

Acknowledgement

This chapter was written while Charles Forsdick was AHRC Theme Leadership Fellow for 'Translating Cultures' (AH/N504476/1). The author records his gratitude for this support.

References

Apter, Emily. 2006. *The Translation Zone: A New Comparative Literature*. Princeton and Oxford: Princeton University Press. [Translated as *Zones de traduction*, trans. by Hélène Quiniou (Paris: Fayard, 2015).]

Bandia, Paul. 2014. 'Postcolonial literary heteroglossia: a challenge for homogenizing translation.' *Perspectives: Studies in Translatology* 20.4: 419–431.

Candler Hayes, Julie. 2012. 'Translation and the transparency of French.' *Translation Studies* 5.2: 201–216.

Casanova, Pascale. 2015. *La Langue mondiale: traduction et domination*. Paris: Seuil.

Cavaillé, Jean-Pierre. 2007. 'Francophones, l'écriture est polyglotte.' *Libération*, 30 March.

Celayo, Armando and David Shook. 2008. 'In darkness we meet: a conversation with Junot Díaz.' *World Literature Today*, March–April: 12–17.

Ch'ien, Evelyn Nien-Ming. 2004. *weird English*. Cambridge, MA and London: Harvard University Press.

Collins, Holly. 2015. 'The littérature-monde vs. the Parisian publishing empire.' *Romance Notes* 55.3: 495–508.

Corcoran, Patrick. 2016. 'The "untranslatability" of culture: Ahmadou Kourouma's *Allah n'est pas obligé*.' *Forum for Modern Language Studies* 52.3: 274–292.

Devi, Ananda and Julia Waters. 2013. 'Ananda Devi as writer and translator: in interview with Julia Waters.' In Kathryn Batchelor and Claire Bisdorff (eds), *Intimate Enemies: Translation in Francophone Contexts*. Liverpool: Liverpool University Press: 117–123.

Doloughan, Fiona. 2016. *English as a Literature in Translation*. London: Bloomsbury Academic.

Dubois, Laurent and Achille Mbembe. 2014. 'Nous sommes tous francophones.' *French Politics, Culture & Society* 32.2: 40–48.

Dutton, Jacqueline. 2016. 'World literature in French, littérature-monde, and the translingual turn.' *French Studies Bulletin* 70.3: 404–441.

El-Shakry, Hoda. 2016. 'Heteroglossia and the poetics of the roman maghrébin.' *Contemporary French and Francophone Studies* 20.1: 8–17.

Forsdick, Charles. 2010. 'From "literature voyageuse" to "littérature-monde": the manifesto in context.' *Contemporary French and Francophone Studies* 14.1: 9–17.

Forsdick, Charles. 2011. '"Worlds in collision": the languages and locations of world literature.' In Ali Behdad and Dominic Thomas (eds), *A Companion to Comparative Literature*. Oxford: Blackwell: 473–489

Forsdick, Charles, and Katy Hindson. 2013. 'France, Europe, the world: *Gulliver*, or the journal as vehicle of literary transformation.' In Charles Forsdick and Andy Stafford (eds), *La Revue: The Periodical in Modern French-Speaking Cultures*. Oxford: Peter Lang: 115–135.

Gauvin, Lise. n.d. 'De tourment de langage à la pensée du Tout-langue,' available at: http://mondesfrancophones.com/espaces/canadas/de-tourment-de-langage-a-la-pensee-du-tout-langue/ [last accessed 20 January 2017]

Gikandi, Simon. 2014. 'Editor's column: provincializing English.' *PMLA* 129. 1: 7–17.

Glissant, Édouard. 1996. *Introduction à une poétique du divers*. Paris: Gallimard.

Gramling, David. 2016. *The Invention of Monolingualism*. London: Bloomsbury Academic.

Hargreaves, Alec G. and William J. Cloonan (eds). 2010. '"Littérature-monde": new wave or new hype?' Special issue of *Contemporary French and Francophone Studies* 14.

Hargreaves, Alec G., Charles Forsdick, and David Murphy (eds). 2010. *Transnational French Studies: Postcolonialism and Littérature-monde*. Liverpool: Liverpool University Press.

Huggan, Graham. 2001. *The Postcolonial Exotic: Marketing the Margins*. London and New York: Routledge.

Kellman, Steven. 2000. *The Translingual Imagination*. Lincoln, NE: University of Nebraska Press.

Kilito, Abdelfattah. 2013. *Je parle toutes les langues, mais en arabe*. Arles: Actes Sud.

Kippur, Sara. 2015. *Writing It Twice: Self-Translation and the Making of a World Literature in French*. Evanston, IL: Northwestern University Press.

Kramsch, Claire. 2006. 'The traffic in meaning.' *Asia Pacific Journal of Education* 5: 99–104.

Kumar, T. Vijay. 2007. '"Postcolonial" describes you as a negative: an interview with Amitav Ghosh.' *Interventions* 9.1: 99–105.

Laifong, Leung. 2006. 'Overseas Chinese literature: a proposal for clarification.' In Maria Ng and Philip Holden (eds), *Reading Chinese Transnationalisms: Society, Literature, Film*. Hong Kong: Hong Kong University Press: 117–127.

Le Bris, Michel et al. 1992. *Pour une littérature voyageuse*. Brussels: Complexe.

Le Bris, Michel and Jean Rouaud (eds). 2007. *Pour une littérature-monde*. Paris: Gallimard.

'Manifeste pour une littérature-monde en français.' 2007. *Le Monde des Livres*, 15 March. [English translation by Daniel Simon: *World Literature Today*, March–April 2009: 54–56.]

Maylaerts, Reine. 2012. 'Multilingualism as a challenge for translation studies.' In Carmen Millán and Francesca Bartrina (eds), *The Routledge Handbook of Translation Studies*. New York: Routledge: 519–533.

Pennycook, Alasdair. 2008. 'English as a language always in translation.' *European Journal of English Studies* 12.1: 33–47

Phipps, Alison. 2013. 'Unmoored: language pain, porosity, and poisonwood.' *Critical Multilingualism Studies* 1.2: 96–118.

Piller, Ingrid. 2016. 'Monolingual ways of seeing multilingualism.' *Journal of Multilingual Discourses* 11.1: 25–33.

Pratt, Mary Louise 1992. *Imperial Eyes: Travel Writing and Transculturation*. New York and London: Routledge.

Pratt, Mary Louise. 2011. 'Comparative literature and the global languagescape.' In Ali Behdad and Dominic Thomas (eds), *A Companion to Comparative Literature*. Oxford: Blackwell: 273–295.

Rosenwalt, Lawrence Alan. 2008. *Multilingual America: Language and the Making of American Literature*. Cambridge: Cambridge University Press.

Said, Edward W. 2001. 'Globalizing literary study.' *Publications of the Modern Language Association* 116.1: 64–68.

Saint-Loubert, Laëtitia. 2016. 'Francopolyphonies in translation.' *Francosphères* 50.2: 183–196.

Salhi, Kamal (ed.). 2009. '"Littérature-monde en français": the literary politics of twenty-first-century France.' Special issue of *International Journal of Francophone Studies* 12.

Singh, Kavita Ashana. 2014. 'Translative and opaque: multilingual Caribbean writing in Derek Walcott and Monchoachi.' *Small Axe* 18.3: 90–106.

Taylor-Batty, Juliette. 2013. 'Modernism and Babel.' In *Multilingualism in Modernist Fiction*. New York: Palgrave Macmillan: 16–38.

Trivedi, Harish. 1999. 'The postcolonial or the transcolonial? Location and language.' *Interventions* 1.2: 269–272.

Walkowitz, Rebecca L. 2015. *Born Translated: The Contemporary Novel in an Age of World Literature*. New York: Columbia University Press.

Yildiz, Yasemin. 2012. *Beyond the Mother Tongue: The Post-Monolingual Condition*. New York: Fordham University Press.

3 Translation studies for a world community of literature[1]

Azucena G. Blanco

In 2013, Lawrence Venuti declared that 'World Literature cannot be conceptualized apart from translation' (Venuti 2013: 193) and what we are now starting to see is how the relationship between World Literature and translation is bringing about the transformation of comparative literature, a transformation which involves cooperation.[2]

This collaborative comparing is based on linguistic limitations, since it is an impossibility that all comparatists can know all the languages and literatures of the world, and this limitation is bound to have epistemological and political consequences. With this in mind, Otmar Ette has reconsidered, in several works,[3] Alexander von Humboldt's model of knowledge: one of relational, dialogical and transdisciplinary knowledge that requires collaborative thinking so as to establish connections through networks. Franco Moretti in 'Conjectures on World Literature' (2000) has similarly stated that in order to analyse world literature, there needs to be collaborative work between comparatists and specialists in particular national literatures. In this process, literary translation studies play a transversal role. Susan Bassnett in 'Reflections on Comparative Literature in the Twenty-First Century' emphasizes the critical role of translation studies. Bassnett considers comparative literature and translation studies to be ways of reading that are mutually beneficial as she argues that 'the crisis in comparative literature derived from excessive prescriptivism combined with distinctive culturally specific methodologies that could not be universally applicable or relevant (Bassnett 2006: 6).

Likewise David Damrosch who noted, in a debate on world literature for the twenty-first century that took place at the Freie Universität Berlin in 2013, that reflecting on the difficulties of translating from one language to another is a discourse that came into being with the idea of the nation state and consequent attempts to distinguish between national literatures. This seems to highlight the need to understand the political and linguistic background of textual analysis that forms the basis of this chapter's proposition: thinking around world literature involves a return to the possibilities of translation in a global and globalized world and in the publishing market. It also involves questioning the stagnation of ideas about national identity, a shift already underway at the end of the twentieth century, as articulated by Claudio Guillén in *Entre lo uno y lo diverso* (1985), who highlights the role that translation plays in our understanding of the world. As Michael Cronin puts it in *Translation and Globalization* (2003):

> If contemporary reality is inescapably multicultural and multinational, then it makes sense to look to a discipline which has mediation between cultures and languages as a central concern to assist us both in understanding globalization and in understanding what it might mean, and why it is sometimes so difficult, to be a citizen of the world.
>
> (Cronin 2003: 6)

A concept of community could occupy a central place in the relationship between world literature and Translation Studies in a cooperative model today. As we shall see below, this concept of community places the relationship between world literature and translation within a frame that traces a principle of *aesthetic equality* that was not part of earlier notions of *Weltliteratur*. In order to understand the factors that have determined these shifts, this chapter will consider the role that translation has played in the transformation of Romantic *Weltliteratur* into world literature as a *pluriversal* [4] community of literature. Literary translation shows that there is a need for cooperation and, as part of its fundamental role, translation creates community.

From *Weltliteratur* to world literature: community and literature

In 'Philology and 'Weltliteratur' (1952), Erich Auerbach underlined the problems of how human life was becoming standardized and losing cultural diversity, a diversity which he considered to be a presupposition for *Weltliteratur*. Auerbach was referring to a fear that was still too close at that time: the movement of an equalizing, unifying mass that Canetti would speak of in *Crowds and Power* (1960). Auerbach denounced one of the most dangerous aspects of the totalization of universal literature, that in its embodiment 'herewith the notion of *Weltliteratur* would be at once realized and destroyed' (1969: 809). Instead, he distinguished two roles that *Weltliteratur* had to play: it should be not only what it is common and human, but humanity itself engaged in fruitful intercourse between its members. 'Our earth,' Auerbach considered must be, 'the domain of *Weltliteratur*'.[5] That is to say, Auerbach showed that world literature was both connected to a concept of plural community and had an aesthetic role to play in the community. World and literature were in this way indisputably connected.

Others have followed the path marked out by Auerbach, such as Edward Said. When in 1975, he joined the debate on the ontology of the work of art in 'The World, the Text and the Critic', he referred to the need to return to setting out the relationship between text and world: 'The point is that texts have ways of existing that even in their most rarefied form are always enmeshed in circumstance, time, place, and society – in short, they are in the world, and hence worldly' (1975: 35).

Meanwhile, Claudio Guillén published *Entre lo uno y lo diverso* (1985). There he pointed out three meanings in relation to world literature as literature of the world: literatures accessible to future readers from a growing number of countries, works that have moved backwards and forwards around the world and poems that reflect the world, which perhaps speak for the most profound, common and endurable human experiences (Guillén, 1985: 57–58). This third meaning is particularly interesting, for it focuses attention on the relationship between the text and the world, and on literature as the vehicle for human experience.

More recently, Ottmar Ette suggested in 'El espacio globalizado del saber. Perspectivas de la ciencia para el siglo XXI' (2007) that knowledge about life and about survival is found in literature. In other words, that literature, in its global nature, is capable of transgressing borders though not avoiding them, with the commitment of making what is in the *in-between* visible, that is to say, that literature is capable of speaking about the excluded and the oppressed. The potentiality of world literature, which is the study of literature for the world, finds its application in the cultural context. This means, according to Ette, that the globalization process requires different cultures to live together, accepting their differences and incentivising reciprocal respect.

While these proposals are based on a humanist ethic, it is important to note that the community models proposed here are closer to those that have been developed since the 1980s. It is therefore timely to revise the concept of community that the above-quoted authors pointed to in the second half of the twentieth century. Jean-Luc Nancy, Giorgio Agamben and Roberto Esposito have sought to rethink community in an open and inclusive manner opposed to the concept of crowd that Canetti described.[6] Considering Auerbach with Nancy, world literature will be analysed as a world community of literature. Thus, 'mondiality' is defined in contrast to the universality, and the community to the crowd.

World literature, translation and community: A mythological relationship

In *The Inoperative Community*, Jean-Luc Nancy analysed the concept of community as *inoperative* and as an *interrupted* myth.[7] Myth acted as a totalizing order for the founding of a modern community and was characterized by the nullification of individual will. Against the myth of modernity, Nancy proposed the myth of a community 'interrupted' by literature. He defines 'interrupted community' as a community without communion. This communion proper to myths would be interrupted by literature in general and, as will be seen, by literary translation in particular: 'Myth is interrupted by literature precisely to the extent that literature does not come to an end' (Nancy 1991: 64.) Hence the relations of literature with the world are framed by the indefinite postponement of the myth of totalizing. Literature would thus show its unfinished nature. According to Nancy, Romanticism fought for the creation of a new humanity that must arise from/in its new myth, and this myth itself must be (according to Schlegel) nothing less than the totalization of modern literature and philosophy, as well as ancient mythology, revived and united with the mythologies of the other peoples of the world. The totalization of myths goes hand in hand with the myth of totalization, and the 'new' mythology essentially consists in the production of a speech that would unite, totalize, and thereby put (back) into the world the totality of the words, discourses, and songs of a humanity in the process of reaching its fulfilment (or reaching its end) (Nancy 1991: 51).

Proposals of universal literature from Goethe to Marx fall into a similar totalizing mould. It could be argued, following Nancy, that this relationship between literature, translation and world is, first, mythological, and only afterwards interpretative or mimetic, if mimesis is understood as modes of historical interpretation of the real and the mythological.

From this perspective, the question is how literature can be a vehicle for an experience of the world in an inoperative community, an unfinished community, after the 'End of Art', that is, as Mariano Siskind puts it in 'Hegel, Saer y el Fin del Arte: Estética y política de los márgenes del universal': 'When art can no longer aspire to represent the world as a totality of reconciled meaning, or be taken as sensible space in which to experience the Absolute, like aestheticity or sublime and sublimated historicity' (Siskind 2012: 31).

The world seen here is no longer a totality of reconciled meaning. From an epistemological viewpoint, at least three different spheres of thought are at play in the word 'world' of 'World Literature' that affect the concept of literature and include literary translation: one spatial, another temporal, and the third normative, which affects the previous two. The spatial includes a geographical reference to the will to overturn the world/nation dichotomy, and therefore to move beyond the study of national literatures in isolation. Overcoming this dichotomy allows for a new reflection on the importance of literatures without a fixed residence, such as migration literature, travel writing, and so on, in the shaping of those identities that have been called national, as Ette declared in his *Literature on the Move: Space and Dynamics of Bordercrossing Writings in Europe and America* (2003). That which enables movement across borders as a 'transfer from one place to another' is, undoubtedly, translation, that is to say, translation as a journey between languages, translation as negotiation, as intercultural mediation or as a transcultural process.

'World' is also a reference to the organic habitable space, to the home, the living space. World Literature becomes a site where knowledge about life, about how to live can be stored. It can be seen as something that acts upon lives and upon the world, also as an ethics of literature as *savoir vivre*, as Ette suggests in *Writing-between-Worlds* (2016). But in the term 'world' we can also read the inhospitable, that is an abstract, commercial, global space, one of colonial identity, exercised through what Joseph Nye (1990) called *soft power*, or of unequal movements of literary influence, as proposed by Lawrence Venuti in *The Scandals of Translation* (1998). Boaventura de Sousa Santos, in *Epistemologies of the South* (2016), argues that marginal literatures enable us to access knowledge excluded by modernity. Modernity, in his view, may have developed concepts of universality, knowledge and law and imposed them through colonialism, but has done so by excluding those subjects that resided in a 'state of nature'.[8] Like Nancy, de Sousa explores the coexistence of different worlds that make up the idea of World. In the words of Nancy in the Spanish preface to *The Inoperative Community*: 'if a world is a network of connected meanings, or, let us say, a symbolic knot, the worlds that make up the world are always several' (Spanish edition 1998: 8; translation mine).

The word 'world' is also a temporal reference. In the recent study by Peng Cheah, *What is a World?* in the Heideggerian tradition, Cheah explains how it is possible to resist capitalism's rational teleology using alternative temporal models and critiques the Aristotelian conception of the fable as the temporal order of a story, governed by the principle of causality. For Cheah, world literature studies offer resistance to the global system of modern capitalism. Through the performative capacity of literature to make the world (*worlding*), marginal postcolonial literatures are drawing up alternative temporalities:

> The theory of world literature I propose suggests that the world is a normative temporal category and not the spatial whole made by globalization. Because world literature has the normative vocation of opening up new worlds, its study cannot merely consist of historiographical or sociological analyses of how literary texts circulate globally and the effects of circulation at the level of form and style.
>
> (Cheah 2016: 16)

World is also a classical reference to order and aesthetic harmony derived from its connection with the term cosmos. In his 'Limits and Method of Exposition of the Physical Description of the Universe', Alexander von Humboldt explains that it was Pythagoras who first used the term 'cosmos' for the order of the universe, and later to designate both the order of the world and the world itself (Miranda 1977: 34–35). As Cheah (2016) notes, since the unitary representation of the world is normative and is given to us by the imagination, not by representation (3) it is therefore an aesthetic or mythological construct. The totalizing concept of *Weltliteratur* has been based on the modern myth of the Absolute. The question is then how to revise the myth of *Weltliteratur* of Romantic origin, in the light of a new myth based on a disrupted community as a pluriversal model of World Literature.

The Babel of Borges, the myth of the inoperative world community

But first, there is another question that is key to answering the previous one: how does translation act to disrupt the myth of a total language? The question of translation is necessary here because the classical myth of total community was founded on its invisibility. This classical myth has been disrupted by a later literary recreation that works as translation-transfer from a totalizing to an inoperative community. This is the classical myth of the Tower of Babel and the rewriting that Borges's 'Library of Babel' created out of it. Both demonstrate the crucial position that translation occupies in the formation of a world community.

Although scholars such as Damrosch and Moretti have shown the impossibility of a world literature that includes all the literatures of the world, we could say that the 'Library of Babel' described by Borges is, in itself, the potential corpus of world literature as 'its bookshelves contain all that is able to be expressed, in every language' (Borges 1998: 112). Nostalgia for the idea of reconstructing the one sole language is at the basis of the myth of the Tower of Babel, justifying aspiration to an original that survives even to modernity, and that was also part of the origin of the classical myth. As Nancy states: 'from its birth (whether one locates this birth in Plato, in Vico, in Schlegel, or elsewhere) myth has been the name for logos structuring itself, or, and this comes down to the same thing, the name for the cosmos structuring itself in logos' (Nancy 1991: 49).

The Borges story, however, works with the myth of the infinite propagation of texts through interpretations, translations, commentaries and so forth. 'The Library of Babel' appears to reproduce the myth of the modern totalization of community (the Library is 'total'), but, conversely, it shows its impossibility. It is always expanding toward the infinite dissemination of texts and of every one of the books on its shelves:[9]

> On some shelf in some hexagon, it was argued, there must exist a book that is the cipher and perfect compendium of all other books, and some librarian must have examined that book; this librarian is analogous to a god. (...) How was one to locate the idolized secret hexagon that sheltered Him? Someone proposed searching by regression: To locate, A, first consult book B, which tells where book A can be found; to locate book B, first consult book C, and so on, to infinity (...) I cannot think it unlikely that there is such a total book on some shelf in the universe.
>
> (Borges 1998: 112–115)

As with language itself, 'unlimited but periodic' (Borges, 1998: 118), the Borgesian library is always 'unlimited'. That is to say, the Library of Babel represents the incompletion of the total community that intended to be *Weltliteratur*. The world literature community, in its relationship with translation, is in the Borges story the disrupted myth of the total community of literature. Otherwise, if a communion of total unity were to emerge, the community of literature would disappear.

The myth of the inoperative community is not an isolated example in Borges' 'Library of Babel'. It can be found also in his stories and essays that deal with translation, among which 'The Translators of *The Thousand and One Nights*' (originally published 1932) stands out. The diverse translations of this work enabled Borges to explore key theoretical questions about translation, such as the issue of the faithfulness or unfaithfulness of a translation with respect to the original text and the diversity of translations produced at differing historical moments.

A recurring text both in his fiction and his essays, *The Thousand and One Nights* is especially suitable for reflection on the status that translation occupies in relation to an original. *The Thousand and One Nights* can be considered as a critique in itself: Scheherazade has to tell a story every night in order to save her life and defy the condemnation that, like the Sword of Damocles, had been laid upon her just for being a woman. The notion that every woman is unfaithful parallels the accusation that every translation is a form of betrayal ('tradutore traditore'). Scheherazade represents in the text the metaphor of the translator/ translation. In her essay, 'Gender and the Metaphorics of Translation', Lori Chamberlain challenges the gendered metaphor of translations as 'les belles infidèles', pointing out that,

> the meaning of the word 'fidelity' in the context of translation changes according to the purpose translation is seen to serve in a larger aesthetic or cultural context. In its gendered version, fidelity sometimes defines the (female) translation's relation to the original, particularly to the original's author (male) of the translation.
>
> (Chamberlain 1988: 461)

But in *The Thousand and One Nights*, every night is a judgement that Scheherazade manages to overcome, not because she proves her faithfulness, but because of her creative proliferation of new texts as new life. This new life is then represented by the baby she and Shahryar have together. We can thus read translation as a new being with a performative condition just like any other original. Scheherazade and Shahryar constitute what Nancy calls 'a community of lovers', pointing out that 'When the infant appears, it has already compared. It does not complete the love, it shares it again, making it pass again into communication and exposing it again to community' (1991: 40).

It is this performative power of translations and the mobile nature of literature that translation makes visible which interested Borges. He challenges the immobility of the original text, which he also criticizes through another comparison, that of the original text as sacred, declaring that 'the concept of the *definitive text* corresponds only to religion or fatigue' (Borges 1999: 69). His essay on the succession of translations of *The Thousand and One Nights* develops this idea. On the one hand, as he explains, there is no 'good-hearted naïveté' of the original text (Borges 1999: 96). On the other hand, because these translations that he calls a 'hostile dynasty' are characterized more by the need to differ from each other than for literal attention to the original, they are attempts to glorify the originality of each translator. The translations cited by Borges are all *unfaithful* to the original. The most acclaimed translations, from Jean Antoine Galland to Richard Burton, are alike in their 'infidelities' toward the original text, the main intention of which was to adapt them for a new target audience, leading on to new aesthetic works in the receiving language. Burton, Borges writes, does not shy away from the glorious hybridization of English: neither Morris' Scandinavian repertory nor Johnson's Latin has his blessing, but rather the contact and reverberation of the two. Neologisms and foreignisms are in plentiful supply: castrato, inconsequence, hauteur, in gloria, bagnio, langue fourree, pundonor, vendetta, Wazir. Each of these is indubitably the *mot juste*, but their interspersion amounts to a kind of skewing of the original. A good skewing, since such verbal – and syntactical – pranks beguile the occasionally exhausting course of the Nights.

(Borges 1999: 101)

As in the essay 'On William Beckford's *Vathek*', Borges could well have declared 'the original is unfaithful to the translation' (Borges 1999: 239). Furthermore, translations as literary texts, according to Borges, become part of the receiving tradition itself by conversing with it. He argues that all the many translations presuppose a rich (prior) process and an enrichment of the target language:[10]

In some way, the almost inexhaustible process of English is adumbrated in Burton – John Donne's hard obscenity, the gigantic vocabularies of Shakespeare and Cyril Tourneur, Swinburne's affinity for the archaic, the crass erudition of the authors of 17th-century chapbooks, the energy and imprecision, the love of tempests and magic. In Mardrus's laughing paragraphs, *Salammbô* and La Fontaine, the *Mannequin d'osier* and the *ballets russes* all coexist.

(Borges 1999: 108)

The ideas explored above allow us to answer the question of how translation acts on the disruption of the myth of a total language. In literary translation two forces converge: a *metaphorical force* that brings together far-off cultures, establishing new relations and linguistic cooperation, and at the same time, a *disseminating force* that produces an opening for texts that are translated and reinterpreted constantly, in each historical context. The translation acts, as with Borges's Library of Babel, to disrupt the myth of the total communion of any linguistic community: on the one hand, by its performative nature, translation *acts* within the linguistic community of which it comes to form a part and, on the other hand, it makes visible the *unfinished* nature of a literary text. Consequently, a literary text can never be read definitively, it is never a totality but a pluriversality.

Mimesis and translation: visualizing world community

It has been already observed that literature comprises community in accordance with two forces: one performative (*normative or metaphorical force*) and the other interpretative (*disseminating force*). The linguistic community of world literature is thus disrupted in Nancy's terms. A metaphorical force can bring together far-off cultures, establish new relations and linguistic cooperation and so rebuild the target language and culture. It is a normative force which configures the world as cosmos, that is to say, as aesthetic construct. Meanwhile, interpretation shows the unfinished nature of literature which must be translated and reinterpreted constantly, in each historical context. Like all literature, literary translations exercise a repressive and a subversive role simultaneously: first as normative and *poietic* constructs of the world through story, and then as subversive mimesis of the ways in which the sensitive is ordered, if we consider mimesis as modes of historical interpretation.

Literary mimesis is defined in this way as a revealing of the different ways in which people have ordered the world, or what Jacques Rancière called 'the distribution of the sensitive' in *Politics of literature* (2011):

> Literature is the deployment and deciphering of these signs written on things themselves. The writer is the archaeologist or geologist who gets the mute witnesses of common history to speak. Such is the principle that brings the so-called realist novel into play
>
> (Rancière 2011: 15)

In this context, translation acts as an essential agent in the modes of visualizing the mimesis of other cultures and, as Bassnett argues in *Constructing Cultures. Essays on Literary Translation* (1998), literary translation helps to build community through texts, by shifting the focus from author to reader and the present. If we accept that translation has the power to rediscover a world for readers, then this is due to its ability to capture what usually remains invisible.

According to de Soussa Santos, what remains silenced in the construction of modernity is an epistemology of colonial difference (for example, social class, gender, colonialism), and the concept of identity as closed entity:

> The theories of the social contract of the seventeenth and eighteenth centuries are as important for what they say as for what they silence. What they say is that modern individuals, that is, metropolitan men, enter the social contract in order to abandon the state of nature to form civil society. What they do not say is that a massive world region given over to the state of nature is thereby being created, a state of nature to which millions of human beings are condemned and left without any possibility of escaping via the creation of a civil society.
>
> (Sousa Santos 2016: 122)

Literary translation can subvert this silence, lodging in national literatures an alien discourse: a literature from other ways of understanding the world. The translation of literary works that in modernity have been silenced may find, in the space offered by world literature, a voice like 'mute witnesses of common history' (Rancière 2011: 15). The role of literary translation in world literature is to seek out other ways for 'the distribution of the sensitive' that includes an epistemology of difference.

The translation of literary works in world literature involves a reorganization of modes of making visible, within the normative capacity of literature. As Venuti argues, translation makes visible the construction processes of the community in a double movement which can be repressive, such as domesticating the foreign, or subversive, such as representing other identities:

> Since translating is always addressed to specific audiences, however vaguely or optimistically defined, its possible motives and effects are local and contingent, differing according to major or minor positions in the global economy. This is perhaps most clear with the power of translation to form cultural identities, to create a representation of a foreign culture that simultaneously constructs a domestic subjectivity, one informed with the domestic codes and ideologies that make the representation intelligible and culturally functional.
>
> (Venuti 1998: 159)

Bassnett has demonstrated how a text such as Ezra Pound's *Cathay* 'highlights the way in which translation can serve as a force for literary renewal and innovation' and not only as domestication of a foreign culture (2006, 8). Like Pound's China or Borges' Iceland, these translations involve simultaneously a kind of domestication of the culturally foreign and a renewal of aesthetic and linguistic forms as part of a process of cultural reinvention.

In this regard, the debates around the translation of Kafka's title, *Die Verwandlungen*, into Spanish highlights how a literary text converses with a pluriversal world experience. In 1999, Jordi Llovet, translator of the complete works of Kafka, claimed that the title should be corrected from *La metamorfosis* to *La transformación*. Then, in 2015, Susana Hernández tackled the translation of the title afresh for the publisher Nórdica, this time citing Goethe as an authority. According to Hernández:

> As a great expert of the classics, I have no doubt that the term he chose, *Verwandlung*, for him evoked the literary-mythological metamorphoses, as *Verwandlung* was the title given in German to the work by Ovid up until the nineteenth century (and is still called so in some cases even today: *Metamorphoseon libri* = Bücher der Verwandlungen). Goethe himself, truly an authority on the German language, used the term *Verwandlungen* in his literary texts, reserving *Metamorphosen* for his scientific studies – such is the usage the German language gives to this pair of terms.
>
> (Hernández and Llovet 2015)

Hernández recovers the canonical title as a calque from Ovid's *Metamorphoses*, so that Kafka's work enters directly into dialogue with the Western mythological tradition. For his part, Jordi Llovet argued that his new translation added greater accuracy and pointed out that it had 'a character of domestic, urban and biographical narration, not mythological'. Llovet thus endeavoured to link Kafka's work with the realism and social criticism of Dickens or Chekhov:

> Kafka is not a pioneer in the tradition of protest against the rule of oppressive law: he is preceded by Kleist, Dickens, by Robert Walser and Chekhov (...) His greatness is having been able to detect and narrate those conflicts between individual and community in accordance with the specific circumstances of an advanced phase of capitalism.
>
> (Hernández and Llovet 2015)

Llovet based the model for his translation on the historical period in which the work was created, and also on the authority of Borges, who had also proposed *La transformación*. However, Borges based his arguments neither on Kafka's debt to Ovid and the Western tradition, nor on it being a more faithful translation. In 1983, when celebrating the 100th anniversary of Kafka's birth, Borges argued:

> We can read Kafka and think that his fables are as ancient as history, that those dreams were dreamed by men from other epochs without needing to link them to Germany or to Arabia. The fact of having written a text that transcends the moment in which it was written is remarkable. One could believe that it was written in Persia or in China, and therein lies its worth.
>
> (Borges 1983)

Borges was drawing attention to the dissemination of a text that could have been written, as he says, in Arabia, in Persia, or in China. But, however, due to its translation, it had been reduced practically to a reading within the Western tradition. Choosing to translate the title as *La transformación* made it possible to put Kafka's work in the context not only of Ovid's work and classical mythology, but also in that of the parables of Hebrew tradition, in relation to Zeno's paradox, and in the context of the *I Ching* or *The Book of Changes* and the apologue of Han Yu, which Borges quotes in 'Kafka and His Precursors' (Borges 1998: 710).

The translation as 'The Transformation' at the same time makes it possible to open up a dialogue between Kafka's text and the criticism of Western capitalism that concerns the tradition of world literature. As Borges declared in 'The Argentine Writer and Tradition', the tradition of the literary text is universal literature, claiming that 'We must believe that the Universe is our birthright' (Borges 1998: 427). For this translation shows us that it belongs to the very nature of a literary text potentially to be of many modes at the same time.[11]

Conclusions: translation and world community of literature

The relationship between world literature and translation has started to transform comparative literature as a cooperative discipline, affecting it in different ways. Firstly, it has been observed how world literature shows that comparative literature and translation studies have to work in together, not only because of the linguistic limits of the comparatist who cannot know all languages, but also because translation will show, in the space of the plural linguistic community, how different traditions engage in dialogue with one another.

Secondly, on an epistemological level, two questions in which translation plays a fundamental role have been answered: how does world literature account for the world, and how to review the myth of *Weltliteratur* in the light of the disrupted myth of world literature? On the one hand, in the meaning derived from 'cosmos', the normative capacity of literature can be seen. This term has gone from being used as a designation of harmonious ordering of the world (normative function) to being used instead for the world itself (representative function). This has had two direct consequences in the modern configuration of the concept of *Weltliteratur*: the usage in the singular of the term as ideal world unity (World Literature instead of world literatures) and the mythological-normative forgetting that acts within the term as an aesthetic construct. On the other hand, as a critique of this totalizing concept, a 'disrupted community' of literature has been proposed, in which translation plays a fundamental role because the classical myth of the total community was founded on its invisibility. The Borgesian Library of Babel shows a community without communion, a disrupted community in Nancy's terms.

As a consequence, translation increases the heterogeneity of literary traditions because the translator's verbal choices amount to interpretive moves that vary the source text. As Venuti pointed out, variations may be determined not simply by the receiving language and culture but also by a reading of the source text that incorporates knowledge of the source culture as well (Venuti 2013: 195). Thus, translations make the ideal of a unique and stable identity impossible, as well as being susceptible to the creation of a new order, as *aesthetics* of equality. The translation of a text that belongs to another culture, once introduced into the receiving culture, acts like a fold between both cultures, transforming the dichotomies 'foreign' and 'local', 'original' and 'secondary', as has been seen with Borges.

The translation is thus incorporated into the host culture, acting in a similar way to Derrida's concept of *supplement*. It appears as something that can be disregarded because it is foreign to the culture that receives it, but which, once introduced, acts like any other original work and can transform the language. Thus, translation introduces the alien, the foreign, into the receiving culture, 'contaminating' it, and therefore making it impossible to return to any idea of an original as pure and total language. Translation, like Borges's antimyth, demonstrates the decentring movement of language and the impossibility of a closed cultural identity. Hence the relations between world literature and translation act as a constitutive and subversive force in a world community that, having the principle of equality as its *a priori*, is a plural and indefinite opening.

The translation also acts, like Borges's Library of Babel, to disrupt the myth of the total communion of any linguistic community, both by its performative nature, that is, how translation *acts* in the linguistic community of which it comes to form a part and by making visible the *unfinished* nature of a literary text. Consequently, the literary text can never be read once and for all; it is not a totality but a pluriversality. A global community of literature does not cease to redefine the limits of our world library.

Consequently, world literature is proposed as a pluriversal model of diverse historical world experiences, making it possible to sketch out the horizon of an aesthetics of equality. This equality has to be understood as an aesthetic of equality, that is to say, according to the normative and mimetic nature of the world, political equality is first an aesthetic potentiality of every literature as part of World Literature. Moreover, due to the plural nature of every text, literature provides a pluriversal experience of the world. Literary translation serves to remind us that there is a common story to be heard, which is infinite and in continuous transformation.

Glossary

Pluriversality	is defined by Walter Mignolo as entanglement of several cosmologies connected today in a power differential, considering the fact that all known civilizations are founded on the universality of his [sic] own cosmology.
Interrupted	is defined by Nancy as 'incompletion'. 'There is no entity or hypostasis of community because this sharing, this passage cannot be completed. Incompletion is its "principle", taking the term "incompletion" in an active sense, however, as designating not insufficiency or lack, but the activity of sharing, the dynamic, if you will, of an uninterrupted passage through singular ruptures. That is to say, once again, a workless and inoperative activity' (Nancy 1991: 35).

The distribution of the sensitive   is defined by Rancière (1999) as different ways in which roles and modes of participation in a common social world are determined by establishing possible modes of perception.

Notes

1 This chapter was written during my stay as Associate Researcher at UC Berkeley, funded by the 'José Castillejo' programme.
2 Collaborative methods have been common in the natural sciences, while human sciences have been based mainly on individual projects. Nevertheless, cooperative proposals have been developed in recent years. This is the case with Stephen J. Collier, Andrew Lakoff and Paul Rabinow, who have developed what they named a 'laboratory' for human sciences, especially for anthropology. Those authors consider this method would be better for analysing norms of knowledge production 'and about shared problems and concepts that might be collectively worked on and developed'. They have been seeking to create a community of knowledge around 'a clearer sense of common problems or debates' (Collier et al. 2006: 3–5).
3 According to Ette (2007), Humboldt's science model is conceived as a response to the second phase of accelerated globalization (after the first, the colonial expansion of Europe during the fifteenth and sixteenth centuries), which had begun with voyages of discovery on the second half of the eighteenth century, and that would still have consequences in our fourth stage of globalization. Humboldt's model opposes that of Hegel or Schlelling, offering an integrated response of knowledge about the world (2007: 60–61). See also Ette (2002, 2004 and 2009).

4 This term is taken from Walter Mignolo (2013), who has stated that: 'pluriversality is not cultural relativism, but entanglement of several cosmologies connected today in a power differential', considering 'the fact that all known civilizations are founded on the universality of his [sic] own cosmology'.

5 Full quote: 'Our earth, the domain of Weltliteratur, is growing smaller and losing its diversity. Yet Weltliteratur does not merely refer to what is generically common and human; rather it considers humanity to be the product of fruitful intercourse between its members. The presupposition of Weltliteratur is a *felix culpa*: mankind's division into many cultures. Today, however, human life is becoming standardized (gemeinsames Leben der Menschen auf der Erde)' (Auerbach 1969: 2).

6 They all share a common project: community would integrate individuals, respecting differences without seeking to dominate them. That is to say, this project would be closer to heterotopy than to an ethical utopia. As Greg Bird (2016) argues, those philosophers rearticulate community not as something that is proper to those who belong and improper to those who are excluded or where inclusion is based on one's share in common property. Instead, they return to the forgotten dimension of sharing, not as a sharing of things that we can contain and own, but as a process that divides us up and shares us out in community with one another.

7 'Interrupted' is defined by Nancy as 'incompletion': 'there is no entity or hypostasis of community because this sharing, this passage cannot be completed. Incompletion is its 'principle', taking the term 'incompletion' in an active sense, however, as designating not insufficiency or lack, but the activity of sharing, the dynamic, if you will, of an uninterrupted passage through singular ruptures. That is to say, once again, a workless and inoperative activity' (Nancy 1991: 35).

8 As Jacques Rancière had already pointed out in *Disagreement. Politics and Philosophy* (1999), this exclusion has the same nature as the one which previously also affected workers who were disqualified due to their perceived 'incapacity to speak and reason'.

9 This textual dissemination is considered in the actual form of the Borges story itself, which has no conclusion. The story ends with a false ending when it makes reference, in a footnote, to another story that is conceived as its double, 'The Book of Sand', which in turn forwards to another infinite story, 'The Zahir'.

10 Undoubtedly Borges overestimates Burton's prose. Although we would like to consider the theory of translation that Borges outlines in these conclusions.

11 According to Agamben in *The Fire and the Tale* (2017), developing one of the meanings of Mannerism as the recreation of original themes 'in the manner of', all literary texts have potentiality for a 'no', which is present even if not developed, that is, that all texts remain in some way unfinished. It is this negative potentiality of a text that, nevertheless, enables it to go on being developed subsequently, and to enable the reader to go on reading.

Bibliography

Agamben, Giorgio (2017) *The Fire and the Tale*, Stanford: Stanford University Press.

Auerbach, Erich (1952) Mimesis. Dargestellte Wirklichkeit in der Abendländischen Literatur, Berna: Francke.

Auerbach, Erich (1969): 'Philology and Weltliteratur'. Translation by Maire Said and Edward Said. *The Centennial Review* 13, 1(Winter): 1–17.

Bassnett, Susan (1998) *Constructing Cultures. Essays on Literary Translation*, Bristol/ Buffalo/Toronto: Multilingual Matters.

Bassnett, Susan (2006) 'Reflections on Comparative Literature in the Twenty-First Century'. *Comparative Critical Studies* 3, 1–2: 3–11.

Bassnett, Susan (2011) *Reflections on Translation*, Bristol/Buffalo/Toronto: Multilingual Matters.

Benjamin, Walter (1996) *Selected Writings Volume 1 1913–1926*. Ed. Marcus Bullock and Michael W. Jennings, Cambridge/London: Harvard University Press.

Bird, Greg (2016) *Containing Community. From Political Economy to Ontology in Agamben, Esposito, and Nancy*, New York: Sunny Press.

Borges, Jorge Luis (1983) 'Un sueño eterno'. Interview in *Babelia. Suplemento cultural*. 3 August. Available at http://cultura.elpais.com/cultura/2015/04/09/actualidad/1428570964_294931.html

Borges, Jorge Luis (1998) *Collected Fictions*. Trans. Andrew Hurley. New York: Penguin.

Borges, Jorge Luis (1999) 'The Translator of Thousand and One Nights'. In *The Selected Non-fictions*, ed. Eliot Weinberger and trans. Esther Allen, Suzanne Jill Levine and Eliot Weinberger. New York: Penguin.

Borges, Jorge Luis (2004) *Obras completes*, vol. 1, Barcelona: Emecé.

Canetti, Elias (1960) *Crowds and Power*, New York: Continuum.

Chamberlain, Lori (1988) 'Gender and the Metaphorics of Translation'. *Signs* 13, 3: 454–472.

Cheah, Pheng (2016) *What Is a World. On Postcolonial Literature as World Literature*, Durham/London: Duke University Press.

Collier, Stephen J., Andrew Lakoff and Paul Rabinow (2006) 'What Is a Laboratory in the Human Sciences?', *ARC Working Paper*, No. 1, 2 February.

Cronin, Michael (ed.) (2003) *Translation and Globalization*, London/New York: Routledge.

Damrosch, David (2012) 'Konzeptlabor "Approaches to World Literature": Podiumsdiskussion' (26 June). Available at www.fu-berlin.de/sites/dhc/zVideothek/980Konzeptlabor_Approaches_to_World_Literature_Podiumsdiskussion/index.html

Esposito, Roberto (2004) *Communitas: The Origin and Destiny of Community*, Stanford: Stanford University Press.

Ette, Ottmar (2002) *Weltbewusstsein: Alexander von Humboldt und das unvollendete Projekt einer anderen Moderne*, Weilerswist: Velbrück Verlag.

Ette, Ottmar (2003) *Literature on the Move*, Amsterdam/New York: Rodopi.

Ette, Ottmar (2004) *ÜberLebenswissen. Die Aufgabe der Philologie*, Berlin:Kadmos.

Ette, Ottmar (2007) 'El espacio globalizado del saber. Perspectivas de la ciencia para el siglo XXI'. In Oliver Kozlarek, *Entre cosmopolitismo y conciencia del mundo: hacia una crítica del pensamiento atópico*, México: Siglo XXI.

Ette, Ottmar (2009) *Alexander von Humboldt und die Globalisierung. Das Mobile des Wissens*, Frankfurt am Main – Leipzig: Insel Verlag.

Ette, Ottmar (2016a) *TransArea. A Literary History of Globalization*. Berlin/Boston: Walter de Gruyter.

Ette, Ottmar (2016b) *Writing-between-worlds. Transarea Studies and the Literatures-without-a-fixed-abode*, Berlin/Boston: Walter De Gruyter.

G. Blanco, Azucena (2014) 'Estética politica y teoria de la literatura: un dialogo abierto' Res publica. Revista de Historia de las Ideas Politicas vol.17, 2: 453–462.

Guillén, Claudio (1985) *Entre lo uno y lo diverso. Introducción a la literatura comparada*, Barcelona: Tusquets.

Hernández, Susana and Llovet, Jordi (2015) 'Traducir a Kafka: ¿"La metamorfosis" o "La transformación"?' *Babelia. Suplemento cultural*, 22 April. Available at http://cultura.elpais.com/cultura/2015/04/22/babelia/1429701387_466414.html

Mignolo, Walter (2013) 'On Pluriversality'. Available at http://waltermignolo.com/on-pluriversality/

Miranda, Miguel Ángel (ed.) (1977) *El cosmos de Humboldt. Selección de textos*, col. Geocrítica, Barcelona: Universidad de Barcelona.

Moretti, Franco (2000) 'Conjectures on World Literature'. *New Left Review*, 1(January/February): 54–68.

Nancy, Jean-Luc (1991) *The Inoperative Community*, Minneapolis and Oxford: University of Minnesota Press. (Spanish trans. Juan Manuel Garrido Wainer, *La comunidad inoperante*, Santiago de Chile: Escuela de Filosofía Universidad ARCIS, 2000).

Nye, Joseph (1990) *Bound to Lead: The Changing Nature of American Power*, New York: Basic Books.

Rancière, Jacques (1999) *Disagreement. Politics and Philosophy*, trans. Julie Rose, Minneapolis/London: Minnesota University Press.

Rancière, Jacques (2011) *Politics of Literature*, Cambridge/Malden: Polity Press.

Said, Edward (1975) 'The Text, the World, the Critic'. *The Bulletin of the Midwest Modern Language Association* 8, No. 2 (Autumn): 1–23.

Siskind, Mariano (2012): 'Hegel, Saer y el Fin del Arte: Estética y política de los márgenes del universal'. In César Domínguez, 'Literatura mundial: una mirada panhispánica', *Ínsula*: 787–788.

Sousa Santos, Boaventurade (2016) *Epistemologies of the South. Justice against Epistemicide*, London/New York: Routledge.

Venuti, Lawrence (1995) *The Translator's Invisibility. A History of Translation*, London/New York: Routledge.

Venuti, Lawrence (1998) *The Scandals of Translation: Towards an Ethics of Difference*, London/New York: Routledge.

Venuti, Lawrence (2013) *Translation Changes Everything: Theory and Practice*. London/New York: Routledge.

4 Translation and cosmopolitanism

Paulo de Medeiros

Gilt eine Übersetzung den Lesern, die das Original nicht verstehen?

Walter Benjamin (1972 [1923])

'Is a translation meant for readers who do not understand the original?' asks Walter Benjamin, practically at the outset of his seminal essay on 'The Task of the Translator' (1968a). This seemingly simple question already points to an irreducible difference inherent in the possible meanings of *gilt*. Harry Zohn's translation, long the standard in English, is a smooth and idiomatic rendering. Yet, it is perhaps too smooth, inasmuch as it covers over the fact that Benjamin's question is also one into the validity of any given translation for those readers without access to the original. Indeed, if one lacks knowledge of the original one must take the translation at face value, on credit, believing it to reproduce the meaning of the original. For Benjamin of course, the question of translation is never simply one of just content or any kind of direct relationship between languages that would somehow allow for a simple passage of meaning. As such, and without at all intending to delve into yet another analysis of what has become one of Benjamin's most often cited essays, I would like to seize on those related questions, of the necessary difference in translation, and of validity, to reflect on the relationship between translation and cosmopolitanism in reference to world literature. In the process I want to avail myself of a number of case studies drawn from literatures written in Portuguese as I think that their placement in the world-system as semi-peripheral, or downright peripheral, can serve well to test a number of contested developments in World Literature studies.

World literature has imposed itself in the last decade as one of the most vibrant and disputed fields of literary studies. Whether one sees it as a renewal, expansion, or concretization of the premises and promises of the discipline of Comparative Literature, or as the global development of postcolonial critique – and it has much of both of course – there is no doubt that translation is fundamental for its existence. However, how to view the relationship of translation to world literature, its positioning, and even its own possibility, remain hotly debated. It would be much easier if at least as regards cosmopolitanism there might be some consensus – the opposite of course is true: not only has cosmopolitanism always been subject to conflicting viewpoints but presently risks being seen as a relic from a different political constellation, superseded by the advent of neo-liberalism, and challenged by the return of xenophobic nationalisms. World literature, understood as a form of resistance to such a narrowing of the mind – indeed, very much so as was always a key aspect of Comparative Literature – as a form to resist the blindness of understanding literary phenomena primarily from the perspective of the nation, is intrinsically cosmopolitan. And translation, I would suggest, must be seen not only as that which enables such a cosmopolitan perspective but also as that which can ensure that difference, linguistic, contextual, and historical, never is elided.

For the moment, but perhaps not much longer, it is still possible to hold a fairly reasonable overview of the varied, competing and complementary critical positions that have been staked out with regards to the key issues affecting World Literature, Translation Studies, and cosmopolitanism. From several overviews of the renewed interest in World Literature and the intense debate surrounding it, two perhaps stand out. One, by Theo D'haen, 'Worlding World Literature' (2016) is a very useful, concise and yet extensive review that pulls in a large number of publications, from Sarah Lawall's early edited volume on *Reading World Literature: Theory, History, Practice* (1994) to one of the latest, Phen Cheah's *What Is a World? Postcolonial Literature as World Literature* (2016). The other, somewhat older but perhaps even more useful in its sharpness and lucidity, is provided by Emily Apter in the 'Introduction' to her polemical *Against World Literature: On the Politics of Untranslatibility* (2013), which manages to slice through the different and sometimes opposed viewpoints on the concept of World Literature in a way that remains very balanced in spite of the author's own deep involvement on the issues.

The debates on cosmopolitanism have also always raged and could be said to constitute a sub-field unto themselves that cuts across political theory, history, economics, and literary studies as the issue of representation in its aesthetic and political senses gets played out most clearly in literary works. In *Cosmopolitanism: Ethics in a World of Strangers* Kwame Anthony Appiah, after warning against a facile view of cosmopolitans as confined to urban elitist globalists, articulates a concise but, in my view, crucial operative definition of cosmopolitanism:

> So there are two strands that intertwine in the notion of cosmopolitanism. One is that we have obligations to others, obligations that stretch beyond those to whom we are related by the ties of kith and kind, or even the more formal ties of a shared citizenship. The other is that we take seriously the value not just of human life but of particular human lives, which means taking an interest in the practices and beliefs that lend them significance. People are different, the cosmopolitan knows, and there is much to learn from our differences.
>
> (Appiah 2006: xiii).

Basic to such a view of cosmopolitanism is the notion of difference, and the respect, tolerance, and curiosity that go with it. Translation necessarily becomes fundamental to such learning from difference as highlighted by Appiah, translation in its various modes, from the cultural to the strictly linguistic. This is something that can be clearly seen in his choice of cultural hero, Sir Richard Burton, who is the main figure in the first chapter and who is presented as a great translator. Writing in the aftermath of 9/11, Appiah is also very clear on how world events were increasingly pointing to a fierce clash between cosmopolitan desires and counter-cosmopolitan forces, driving a wedge of fear between people and nations across the world. However, ten years later, and given the rapid, explosive turn to the right across various parts of the world and most noticeably so in Europe and the USA, it almost seems as though Appiah's understanding of those forces – a series of various fundamentalisms – was naïve or innocent. Indeed, who would have predicted that by 2017 the UK Prime Minister would seemingly reject Enlightenment values and declare at the Conservative's 2016 convention in Birmingham that 'if you believe you are a citizen of the world, you're a citizen of nowhere' (May 2016). If the notion of cosmopolitan Europe always was more of a myth or an ideal than actual reality at one point, especially after 1989, it did appear as if it might come to be. The danger then was that any vision of Europe as a cosmopolitan polity risked excluding those deemed foreign to this 'imagined community'. The danger now has shifted inwards and, just as the succeeding crises surrounding the massive numbers of migrants and dislocated people showed the cracks in 'Fortress Europe', rabid and xenophobic nationalism has displaced what intellectuals, following Michael Billig, used to call 'banal nationalism' (Billig 1995). In the light of such threats what translation and Translation Studies can offer is a renewed and transnational understanding of culture that, without eliding difference, can serve as the indispensable grounding for an effective cosmopolitanism.

The interconnectedness of translation and cosmopolitanism has been examined from a variety of angles, especially as Translation Studies have followed what one could refer to as a globalization turn (Snell-Hornby 2006) that has become more and more evident in the last decade. This can be clearly seen in Emily Apter's guest edited special issue of *Public Culture* on *Translation in a Global Market* (2001), in Esperança Bielsa and Susan Bassnett's focused *Translation in Global News* (2009), and in more recent work also by Esperança Bielsa. In *Cosmopolitanism and Translation: Investigations into the Experience of the Foreign*, Bielsa traces a fine and substantive history of the multiple intersections between cosmopolitanism and translation studies across the Humanities and the Social Sciences. Drawing on the work of a large number of theorists, she refers repeatedly to the seminal work of Ulrich Beck, quoting for instance from his *Cosmopolitan Vision*:

> Cosmopolitan competence, as a fact of everyday and of scientific experience, forces us to develop the art of translation and bridge-building. This involves two things: on the one hand, situating and relativizing one's own form of life within other horizons of possibility; on the other, the capacity to see oneself from the perspective of cultural others and to give this practical effect in one's own experience through the exercise of boundary-transcending imagination
>
> (Beck 2006: 89; in Bielsa 2016: 6)

The world-bridging capacity of translation is something that Ursula K. Le Guin had already focused on in her 1976 dystopian novel *The Word for World is Forest*. There she equates the figure of the translator with that of a 'god', Selver, the Atshean warrior responsible for defying the colonization and enslavement at the hands of the Terrans bent on cutting all of the planet's trees to ship back to a desert-like planet Earth:

> What did *sha'ab* mean, though? (...) *Sha'ab* meant god, or numinous entity, or powerful being; it also meant something quite different, but Lyubov could not remember what. (...) Of course: *sha'ab*, translator. (...) And the translator is the god. Selver had brought a new word into the language of his people. (...) Only a god could lead so great a newcomer as Death across the bridge between the worlds.
>
> (Le Guin 2015: 84)

Attuned to the power of translation, Le Guin is also realistic as the reach across cultures ultimately fails: even though the Ashteans manage to escape extermination, the price paid, learning the meaning of killing other human beings, is a heavy and irreversible charge. Basing herself on a number of statistical studies, Bielsa is also realistically sobering when she notes the profound asymmetry between cultures:

> Moreover, current geopolitical inequalities are directly mirrored in translation (...) Thus, some accounts of globalization have pointed to the number of book translations from English and into English as an indication of the power distribution in global information flows, where those at the core do the transmission and those at the periphery merely receive it.
>
> (Bielsa 2014: 2)

Realizing the perniciousness of such an asymmetry is key to understand both the fundamental importance of translation for a cosmopolitan understanding of the world and one's place in it; but it reveals not only the limitations of translation but, more importantly, the way in which translation can, however unwittingly, serve as a tool for the further perpetuation of the imbalances it might want to redress.

Some might object that such a view places undue emphasis on material conditions and on a particular *a priori* political perspective. As much as I recognize that aesthetic considerations play as important a role as any other, be they ethical or political, when discussing literature or any other art form, the attempt to separate them seems to be misguided. Indeed, I find it especially strange that in a whole chapter dedicated to 'cosmopolitanism and world literature' Bielsa would come to the conclusion that 'Notions of aesthetic cosmopolitanism and world literature provide a corrective to a concept of cosmopolitanism that is predominantly conceived in moral and political terms' (Bielsa 2016: 85). On the contrary, I would suggest, it is precisely the relative political urgency of world literature that allows for an ethical response. Moreover, as we all know, singling out aesthetics by itself in no way precludes their being co-opted by the political. As Walter Benjamin also pointed out a long time ago, 'The logical result of fascism is the introduction of aesthetics into political life' (Benjamin 1968b: 241). Should there be any doubts about how insidious such a process can still be in the present one has only to read the recent solicitation (2017-JC-RT-0001) issued by the US Department of Homeland Security, concerning bids for the building of prototypes for the infamous wall between Mexico and the USA which, as reported by T. Christian Miller in *ProPublica*, 'will meet requirements for aesthetics, anti-climbing, and resistance to tampering or damage' (Miller 2017).

Obviously Bielsa is more than aware of Benjamin's position – indeed, a significant part of her chapter concerns an attempt at reconsidering some of Benjamin's views and wanting to see them in the light of today's globalising forces. And I, for one, would readily subscribe to Bielsa's call for more attention to the material circumstances of production and distribution (Bielsa 2016: 72). Ultimately, however, if there is a stable conclusion proffered by Bielsa concerning the relation between World Literature, translation, and cosmopolitanism it seems to waver between a reading of some of the prominent names in the debate on World Literature – David Damrosch, Pascale Casanova, and Pheng Cheah – and a harking back still to Goethe; or rather to the views of Goethe as expressed in the famous conversations with Eckermann. After citing at some length from Eckermann, Bielsa concludes:

> This constitutes the most persuasive argument about the cosmopolitan potential of foreignising translation: to serve as a vehicle for an experience of the foreign, potentially to all contemporaries, as opposed to a narcissistic experience of the recognition of dominant cultural values of one linguistic group.
>
> (Bielsa 2016: 76)

In and of themselves such comments appear not only fair, balanced, and enlightened, but even desirable. Indeed, Bielsa manages to navigate a number of very significant, and not infrequently divergent, positions around the question of cosmopolitanism, translation, and world literature. Nonetheless, in spite of such virtuosity, there is a certain degree of, perhaps inevitable, avoidance of the political import of such considerations. As such, in spite of all its attention to fashionable critical buzzwords, Bielsa's argument ends up reifing a certain abstract quality of aesthetics in detriment of the more concrete materialities that would demand another reading of the various inequalities inherent in translation and culture often pointed to but quickly left without further analysis.

At this moment I would like to propose two perspectives which, even though significantly divergent, when pulled together might begin to touch upon some of the blind spots inherent in a traditional reading of the relation between cosmopolitanism, translation, and world literature such as Bielsa's. The first can arguably be seen best as developed by Graham Huggan in his study of the *Postcolonial Exotic*. Huggan is very clear at the very onset when he states:

When creative writers like Salman Rushdie are seen, despite their cosmopolitan background, as representatives of Third World countries; when literary works like Chinua Achebe's *Things Fall Apart* (1958), are gleaned, despite their fictional status, for the anthropological information they provide; when academic concepts like postcolonialism are turned, despite their historicist pretensions, into watchwords for the fashionable study of cultural otherness – all of these are instances of the *postcolonial exotic*, of the global commodification of cultural difference

(Huggan 2001: vii)

Although Huggan builds on a number of insights taken from the seminal work of Edward Said he also is careful to show how some of Said's own points in *Culture and Imperialism are* still reflected in what one might consider a more benign approach to the question of exoticism: 'For Said, exoticism functions in a variety of imperial contexts as a mechanism of aesthetic substitution which "replaces the impress of power with the blandishments of curiosity" (Said 1993: 159)' (Huggan 2001: 14). Huggan's corrective is one I fully agree with as he notes that 'it is not that exotic spectacle and the curiosity it arouses replaces power, but rather that it functions as a decoy to *disguise* it' (Huggan 2001: 14). Since then others, like Ana Margarida Martins (2012), have also looked at how Huggan's critique still operates from a fairly canonical and Anglophone perspective while sidelining most issues relating to gender. Nonetheless, recognizing the sort of erasure operated by such an exoticizing of Otherness as analysed by Huggan, its 'decoy effect' as it were, I would suggest, is crucial to understand the complex relationships between translation, cosmopolitanism and world literature. Falling into a plea for 'aesthetics' in my view is nothing more than yet another instantiation of precisely such a diversion.

The second might be seen in the critical call to recognize processes of marginalization that effectively render certain cultural products as invisible and how translation both serves to re-inscribe such invisibility and to expose it. This is made very explicit by Emily Apter as she reflects on the motives behind a special issue of *Public Culture* dedicated to 'Translation in a Global Market' she edited:

The constraints imposed by what is available in translation in part determine the content of the transnational canon, which contributes another layer of complexity to the value-laden selection of authors and serves as partial explanation for why 'global lit' courses tend to feature similar rosters of non-Western authors.

(Apter 2001: 2)

So it is not for a lack of self-awareness and even self-critique that the forms of invisibility ascribed to certain literatures keep on being reproduced. On the one hand one could say that the seemingly emancipatory critical moves at the basis of seminal works such as Gilles Deleuze and Félix Guattari's well-known study of *Kafka: Toward a Minor Literature* (1975; 1986) simply get co-opted, even as they are often fundamentally misinterpreted, resulting in a reinforced doubling of the exclusionary politics inherent in the categories of major and minor. And of course, even if Kafka's reception in the beginning was hesitant as Ritchie Robertson has noted, a decade or so after *The Castle*'s initial translation into English, Kafka had become widely recognized as a key modernist author (Robertson 2003: viii). The result, even if unwittingly, more often than not is a reification of the traditional canon that domesticates even the most subversive of writers.

The tensions inherent in the use of terms such as 'major' and 'minor' when applied to literatures and languages have been scrutinized for some time now. Personally I remember well the sense of surprise when first encountering a Dutch view of Portuguese and German as minor literatures (as part of the institutional designation of 'kleine letteren' for university studies enrolling less than twenty students a year at Dutch universities; for a discussion of such issues see Rapport van de adviescommissie Kleine Letteren 2002). One could have thought that with about 23 million speakers world-wide there might have been some sensitivity about the issue of 'minor' languages, certainly when referring to German, which is the tenth most spoken language in the world (over 76 million native and 52 million second speakers) and Portuguese, ranked sixth in the world (over 218 million native and 11 million second speakers according to Ethnologue 2017). Obviously, the criteria are vague and pragmatically linked to questions of financing in times of crisis; but the very designation, its asymmetry, to say nothing of the ironies of scale involved, also contribute to yet a further process of rendering some literatures more invisible than others. These and many other, related, issues have been exposed in various ways, and the recent volume on *Major versus Minor? Languages and Literatures in a Globalized World* (D'haen et al. 2015) represents arguably one of the most extensive offerings. Attempts at expanding the framework of the discussion, however, more often than not never even scratch at the surface of the question as, in my view, the issue is not so much one of just expanding the canon or the geographical and linguistic coverage, but rather the urgent need to question the power imbalances that have always accompanied any discussion of world literature, since Goethe's time, right down to the present. The failure to do so can become even more noticeable precisely when some claim is made to go against it. For instance, Theo D'haen, in one of his multiple recent interventions on the topic, seems to argue against the homogenizing, flattening out of categories that produces an even greater degree of invisibility for so-called 'minor literatures' in an essay in which he refers to the case of literature written in Dutch as 'the most minor of the minors, the most peripheral of peripherals' (D'haen 2013: 4). Perhaps this should be read as if it were tongue in cheek, an ironic nod to those in the know. However, given that it seems especially directed at a much earlier, and, arguably theoretically more coherent, essay on 'Theorizing the European Periphery' (Klobucka 1997), it is difficult to see any irony in that complaint.

This problematic, what one could see as a sort of blind rush towards exposing eurocentrism, which was crucial for most postcolonial criticism and its reshaping of comparative literature as a discipline, was already discussed specifically in relation to translation issues by Susan Bassnett, Maria Tymoczko, and Harish Trivedi to name a few (Bassnett and Trivedi 1999). In 2003 Michael Cronin, building in part on that work, put it perhaps most succinctly in his book on *Translation and Globalisation*. At some point Cronin takes his argument towards what he names as 'Invisible Minorities' as he presents relentless statistics that make clear the power imbalance in the field of translation studies among different, 'major' and 'minor' languages and literatures. As he points out,

> [i]f we take children's literature for example, 3 percent of the output in Britain and the United States are translations. This compares with 70 percent in Finland, 50 per cent in the Netherlands, 50 per cent in Italy, and 33.5 per cent in Germany.
>
> (Cronin 2003: 139)

Reflecting on the sort of ease with which different countries and languages can become all rolled into a generic designation of European, Cronin points out that in effect that can lead to a silencing of those countries and languages that were not directly involved in 'the colonial enterprise' (Cronin 2003 140). Even if this claim might appear as somewhat of an exaggeration, his subsequent reflection is one I find important: 'if translation has traditionally suffered from lack of visibility then there is a sense in which translators working in minority languages are doubly invisible at a theoretical level' (Cronin 2003 140).

There are several points at stake here, although they are not mutually exclusive in any way I would like to specify: on the one hand, the issue of how differences between the various European nations and languages, when viewed strictly from an outside perspective, are often elided, which in effect means that the smaller or less influential ones are rendered invisible. On the other, however, is the fact that the very act of translating, which traditionally had always involved a certain form of effacement already – even literally as often the names of the translators would be left out of publishing data – undergoes yet another process of erasure – a double invisibility – when the languages and literatures in question are less than central. And, in the European case the most central languages, at least from the 19th century onward, were English and French, with German trailing and others usually ignored. Also, seeing this from an historical perspective, it becomes clear that what leads to such processes of exclusion is extrinsic to the languages themselves and fully dependent on the specific power and influence yielded by a given nation at a given time.

The process of making a language invisible is not just a metaphorical one as Cronin also argues, basing himself on data from Stephen A. Wurm (2001) concerning the actual disappearance of languages in a colonial situation. One of the examples given for instance is that of Brazil, which, even though it is said to preserve the largest number of native languages today, around 170, also has lost about the same number since Portuguese colonization started in the 16th century (Cronin 2003: 142). I am calling attention to this because I want now to try to develop Cronin's insight and to do so I want to refer specifically to literary works written in Portuguese. My argument is simple: if translation working with 'minor literatures' always already suffers from a process of double invisibility, works written in a language, such as Portuguese, which, in spite of its large number of speakers and its role in imperialism and colonialism, no longer can be seen as hegemonic, or indeed as central bearer of cultural capital, suffer at least from such a double invisibility, if not even more. But this is not due to the language – and in the case of Portugal at least, the nation as well – never having been directly involved in imperialism as the 'colonial enterprise'. Rather, it must be understood as directly linked to the capital flows and market forces that have shaped the world leading up to the current phase of capitalism.

In order to avoid possible misunderstandings I would like to further note that referring to literatures written in Portuguese does not imply at all that one could draw any inference of exceptionality from such a move. Having in mind the complaint about the supposed extreme marginalization of literature written in Dutch, whether from the Netherlands or Belgium, one could say that in the case of both the issues of their respective nations having been deeply and directly involved in imperialism and colonialism is beyond a doubt. The radical differences between the historical employment of Dutch and Portuguese should be kept in mind, but ultimately what their discrepancy points to is that these issues are complex and never just a question of simplistic dichotomies. So, although there will be specific texts to be drawn upon, and cases to be made out of Dutch and Belgian literature, they would have to be examined individually. Just think of Multatuli's *Max Havelaar* (1860), for instance, which was written as a response to the cruel conditions imposed by the colonial system in the then Dutch East Indies. It was almost immediately translated into English in 1868, and had enormous influence for denouncing colonialism in general and the Dutch rule in Indonesia in particular. *Max Havelaar* has enjoyed wide circulation, benefiting from having been translated into some forty languages and in a sense, it can be said to have embodied a form of critique that bears directly on cosmopolitanism. But no one would claim that it has been invisible, except, that is, in the one other country besides the Netherlands that was directly concerned, Indonesia, where it was only translated in 1978. What makes the case for considering Portuguese-language literatures more relevant for a discussion on cosmopolitanism and translation is not their singularity or isolated cases but rather the fact that given the sheer range, scope, and diversity, literatures written in Portuguese allow for a consideration of the connections between both translation and cosmopolitanism that not only avoids the straight dichotomies of major versus minor – indeed could be said to reveal the fallacies of such binaries – but also points to other ways of relating. Several reasons can be adduced: on the one hand, the fact that although at least since the 18th century Portugal has been relegated to a semi-peripheral role on the world stage but was, alongside Spain, one of the two hegemonic powers leading Europe into modernity in the 16th and 17th centuries; on the other hand, the fact that Brazilian literature, as rich as it is, has not yet managed to completely break through worldwide and, indeed, even in Portugal, many will not be aware of major developments in Brazil. Added to that is the fact, perhaps the most important element in this, that the new literatures being written in the former African colonies, especially in Mozambique and Angola, represent some of the most vibrant aspects of Portuguese-language literary writing and enjoy widespread attention in Portugal, Brazil, and worldwide. In other words, one of the key reasons to look at Portuguese-language literatures is because they form a sort of system unto themselves through the shared language and yet, at the same time, fail to perform as such, even in terms of distribution and circulation so that it is in their relationship to other literatures, in translation, that their specific form, and their cosmopolitan claims, can perhaps best be realized.

A salient example can be provided by Portuguese modernist Fernando Pessoa and the contemporary Mozambican author Mia Couto, as both can be said to embody deep cosmopolitan views, both have been widely translated, and both have been entered into the canon of world literature. At the beginning of the 20th century Portugal was a backward country, still nominally an imperial nation but left reeling from the enormous blow to its national pride by the British Ultimatum of 1890, which had definitively thwarted Portugal's ambitions in Africa and irrevocably pricked its delusional bubble. Although Portugal was torn apart by turmoil – the assassination of the King and Crown Prince in 1908, the proclamation of the Republic in 1910, successive political and financial crises – it was also deeply provincial and its small middle class especially so. In a sense this does not seem promising for the development of avant-garde cultural movements and yet Fernando Pessoa would rise from precisely such an environment and produce an astonishing body of work which would make him come to be considered as one of the most important modernist writers. Alain Badiou expresses perhaps this most intensely when, in his *Handbook of Inaesthetics* he states:

> Fernando Pessoa, having died in 1935, only came to be more widely known in France fifty years later. I, too, participated in this scandalous deferral. I regard it as a scandal because we are dealing with one of the decisive poets of the century, particularly if we try to think of him as a possible condition for philosophy.
>
> (Badiou, 2005: 36)

There will always be a combination of different reasons to be invoked that might contribute to Pessoa's preeminence and indeed to his cosmopolitanism. From those I would especially focus on his upbringing in colonial Durban, South Africa where he was constantly confronted by the double contradictions of both British and Portuguese colonialisms; his immersion in the English language, that led him to win the Victoria Prize at his secondary school and a scholarship to Oxford he did not take up, as well as continuously writing some pieces in English even after he stopped wanting to make a name for himself as an English poet; and his work as a commercial translator for several Lisbon trading houses. Pessoa has been subject to many different studies and interpretations and even though much of it is in Portuguese, there are salient studies available in English to which I would refer readers possibly curious about his works and legacies (Jackson 2010, Maunsell 2012, Medeiros 2013, Ramalho 2003, Sadlier 1998). At the moment I want simply to focus briefly on two points: one, the fact that Pessoa's writing cannot be seen outside of issues of translation even though that is one of the least studied of his facets. This does not mean at all that one should conflate Pessoa's writing, in all of its different guises and heteronymic proliferation, with translation; rather, it is a call to pay attention to how translation was also a constant activity of Pessoa and that some of his literary translations, as for instance from Poe, are of great importance to understand his aesthetics as well as his imbrication in World Literature. A few handful of brief studies of Pessoa and translation do not fail to signal some of its contradictory aspects but for the moment I would simply call attention to how Pessoa, besides practising literary translation also attempted a theoretical reflection on translation, as, for instance, in the essay on 'The Invisible Translator [O traductor invisível]', which Teresa Rita Lopes first published in 1993, a small essay in which Pessoa both anticipates the title and views of Lawrence Venutti in his *The Translator's Invisibility* (1995) and veers off into a more metaphysical, even Platonic (Barrento 2002) view of translation as the ability to understand the ideals conveyed by great literature.

Pessoa's international renown grew slowly if steadily with France and Germany spearheading it. English translations took perhaps a little longer to take hold, in spite of some excellent ones, as if the strangeness – and there are many aspects to Pessoa's poetry and prose that are suffused with a profound sense of alienation – were too difficult to place. That changed radically with the translation of his *Book of Disquiet* by Richard Zenith in 2001 – the earlier (1991) and exquisite one by Margaret Jull Costa somehow missed reaching the greater public, perhaps because, not unlike Pessoa himself, it was ahead of its time. The recently released and altered version (2017), based on the critical edition of Jerónimo Pizarro, being published simultaneously in England (Serpent's Tail) and the United States (New Directions) might signal a new shift and may become a new standard. The *Book of Disquiet* [Livro do Desasocego 2010], a vast fragmentary fictional diary, had only been published in Portuguese in 1982 and it had then already signalled a shift in the reception and critical understanding of Pessoa. But Zenith's translation, in the Penguin series on *Modern Classics*, which received a very perceptive and glowing review by George Steiner in the *Observer* (2001), can be seen as the breaking point inaugurating Pessoa's full entry into the cosmopolitan pantheon of World Literature. Was Pessoa less of a writer before, or one more marked by petty concerns rather than espousing a cosmopolitan view? Obviously we can rest assured that was not the case. That an earlier translation, in spite of its qualities, had somehow not propelled Pessoa in the same fashion does not present a paradox at all but does point, instead, to the complexities at work in the adoption of any given literary work. Although we may never be able to pinpoint exactly which factors were determinant in any given case, I would like to suggest viewing a combination of factors having to do both with the public's receptivity at a given historical time as well as the very mundane, material, considerations of production, circulation, and marketing.

At another end of the spectrum, Mia Couto raises similar questions concerning the interaction of cosmopolitan tendencies, the role of translation, and the inadequacy of the major and minor labels regarding world literature. African literatures written in Portuguese can be seen truly as suffering from that double, or triple form of invisibility previously mentioned: the publishing world's attention to Africa tends to be significantly muted, writing in Portuguese and circulating through Lisbon based editions almost seems an assurance for remaining within a close and small audience as the dialogue between Portuguese and Brazilian publishers is still very limited; and to top it off Mia Couto is an inveterate experimenter and innovator of the Portuguese language so that his works are absolutely full, and depend on, a profusion of invented neologisms or portmanteau words cobbled together from several, in a fantastical and powerful deployment of creativity that poses enormous challenges to any translator. Mia Couto has produced by now a vast oeuvre in a variety of genres and he has attracted a growing number of critics who have addressed his great significance within Lusophone letters (see for instance Rothwell's important monograph, 2004 and the recent *Companion* edited by Hamilton and Huddart, 2016). His position as one of the leading writers in Portuguese is firm, having received the most prestigious Camões Prize in 2013. This was followed by the Neustadt International Prize in 2014, confirming Mia Couto as one of the important figures in World Literature.

Much more reflection would be needed on the persistent difficulties of circulating Portuguese-language books among the various countries that use it as an official language in spite of the synergies that exist on a cultural and even historical level. For the moment let me just note that even if historical reasons can be adduced to explain this anomaly, much of it also can be attributed to fierce competition and protectionist measures even in the era of digital publication and online services. Leaving aside isolated publishing ventures (Europa-América series in the past in Portugal, or the more recent effort to publish classic modernist fiction by Brazilian authors in Portugal by Relógio D'Água), it was almost impossible to find texts by Brazilian authors in Portuguese bookshops and a similar difficulty, even if somewhat attenuated, would be met by Brazilian readers interested in the other Portuguese-language literatures. Change is perhaps possible, as since Penguin bought 45% of the renowned Brazilian publisher *Companhia das Letras* in 2011, its titles are now more readily available at some Lisbon bookstores. Mia Couto however, in spite of coming from Mozambique, performing complex linguistic games, and having his books published in Lisbon (as other well-known African Lusophone writers, given the still incipient publishing industry in Angola and Mozambique due to the countries' devastation in over two decades of civil wars) is widely recognized in Brazil and indeed in the world at large.

In a way, reading Mia Couto always presupposes a form of translation, even if one reads him in the original. And when one reads him in, say, English translation, in a sense we are also always already reading a translation of a translation. The figure of the translator – specifically in this case David Brookshaw – becomes especially salient because for a work such as Mia Couto to succeed it can never be domesticated and rendered familiar through the translation. The extremely difficult balancing act of the translator then, perhaps even more so than in the case of more conventional writers, must be seen as a profound cosmopolitan gesture as well, as the translator must simultaneously attempt to translate the radical difference of the original, without falling into a vulgar exoticizing, and that can only be achieved through an intense form of creation as well. In a sense of course, that is always the case with any form of translation beyond the mechanical. In the case of a writer with Mia Couto's complexity – one could imagine perhaps the complexities of a work like *Ulysses* or *Finnegan's Wake* but then stemming from an African context – the cosmopolitan dose of translation though, is multiplied. Elena Brugioni, in an essay where she begins a very useful reflection on the imbrications of postcolonial issues with translation studies with reference to the African Lusophone literatures, remarks aptly that Mia Couto's writing always involves already a form of inner translation 'neutralizing the logic of linguistic and cultural authenticity, and underlying the coexistence of different symbolically and politically connoted languages that are inscribed within the literary text written in Portuguese' (Brugioni 2017: 79). Just like Fernando Pessoa, yet very differently, Mia Couto embodies a form of cosmopolitanism that is as demanding as it is transformative. Moreover, whereas in the case of Pessoa one could still see an imbrication of his startling projects within a larger framework of a European avant-garde – however surprising that might have seemed to those inclined to only look at the central core of Anglo-American modernism – Mia Couto's writing forces a reconceptualization of traditional notions of World Literature which, even if steadily adapting to accept the rising influence of countries like China, still tends to ignore African literatures. In one of his recent essays, Mia Couto reflects precisely on the growing unease young Mozambicans from the capital, Maputo, feel about the rural parts of their own country and about their lack of knowledge of its various languages. Mia Couto expresses pride about Mozambique not on being in any way better than other nations but on its cosmopolitan mode of being: 'Our richness derives from our willingness to carry out cultural exchanges with others (...) This magic originates in our ability to exchange culture, to produce hybridities' (Couto 2015). There is perhaps no better expression of the relation between translation and cosmopolitanism.

Works cited

Appiah, Kwame Anthony. 2006. *Cosmopolitanism: Ethics in a World of Strangers*. New York: W. W. Norton. London: Allen Lane.

Apter, Emily. 2001. 'On Translation in a Global Market'. *Public Culture* 13. 1. Special Issue on Translation in a Global Market. Guest Ed. Emily Apter. 1–12.

Apter, Emily. 2013. *Against World Literature: On the Politics of Untranslatability*. London: Verso.

Badiou, Alain. 2005 [1998]. *Handbook of Inaesthetics*. Trans. Alberto Toscano. Stanford: Stanford University Press.

Barrento, João. 2002. 'Fernando Pessoa: o tradutor invisível'. In *O Poço de Babel: Para uma poética da tradução literária*. Lisbon: Relógio D'Água.

Bassnett, Susan and Harish Trivedi, Eds. 1999. *Post-Colonial Translation: Theory and Practice*. London and New York: Routledge.

Beck, Ulrich. 2006. *The Cosmopolitan Vision*. Trans. Ciaran Cronin. Cambridge: Polity Press.

Benjamin, Walter. 1972 [1923]. 'Die Aufgabe des Übersetzers'. In *Gesammelte Schriften*. Eds Rolf Tiedemann and Hermann Schweppenhäuser. Frankfurt a.M.: Suhrkamp. 9–21.

Benjamin, Walter. 1968a. 'The Task of the Translator'. In *Illuminations*. Trans. Harry Zohn. Intro. Hannah Arendt. New York: Harcourt, Brace, Jovanovich. 69–82.

Benjamin, Walter. 1968b. 'The Work of Art in the Age of Mechanical Reproduction'. In *Illuminations*. Trans. Harry Zohn. Intro. Hannah Arendt. New York: Harcourt, Brace, Jovanovich. 217–251.

Bielsa, Esperança. 2014. 'Cosmopolitanism as Translation'. *Cultural Sociology* 8. 4. 392–406. doi:10.1177/1749975514546235.

Bielsa, Esperança. 2016. *Cosmopolitanism and Translation: Investigations into the Experience of the Foreign*. London and New York: Routledge.

Bielsa, Esperança and Susan Bassnett. 2009. *Translation in Global News*. London and New York: Routledge.

Billig, Michael. 1995. *Banal Nationalism*. London: Sage.

Brugioni, Elena. 2017. 'Writing From Other Margins. Difference, Exception, and Translation in the Portuguese-Speaking World: Counterpoints Between Literary Representations and Critical Paradigms'. *Cadernos de Tradução (Florianópolis)* 27. 1. 65–89.

Cheah, Pheng. 2016. *What Is a World? Postcolonial Literature as World Literature*. Durham, NC: Duke University Press.

Couto, Mia. 2015. *Pensativities*. Trans. David Brookshaw. Windsor, Ontario: Biblioasis.

Cronin, Michael. 2003. *Translation and Globalisation*. London and New York: Routledge.

Deleuze, Gilles and Félix Guattari. 1975. *Kafka: Pour une littérature mineure*. Paris: Les Éditions de Minuit.

Deleuze, Gilles and Félix Guattari. 1986. *Kafka: Towards a Minor Literature*. Trans. Dana Polan. Minneapolis: University of Minnesota Press.

D'haen, Theo. 2013. 'Major Histories, Minor Literatures, and World Authors'. *CLCWeb: Comparative Literature and Culture* 15. 5. doi:10.7771/1481-4374.2342.

D'haen, Theo. 2016. 'Worlding World Literature'. *Recherche Littéraire/Literary Research* 33. 7–23.

D'haen, Theo, Iannis Goerlandt and Roger D. Sell, Eds. 2015. *Major Versus Minor? Languages and Literatures in a Globalized World*. Amsterdam and Philadelphia: John Benjamins. Ethnologue. 2017. *Languages of the World*. www.ethnologue.com/language/nld.

Hamilton, Grant and David Huddart, Eds. 2016. *A Companion to Mia Couto*. Woodbridge and Rochester, NY: James Currey and Boydell & Brewer.

Huggan, Graham. 2001. *The Postcolonial Exotic: Marketing the Margins*. London and New York: Routledge.

Jackson, K. David. 2010. *Adverse Genres on Fernando Pessoa*. New York: Oxford University Press.

Klobucka, Anna. 1997. 'Theorizing the European Periphery'. *Symplokē* 5. 1–2. 119–133.

Lawall, Sarah. 1994. *Reading World Literature: Theory, History, Practice*. Austin, TX: Texas University Press.

Le Guin, Ursula K. 2015 [1976]. *The Word for World is Forest*. London: Gollancz.

Martins, Ana Margarida. 2012. *Magic Stones and Flying Snakes: Gender and the 'Post-colonial Exotic' in the Work of Paulina Chiziana and Lídia Jorge*. Oxford:Peter Lang.

Maunsell, Jerome Boyd. 2012. 'The Hauntings of Fernando Pessoa'. *MODERNISM/ Modernity* 19. 1. 115–137.

May, Theresa. 2016. 'The New Centre Ground'. Speech delivered at the Conservative Conference in Birmingham. *The Independent*. 5 October.www.independent.co.uk/news/ uk/politics/theresa-may-speech-tory-conference-2016-in-full-transcript-a7346171.html.

Medeiros, Paulo de. 2013. *Pessoa's Geometry of the Abyss: Modernity and the Book of Disquiet*. Oxford: Legenda.

Miller, T.Christian. 2017. 'Trump Invites Bids to Build Wall, Cites Importance of "Aesthetics"'. 8 March. www.propublica.org/article/trump-invites-bids-to-build-wall-ci tes-importance-of-aesthetics.

Pessoa, Fernando. 1991. *The Book of Disquiet*. Trans. Margaret Jull Costa. London: Serpent's Tail.

Pessoa, Fernando. 1993. 'O traductor invisível'. In *Pessoa Inédito*, ed. Teresa Rita Lopes. Lisbon: Livros Horizonte. 285–286.

Pessoa, Fernando. 2001. *The Book of Disquiet*. Ed. and trans. Richard Zenith. London: Penguin.

Pessoa, Fernando, 2010. *Livro do Desasocego. Edição Crítica de Fernando Pessoa, Vol. XII, Tomo 1*. Ed. Jerónimo Pizarro. Lisboa: Imprensa Nacional – Casa da Moeda.

Pessoa, Fernando. 2017. *The Book of Disquiet. The Complete Edition*. Ed. Jerónimo Pizarro. Trans. Margaret Jull Costa. New York: New Directions. London: Serpent's Tail.

Ramalho, Maria Irene. 2003. *Atlantic Poets: Fernando Pessoa's Turn in Anglo-American Modernism*. Hannover and London: Dartmouth College/University Press of New England.

Rapport van de adviescommissie Kleine Letteren. 2002. *Vensters op de wereld: de studie van de zogenoemde 'Kleine Letteren' in Nederland*. Amsterdam. Koninklijke Neder-landse Akademie van Wetenschappen.

Robertson, Ritchie. 2003. 'Introduction'. In Klaus Wagenbach, *Kafka*. London: Haus Publishing.

Rothwell, Phillip. 2004. *A Postmodern Nationalist: Truth, Orality, and Gender in the Work of Mia Couto*. Lewisburg, PA: Bucknell University Press.

Sadlier, Darlene J. 1998. *An Introduction to Fernando Pessoa: Modernism and the Paradoxes of Authorship*. Gainesville: University Press of Florida.

Said, Edward E. 1993. *Culture and Imperialism*. London:Vintage.

Snell-Hornby, Mary. 2006. *The Turns of Translation Studies: New Paradigms or Shift-ing Viewpoints?*Amsterdam and Philadelphia: John Benjamins.

Steiner, George. 2001. 'A Man of Many Parts', *The Observer*, 3 June.www.guardian.co. uk/books/2001/jun/03/poetry.features1.

Venutti, Lawrence. 1995. *The Translator's Invisibility: A History of Translation*. New York and Oxford: Routledge.

Wurm, Stephen A. and Ian Heyward. 2001. *Atlas of the World's Languages in Danger of Disappearing*. Second Edition. Paris: UNESCO. http://unesdoc.unesco.org/images/ 0012/001236/123609e.pdf.

5 Gualterio Escoto—a writer across world-literatures

César Domínguez

In a recent discussion on the reception of Walter Scott in Spain, José Enrique García-González and Fernando Toda claim that on the grounds of the number of results returned by the online catalogue of the Biblioteca Nacional de España, 'Scott has certainly been popular in Spain and continues to be so' (2006, 45). In more specific literary terms than mere quantification, they argue that '[t]he reasons for Scott's popularity in nineteenth-century Spain', whose first half is the period I will focus on here, 'are probably similar to those which made him such a favourite with readers in Britain and elsewhere in Europe' (2006, 57).

As the collective volume that includes García-González and Toda's survey focuses on Europe, it would be out of place to note that there is no reference made to the reception of Walter Scott in Spanish America. But what I do want to pinpoint is that Scott's reception in Spanish America during the first half of the nineteenth century, and later, remains an uncharted field, except for vague statements about both his general influence on Spanish American literature and his individual impact on specific writers. As for the former, critics have made contradictory statements. In her seminal book on the national romances of Latin America, Doris Sommer (1993, 26) claimed that Scott's influence was negligible because his "'middle-brow' exemplarity becomes inimitable', whereas, eight years later, Raúl Ianes (1999, 27), in a monograph on the Latin American historical novel, claimed that 'in relation to narrative, mid nineteenth-century Latin American literature is not alien to the influence of Scott's modern historical novel, whose influence since *Waverley* (1814) extended to all western literature'.[1] As far as Scott's influence on specific writers of this period of Latin American literature is concerned, the names of Gertrudis Gómez de Avellaneda, José Antonio Echevarría and José Joaquín Olmedo, among others, have been listed without further elaboration.

Two inter-related facts, however, make the absence of reception studies of Scott in Spanish America intriguing. First, consider both a classical characterisation of the genre and the widely accepted claim about its role in nation building. As for the former, Georg Lukács (1962, 35) famously argued that 'Scott's greatness lies in his capacity to give living human embodiment to historical-social types. The typically human terms in which great historical trends become tangible had never before been so superbly, straightforwardly and pregnantly portrayed'. As for the latter, Benedict Anderson (1991, 26n38) advocated that '[t]he idea of a sociological organism moving calendrically through homogeneous, empty time', embodied best by the historical novel, 'is a precise analogue of the idea of the nation' (1991, 26). As Spanish America gained its independence between 1820 and 1825, it thus seems likely that Scott was adopted into the debate over the national self. Secondly, in Spanish American postcolonial societies 'social classes were not so much defined by the individual's relationship to the means of production but by their patterns of consumption'. It seems consequential that also the Creole readership mimicked the literary habits of the (former) metropoles, including their devotion for Scott.

Against the background of these two facts I want to stress a shared unique historical moment, the one resulting from the Napoleonic wars, which, in Lukács' words, 'everywhere evoked a wave of national feeling, of national resistance to the Napoleonic conquests, an experience of enthusiasm for national independence' (1962, 25). In the specific case of Spain and Spanish America, this enthusiasm for national independence needs to be contemplated across intersecting, post-imperial and postcolonial lines. On the one hand, the occupation of Spain by French forces led to the Peninsular War (1808–1813) and the establishment of *juntas*, a model replicated in Spanish America. When the status of Spain as a client state of the First French Empire ended in 1813, Ferdinand VII revoked all the changes made by the independent Cortes in Cádiz and restored absolute monarchy. On the other hand, for the autonomous governments in Spanish America, Ferdinand's actions led to a definitive de facto break, which extended to the Spanish liberals' efforts to create a representative government for both sides of the Atlantic. After Ferdinand VII died in 1833, Cuba and Puerto Rico remained the only two Spanish colonies in the Americas. Consequently, it is my contention that the study of Scott's reception in Spanish-speaking areas should not be limited by either national or continental borders, but needs to be carried out across a wider area, which I call the postcolonial, transatlantic Spanish world-literature.[2]

A study of Walter Scott's (here, Gualterio Escoto's)[3] reception in both Spanish America *and* Spain, even if restricted to the first half of the nineteenth century, is well beyond the limits of this chapter. Instead I will focus on a specific stage of what Robert Darnton (1982) has called the 'communications circuit' of book history, namely, the one that runs from the author to the publisher, the shipper and the bookseller. Such a communicative perspective is part and parcel of a reception analysis, though reception critics tend to concentrate on how the reader completes the circuit without paying due attention to the manipulation of the literary work by the above-mentioned mediating agents. Conversely, polysystem theorists have paid greater attention to mediating agents, that is, agents who institutionalise a certain idea of what literature is, but from the perspective of literature as a whole, disregarding the peculiarities of certain works in specific times and places. Furthermore, this communicative perspective may provide stronger foundations to current definitions of world literature on the grounds of circulation, for they tend to obliterate the role of mediating agencies, as when David Damrosch (2003, 4) claims that world literature encompasses 'all literary works that circulate beyond their culture of origin, either in translation or in their original language'. Such a definition, in turn, highlights the need to include a further mediating agent, this time between author and publisher, namely, the translator, who is not taken into account in Darnton's circuit.

World-literature

To my knowledge, the first mention of the term 'world-literature' in English is found in Hutcheson Macaulay Posnett's 1886 textbook *Comparative Literature*, within a framework of surveying 'the gradual expansion of social life, from clan to city, from city to nation, from both of these to cosmopolitan humanity, as the proper order of our studies in comparative literature' (1886, 86). In such gradual expansion, world-literature is defined as 'the severance of literature from defined social groups—the universalising of literature' (1886, 236). Though not explicitly stated, it is obvious that 'world-literature' represents Posnett's way of translating Goethe's coinage of *Weltliteratur*, as when Posnett claims that 'Goethe is the admirer of world-literature' (1886, 342).

My use of 'world-literature', however, does not follow Posnett's old spelling for translating the German *Weltliteratur*, but rather makes reference to the body of literary works in a single world language. My proposal draws directly on Fernand Braudel's concept of *économie-monde* (world-economy)[4] and, consequently, my definition reads as follows: world-literature is a fragment of world literature, a literary section in a world language to which its internal links and exchanges give a certain organic unity. This is not to say that 'world-literature' has not been used, more or less independently of the Goethean tradition, in more recent discussions of world literature. Three cases are especially relevant for my purposes.

The first case is a kind of *argumentum a contrario*. Alexander Beecroft (2008, 88) deprecates the concept of world-literature on the grounds that 'it has the perhaps unintended effect of re-inscribing a hegemonic cultural centre'. Although I agree with Beecroft that this negative effect is most conspicuous in Pascale Casanova's (2004) and (to a lesser extent) Franco Moretti's (2000 and 2003) models of world literature, I think Beecroft's non-intentionality, which he himself acknowledges, is an important reason not to dismiss a concept which does not convey a 'mono-centric' meaning *per se*.

The second case results from an internal discussion in non-scholarly French fields about the ongoing acceptability of the concept of *Francophonie*, due to its imperial overtones, and its replacement by *littérature-monde* (world-literature). Originally coined in 1992 by Michel Le Bris with the occasion of the activities promoted by the festival Étonnants Voyageurs, *littérature-monde* reappeared fifteen years later in the manifesto 'Pour une littérature-monde', published in *Le Monde* in March 2007, and, that same year, as a collective book edited by Michel Le Bris and Jean Rouaud. Though an exact definition of the concept is not provided, the most elaborate description reads as follows:

The end of 'francophonie' and the birth of a world-literature in French: these are the stakes, to whatever degree writers accept them.

[We use the term] World-literature, because it is clear that the French literatures spread all over the world today are multiple and diverse, forming a huge network whose ramifications enlace several continents. [...] So it seems a renaissance has arrived, of a dialogue in a vast polyphonic ensemble, without worrying over who knows what struggle for or against the pre-eminence of this or that language or of any such 'cultural imperialism'.

(Le Bris, 2014, 274)[5]

In a more recent and scholarly definition, which enters into dialogue with the Anglophone discussions on world literature, *littérature-monde* is understood as 'an inter-systemic network of exchanges within which French-speaking areas from the periphery establish institutional and discursive relationships' (Francis and Viau, 2013, 5–6).

And the third case is eclectic in its links to the conceptual genealogies and elaborations so far mentioned. On the one hand, Helena Buescu (2013, 34) uses *literatura-mundo* (world-literature) as a translation of the Goethean concept of *Weltliteratur* (like Posnett) and posits a further synonymic relation with 'word literature'. On the other hand, 'my choice when using the concept of *literatura-mundo*', Buescu claims, 'implies accepting it as an adaptation of the concept of *littérature-monde*, proposed in 2004 by a group of French writers and intellectuals' (2013, 54). *Literatura-mundo* is hence defined as the 'simultaneous experience of what is shared and not shared, an archive of potential similarities, but also of differences and endless variations' (Buescu, 2013, 56) within and across Portuguese.

Interestingly, neither of these authors claims the influence of any of Immanuel Wallerstein's world-concepts,[6] except for Beecroft (2008, 87), who precisely rejects the relevance of world-literature and, paradoxically, sees in Wallerstein 'a more immediate point of origin' for current discussions on world literature.

My proposal, therefore, bears no resemblance to the aforementioned three cases. In my understanding of 'world-literature', the economical autarky present in Braudel's and, to some extent, Wallerstein's definition has been replaced by a linguistic component (world language), which nonetheless does not imply linguistic autarky at all. In fact, in a world-literature works originally written in the language in question and works translated into said language cohabitate to the point that both are instrumental for its planetary impact. As defined by Colin Baker and Syvia Prys Jones (1998, 302), world languages traverse 'the boundaries of the regions or countries where they were originally spoken, and are used internationally, either as first or second languages'. On top of that, world languages may achieve a global status when they are 'taken up by other countries around the world' and given 'a special place within their communities' (Crystal, 2003, 4).

Across political, cultural and social differences, a world-literature has a certain unity, one imposed upon it from above (here I am rephrasing Braudel, 1984, 22) on linguistic grounds. A partial example of a world-literature familiar to the English-speaking reader is 'Commonwealth literature', a concept in currency since the 1960s that makes reference to 'the literatures (written in English) of colonies, former colonies (including India) and dependencies of Britain, *excluding the literature of England*' (Ashcroft, Griffiths and Tiffin, 2000, 51; emphasis added).[7] The above-mentioned imposition is quite literal, for language spread is mainly a result of colonialism. And yet this does not imply in any way a monolingual homogeneity. It is at this point that I need to come back to the communicative perspective in order to add a further layer. The traditional view holds that translation mediates between two literatures in different languages. Udo Schöning (2000, 24–25), for instance, claims that transfer, within which translation is of key importance, is an intercultural process, whereas mediation is an intracultural one. My point is, however, that translation is equally instrumental within a single world-literature due to its, however paradoxical, monolingual heterogeneity. It suffices to mention here in this respect that several translations of a single work may circulate simultaneously during a single timespan within a world-literature to meet the standards of different reading communities, as shown from ad hoc prefaces and other editorial notes to intralingual translation. As posited by Buescu for the case of Portuguese, both works written in a world language and works translated into said world language constitute the 'literary heritage available in this language in its several varieties and made of different cultures' (Buescu, 2013, 56). This leads me, similarly as with the case of translation, to question another disciplinary divide, this time the one that identifies comparative literature with interlingual research. The monolingual heterogeneity of world-literatures also requires a multiple comparative perspective in order to address what Buescu has called the 'archive of potential similarities, but also differences and endless variations' (56).

By 1850, it is estimated that the population of Latin America was 30 million (Brea, 2003, 5) and that the population of Spain was 15 million (Maluquer de Motes, 2008, 141), with a literacy rate of 15% in the first case (Roldán Vera, 2003, 34), a figure that varies from country to country, and 20% in the second case (Gabriel, 1997, 201). This is the human background for Gualterio Escoto's circulation across the postcolonial, transatlantic Spanish world-literature, in which Spanish established itself within a single 'inner circle' resulting from what B.B. Kachru (1992) has termed 'first diaspora', namely, the establishment of Spanish in areas subject to colonisation.

Gualterio Escoto across the postcolonial, transatlantic Spanish world-literature, 1823–1850

For the period 1823–1850, my corpus comprises 109 works by Walter Scott, including titles translated into Spanish and/or reprinted several times, one wrongly attributed work (*Clorinda*, by Constantine Henry Phipps) and two forgeries, one by Jules David (*La Pythie des Highlands*, translated as *La maga de la montaña*) and one by Javelin Pagnon and Auguste Callet (*Allan Cameron*). What I am analysing here is Scott's circulation across Spanish world-literature, and all these 109 works have circulated and reached readers as authored by Scott. Of them, only 5 – *El enano misterioso* (1832), *El cuarto entapizado* (1838), *Guy Mannering; o, El astrólogo* (1850), *El oficial aventurero* (1850) and *El Lord de las islas* (1850) – have no information regarding their publishing houses and neither have they been located in a library, so their inclusion is based only on indirect references. Of these 109 works, copies that have circulated in English and in French translation across Spanish world-literature should be taken into consideration as well, but this aim is set aside for the time being.

The circulation of Scott's work began in 1823 with a fragmentary translation of *Ivanhoe* by José María Blanco White, which places Spanish in the tenth position as target language after, in chronological order, German (1810), Portuguese (1811), French (1813), Danish (1817), Italian, Polish and Swedish (1821), Dutch and Russian (1822; Barnaby, 2006). Blanco White, a Spanish exile in London since 1810, translated eight passages from *Ivanhoe* and published them between January 1823 and April 1824 in the magazine he himself edited – *Variedades; o, Mensagero de Londres*. In the preface to the translation, Blanco White (1823, 32) mentions the existence of a French translation of all the 'Scottish novels' and claims that 'English writers are much more difficult to translate into Spanish than Greek or Latin'. Furthermore, he calls attention to the supremacy of Scott in this genre (1823, 32), which is not identified as yet.

As *Variedades* is the magazine that Rudolph Ackermann, a German publisher established in London around 1786, produced for the Spanish American republics (Durán López, 2015, 24), there is no doubt that Blanco White's translation was addressed to Spanish American readership. Tellingly, the first excerpt of Scott's translation was included in the first issue of *Variedades*, which opens with a 'Noticia biográfica de Don Simón de Bolívar' (A Biography of Simón de Bolívar). In fact, there is no trace of *Variedades* circulating in Spain, where the first critical reaction to Scott after Blanco White's translation did not take place until 1829, when Juan Donoso Cortés recommended Scott to students at the Colegio de Humanidades in Cáceres (Peers, 1967, 2, 150).

But the key text for the construction of a postcolonial, transatlantic literary community is 'Literatura anglo-hispana', also authored by Blanco White and included in year 2, issue 8, 1825 of *Variedades*. Under this category (Anglo-Hispanic literature) Blanco White gathered all the works published in Spanish by Ackermann since the seventh issue of *Variedades* in April 1825, including Leandro Fernández de Moratín's *Obras líricas*, José Joaquín de Mora's *No me olvides*, William Paley's *Teología natural*, José Canga Argüelles' *Elementos de la ciencia de hacienda* and José María de Urcullu's *Catecismo de mitología*. In 1825 and 1826 two book-length translations into Spanish were also published by Ackermann for the first time—*Ivanhoe* and *El Talismán* (five years and one year after the originals, respectively). The translator is another Spanish exile, José Joaquín de Mora, whom Blanco White (1825, 253) had praised in 'Literatura anglo-hispana' for his linguistic skills 'among the ones who write in Spanish in non-Spanish speaking countries'.

As for Spain, the first translation of Scott – *El Talismán; o, Ricardo en Palestina: novela histórica del tiempo de las cruzadas* – was published in 1826 (one year after the original) by the publisher J.F. Piferrer in Barcelona. The translators were Juan Nicasio Gallego and Eugenio de Tapia (Churchman and Peers, 1922, 269), though the text is presented without names. The fact that Gallego was later in contact with Ignacio Sanponts and Buenaventura Carlos Aribau's circle (Freire López, 1999) and that their project was translating Scott's novels (Freire López, 2005) should be related to this first translation. The translation, presented as direct from English into Spanish, does not include any kind of editorial notes.

The timespan I am focusing on here for the circulation of Scott's works across Spanish world-literature closes in 1849, when Mora's 1826 translation of *The Talisman* was reprinted by the publisher Juan Oliveres in Barcelona. The translation is bound with the translation of Comtesse de Genlis' *Le Siège de La Rochelle*. In this period, the last translation of Scott published in Spanish America was in La Habana in 1838 by the publisher Ramón Oliva (see Sánchez Baena, 2009, 182).

Between 1823 and 1850 there were a total of 109 works by Scott published, consisting of 38 different titles (see Figure 5.1). They were published in six countries (Cuba, England, France, Mexico, Spain and the US) by 37 publishing houses (see Figure 5.2). In terms of the number of titles published, Spain and France represent the two main publishing countries, followed at a great distance by England. As for cities, Madrid (31), Barcelona (26) and Paris (18) stand in the three top positions, followed by Bordeaux (7) and Perpignan (4). The main publishing house was Moreno (16) in Madrid, closely followed by Bergnes de las Casas (15) in Barcelona and Rosa (11) in Paris. A total of 33 translators have been identified, 10 only by their initials. A total of 46 items remain anonymous in terms of their translators. The closest equivalent for Spanish to the role performed for French by Auguste-Jean-Baptiste Defauconpret is Pablo de Xérica, who translated seven works by Scott for several French publishing houses. Xérica is followed by Francisco Altés y Gurena (3) and Eugenio de Ochoa (3). Most translators, however, translated just one work by Scott.

This numerical hierarchy is nonetheless inconsequential when it comes to understanding the circulation of Scott across Spanish world-literature. Such an understanding requires a re-reading of all these data against the background of Darnton's communications circuit by focusing on the mediating agents between printers and readers, namely, shippers and booksellers.

Let us begin with one case, which in every category is placed in the lowest position: the publisher Ackermann in London, with only two works by Scott (*Ivanhoe*, either fragmentary or book-length, and *The Talisman*) and two translators (Blanco White and Mora). In the 'Boletín bibliográfico' of *El Repertorio Americano* (August 1827), the Venezuelan humanist Andrés Bello (1827, 310–311), at that moment secretary to the legation of Gran Colombia in London, writes in relation to the Spanish translation of Samuel Richardson's *Clarissa* that:

this excellent novel, one of the few that should not only be allowed but recommended to young female readers, was as difficult to find in the Spanish version published in Madrid in 1796 as looked after by the audience both in Spain and Spanish America.

The quote is telling in every respect. *Clarissa*, one of the few readings approved for a female audience, had been translated into Spanish by José Marcos Gutiérrez, through Pierre Le Tourneur's French translation, and published in two volumes in Madrid by Benito Cano in 1794–1796. Due to its success, it was difficult to acquire copies for over thirty years, after which Ackermann decided to reprint it and, according to Bello's words, correct it in light of the English original, resulting in a more beautifully typographical volume (Bello, 1827, 311).

Published in London by Bossange, Barthés & Lowell, a firm specialising in selling books in French, Italian, Spanish and Portuguese in 'elegant bindings' (Anon, 1830, n.p.), *El Repertorio Americano* was another instrumental magazine for building a transatlantic Spanish-speaking community and addressed mainly a Spanish American readership, as explicitly stated in the initial 'Prospecto': 'Lovers of Spanish American civilisation wished to see a journal that advocated the independence and freedom of the new republics as its own cause' (Bello, 1826, 1). For such a community, London was called to play a key role: 'London is the most suitable place for the publication of such journal. Its commercial relations with the transatlantic countries make of the city their centre' (Bello, 1826, 1–2).

In a similar vein to Bello's admonition, in 1845–1846 the Mexican writer and diplomat Manuel Payno presented his female characters in *El fistol del diablo* as readers of Scott, for his novels are adequate for women. These gender codes have been also advocated for 'real' readers. The *Semanario de las señoritas mejicanas*, for instance, whose first issue was published in December 1840, presented Scott's characters – such as *Ivanhoe*'s Rebecca, *The Betrothed*'s Eveline Berenger, *Waverley*'s Flora Mac Ivor and *The Bride of Lammermoor*'s Lucia – as models for female education (Galí Boadella, 2002, 195–196). If one takes into consideration the approximate timespan between October 1826, when Mora's Spanish translation of *Ivanhoe* was praised in *El Repertorio Americano* by Bello, and the mid-1840s, when Payno recommended to read Scott, and wonders which publishers, shippers and booksellers could have provided Mexican readers with access to Scott's novels, the list will include mainly Rudolph Ackermann and Frédéric Rosa.[8]

As already noted, Ackermann published a fragmentary translation of *Ivanhoe* (by Blanco White) in 1823 and book-length translations of *Ivanhoe* and *The Talisman* (both by Mora) in 1825 and 1826. Already in 1825, Ackermann had sent his second son, George, to Mexico City to open a branch of the bookstore (Roldán Vera, 2003, 105). Beyond the commercial borders of Mexico, Ackermann could sell his books through a network of shippers and booksellers that reached Gran Colombia (present-day Colombia, Venezuela, Ecuador, Panama, northern Peru, western Guyana and northwest Brazil), the United Provinces of the Rio de la Plata (present-day Argentina, Bolivia, Paraguay and Uruguay), Chile, Peru and Guatemala.

Between 1835 and the mid-1840s, the French firm Rosa published nine translations into Spanish of Scott: *El día San Valentín* (1835, by José María Moralejo), *Las aventuras de Nigel* (1836, by Pablo de Xérica), *Perevil del Pico* (1836, by W. Montes), *Guy Mannering; o, El astrólogo* (1840, by Eugenio de Ochoa), *El monasterio* (1840, by Eugenio de Ochoa), *El abad* (1840), *Los desposados; o, El conde de Chester* (1840, by Pedro Mata), *El castillo peligroso* (1840, by Pedro Mata) and *Las aguas de San Ronan* (1841, by Eugenio de Ochoa). Similarly to Ackermann, Rosa had affiliate companies in Spanish America. In Mexico City, Rosa's books were sold by the most important bookseller in the 1820s and 1830s, Mariano Galván (Suárez de la Torre, 2011); in Argentina, by the firm Larrea Hermanos (Leiva, 2005; Parada, 1995).

It should also be noted that the Mexican firm Galván was the first to commission not only a translation into Spanish of Scott to be published in Spanish America, but one of a novel that had yet to be translated—*Waverley* (1833). It was translated by the Cuban poet José María Heredia, who one year before had published a seminal study on the historical novel for Spanish America (Algaba, 2005, 288).

Conversely, publishing houses with higher numbers of titles by Scott reached only local audiences. This is the case of the firms Oficina de Federico Moreno[9] and Librería de Tomás Jordán in Madrid, with 16 titles, and Bergnes de las Casas in Barcelona, with 15. Jordán was a versatile businessman active since around 1832 (Rubio Cremades, 1995, 14) who worked in the fields of production and commerce of paper, printing, editing and bookselling (Morán Orti, 2011, 86). Though I have not been able to establish the exact connection between Jordán and Moreno, it is most probable that after a certain point, the books were printed by Moreno and sold at Jordán's bookstore. There is no doubt that Jordán was one of the most important printers of the period in Madrid, as proven by the many magazines and journals he published and the contributors to his publications (Rubio Cremades, 1995, 15). However, he lacked a distribution network outside Spain.

Antonio Bergnes de las Casas, in turn, was a philologist who between 1830 and 1843 directed a publishing house in Barcelona. A translator himself of Goethe and Chateaubriand, he was a friend of Scott, whom he met in London. His catalogue was extensive and in accordance with his literary training, but he did not have an equal ability for business, and declared bankruptcy in 1843 (Elías de Molins, 1889, 274). Bergnes de las Casas' books were sold in Madrid at the Librería Europea, which distributed throughout Spain. As in the case of Jordán, he also lacked a distribution network outside Spain.

Between the transatlantic business of Ackermann and Rosa and the local Spanish business of Jordán and Bergnes de las Casas, the French printers Jean Alzine and Pierre II Beaume attained an intermediate, bilateral position between France and Spain. Alzine printed four Spanish translations of Scott between 1826 and 1827, though in October 1824 he announced the publication of all Scott's novels in Spanish translation in 82 volumes (Marrast, 1988). Had this

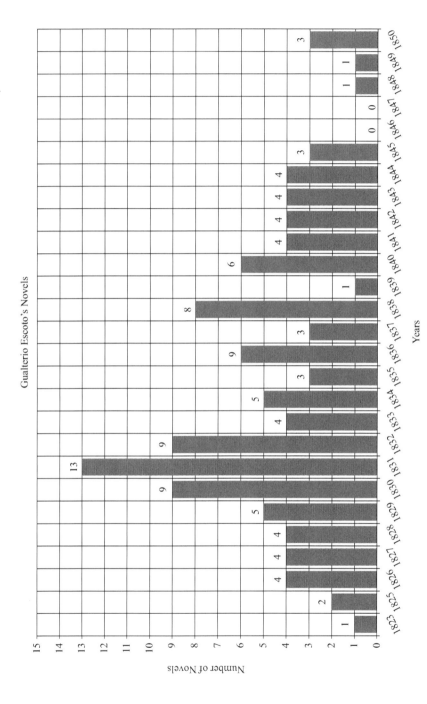

Figure 5.1 Number of Gualterio Escoto's novels per year, 1800–1850.

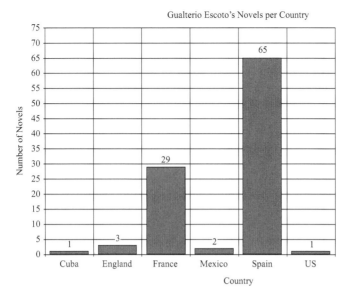

Figure 5.2 Production of Gualterio Escoto's novels per country, 1800–1850.

publication materialised, Alzine would have been responsible for the most ambitious translation project across Europe in the 1820s, which would have dramatically flooded the Spanish literary market with 22 titles between February 1825 and, approximately, August 1827, at a rate of four volumes every six weeks.[10] Robert Marrast (1988, 69) claims in this respect that Alzine was impelled by the success of the French translations, which sold 1,400,000 copies in five years. Spanish readers would have been secured in collaboration with Oliva, a printer and bookseller in Barcelona (Marrast, 1988, 74). But the project did not materialise mainly, according to Marrast (1988, 77), due to the competence of French and English printers, not to mention the problems resulting from publishing forbidden writers such as Rousseau, Constantin François de Chassebœuf, Pigault-Lebrun or Antoine Destutt de Tracy, to name but a few.

Pierre II Beaume, a printer and bookseller established in Bordeaux, published between 1827 and 1835 seven Spanish translations of Scott, three of which were made by the Spanish exile, Pablo de Xérica. He specialised in publishing books in Spanish (in fact, he signed his books as Pedro Beaume) for a readership mainly in Spain. I have not been able to trace any commercial relation with Spanish America.

*

Whereas literary critics conventionally define writers' achievements in aesthetic terms, for book historians, the circulation of books is a matter of trade, investment and commercial speculation that makes book production, as Mark Rose (2002, 13) has argued, 'one of the most capitalistic of early industries'.

Acute observers, however, see both dimensions intertwined, as when the Irish clergyman Robert Walsh, while crossing the plains of Transylvania in 1827, stopped at a bookseller's shop in Hermannstardt (today Sibiu) to buy a map of Hungary and described his coming across Scott's novels in the following terms.

> While looking about the shop, the bookseller, who spoke French, directed my attention to a portrait which he had just hung up. I asked who it was, and he replied, 'Le Sieur Valtere Skote, l'homme le plus célèbre en toute l'Europe'. It was certainly no small proof of his celebrity to have his picture thus exhibited in an obscure town at the remotest confines of civilized Europe: his novels, translated in French and German, formed a considerable part of the books in the shop.
>
> (Walsh, 1828, 335)

My analysis of the data relative to the 109 works by Scott that have circulated across Spanish world-literature during the first half of the nineteenth century shows that the best placed mediating agents between the writer and his readers are not the ones with a higher number of 'Scott holdings', but the ones with a truly international distribution network. From such a perspective, the global capital cities of the postcolonial transatlantic Spanish-speaking community were London, with Rudolph Ackermann, and Paris, with Frédéric Rosa. Both printers took advantage of a group of Spanish liberal exiles for translating Scott's works and addressed the big Spanish American audience and, to a lesser extent, speakers of Spanish across Europe, with the exceptions of those in Spain. This country, in turn, had its own publishing centres, such as Madrid with Jordán and Barcelona with Bergnes de las Casas, which were extremely important locally but held a completely secondary importance within the bigger frame of the transatlantic world. Furthermore, Spain was also served by foreign publishing centres located in Perpignan (with Jean Alzine) and Bordeaux (with Pedro Beaume).

Whereas Scott's products for Spain usually lacked mediating editorial texts, the ones for Spanish America were richer in this respect due to a concern for the audience of the new republics and the role Scott's works might play. Mora's prefaces for his translations of *Ivanhoe* and *The Talisman* are key examples. In short, Scott's works represented an invitation to re-write the history of the 'American countries that once were Spanish' (Preface, *El Talismán*, reproduced in Durán López, 2015, 189).

A further factor for the global role of London and Paris is that they were in the position to provide Spanish American republics with the education materials they so badly needed. The Spanish American republics, in turn, made of these two cities a source of enlightenment and modernity, in contrast to the former metropoles. In translation terms, this correlates to what may be called 'translation packets', meaning that when a source item is selected for being either translated or circulated, literary texts are placed next to non-literary texts. Of the nearly 80 titles in Spanish by Ackermann for being distributed in Spanish America, around 10% were fiction. The following quote by Domingo

Faustino Sarmiento[11] – a reader of the complete collection of Scott's novels in English (Roldán Vera, 2003, 188) – while in San Luis around 1825 shows extremely well how accurately Ackermann met the needs of the market.

> there should be books, I said to myself, that deal with these issues, that teach children. When understanding well what one reads, one may learn without the help of teachers. I embarked on the search of such books and, in that distant province, in the moment I took my decision, I found what I was looking for, just as I have imagined it. Patriots, who loved Spanish America and who perceived this need of educating South America, answered my requests and sent Ackermann's *catecismos* [textbooks], which were introduced in San Juan by don Tomás Rojo.
>
> (Sarmiento, 2017, 139)

But the success of these transcontinental entrepreneurs was also due to a further factor – political lobbying. I have argued elsewhere that on or around 1838, the history of world literature changed due to a historic change in the mastery of circulation (Domínguez, forthcoming). This change resulted from a series of bilateral agreements that established that the flow of books, as materialised in printing, reprinting, translation and vending, should be protected under copyright laws. In my previous research, I focused on circulation across Europe and between the British empire and its colonies. Whether 1838 represented an inflection point also for literary circulation in general and Scott's works in particular across Spanish world-literature is a matter that deserves further study. But in the light of Ackermann's many requests to the Colombian, Mexican and Guatemalan governments for the protection of his books (Roldán Vera, 2003, 39), one may conclude that the transatlantic circulation of Gualterio Escoto during the first half of the nineteenth century was also a part, however minor, of a not altogether different dimension of the national self, namely, national literatures, for their emergence is equally linked to the rights of writers, publishers and readers.

My study shows the need to move beyond a dichotomous view that separates national literatures and world literature. Literary works simultaneously circulate across literary contexts of varying scales, and one of these contexts is 'world-literature', i.e., the body of literary works in a world language. Between 1823 and 1850 the first transfer of Walter Scott's work took place between two world-literatures, namely, world-literature in English and world-literature in Spanish. Such transfer included circulation in the source world language, which has not been analysed here, and circulation in translation into the target world language. In the latter case, translation includes the particularities proper of interlingual translation (from English into Spanish), mediated interlingual translation (from English into Spanish through French) and intralingual translation, as shown by the adaptation process to the different Spanish-speaking audiences. Contrary to expectations, a cultural centre within a world-literature does not necessarily need to be located in the target language area. Here, the circulation of Walter Scott (packaged as 'Gualterio Escoto') across Spanish America was made possible by the global role of London and Paris, whereas cities such as Madrid and Barcelona played a more restricted and local role. Translation, in short, is not only instrumental for communication between literatures in different languages (including world-literatures), but also *within* world-literatures due to their, however paradoxical, monolingual heterogeneity.

Notes

1   Unless otherwise stated, all translations are mine.
2   For the sense in which I use the concept of 'world-literature', in contradistinction to the concept of 'world literature', see Section 1.
3   Gualterio Escoto is the Spanish name given to Walter Scott in some nineteenth-century translations. Beyond the usual Spanish translation rule for proper names which Miguel de Unamuno called 'castizo transcripcionismo' (traditional transcription), I symbolically take the name of 'Gualterio Escoto' to embody all the transformations needed for making possible the circulation of Scott's works across the Spanish world-literature.
4   Braudel (1984, 22) defines *économie-monde* (world-economy) as 'a fragment of the world, an economically autonomous section of the planet able to provide for most of its own needs, a section to which its internal links and exchanges give a certain organic unity'.
5   Though in the title of the English translation of Le Bris' essay *littérature-monde* is rendered as 'world-literature', in the body it is translated as 'world literature'. In order to avoid further confusion, I have re-introduced the hyphen in the quoted passage.
6   Wallerstein (1974, 15), in turn, draws on Braudel's concept of *économie-monde* (world-economy) for his own concept of 'world-system', which he defines as 'an economic [...] entity' which: 'encompasses within its bounds [...] empires, city-states, and the emerging "nation-states". It is a "world" system, not because it encompasses the whole world, but because it is larger than any juridically-defined political unit. And it is a "world-*economy*" because the basic linkage between the parts of the system is economic, although this was reinforced to some extent by cultural links and, eventually, [...] by political arrangements and even confederal structures.'
7   I consider Commonwealth literature to be a 'partial' example of world-literature due to the exclusion of 'the literature of England'. In my view, a world-literature comprises all the works in the global language in question regardless of their provenance. Interestingly, since its foundation in 1965 the *Journal of Commonwealth Literature* – a leading publication still today – has claimed that 'Commonwealth literature' should not be understood as 'a perverse underwriting of any concept of a single, culturally homogeneous body of writings'. And yet, the areas covered are exclusively Australia, Canada, the Caribbean, East and Central Africa, India, Malaysia and Singapore, New Zealand, Pakistan, South Africa, Sri Lanka and West Africa.
8   Bello (1827, 319) recommended Mora's translation of *Ivanhoe* in the following terms: it includes 'almost all the beauties of the original and takes us magically to the heroic and violent centuries of chivalry'.
9   'Moreno's press, which was located in the Plazuela del Cordón, has been relocated to Afligidos, 1, the property called of the Ánimas. The owner has made his best so customers find fairness and efficient service' (*Diario de avisos de Madrid*, 7 March 1830, 263).
10 Alzine made clear in his 'Prospecto' that his translation project addressed the Spanish readership, and not the Spanish American one: 'We are certain that these translations

will fulfill the desires and expectations of the most meticulous and demanding reader. Renown men of letters in Spain are in charge of this job with the only aim of enriching their nation with this new treasure' ('Prospecto', reproduced in Marrast, 1988, 70).

11 'I translated the sixty books of the whole series of Walter Scott's novels, one per day, and many others thanks to the good offices of Mr. Eduardo Abott' (Sarmiento, 2017, 145).

Works cited

Algaba, L. (2005). Por los umbrales de la novela histórica. In: Clark de Lara, B. and Speckman Guerra, E. eds. *La República de las Letras. Asomos a la cultura escrita del México decimonónico*. México: Universidad Nacional Autónoma de México, Vol. 1, pp. 287–302.

Anderson, B. (1991). *Imagined Communities. Reflections on the Origin and Spread of Nationalism*. Rev. edn. London: Verso.

Anon (1830). *Catalogue des livres français, italiens, espagnols, portugais, &c. qui se trouvent chez Bossange, Barthés & Lowell*. London: G. Schulze.

Ashcroft, B., Griffiths, G. and Tiffin, H. (2000). *Post-Colonial Studies: The Key Concepts*. London: Routledge.

Baker, C. and Prys Jones, S. (1998). *Encyclopedia of Bilingualism and Bilingual Education*. Clevedon: Multilingual Matters.

Barnaby, P. (2006). Timeline of the European Reception of Sir Walter Scott, 1802–2005. In: Pittock, M. ed. *The Reception of Sir Walter Scott in Europe*. London: Continuum, pp. xxiv–lxxiv.

Beecroft, A. (2008). World Literature without a Hyphen: Towards a Typology of Literary Systems. *New Left Review*, 54, 87–100.

Bello, A. (1826). Prospecto. In: *El Repertorio Americano. Londres, 1826–1827*. Reprint 1973. Caracas: Presidencia de la República, Vol. 1, pp. 1–6.

Bello, A. (1827). Boletín bibliográfico. In: *El Repertorio Americano. Londres, 1826–1827*. Reprint 1973. Caracas: Presidencia de la República, Vol. 2, pp. 296–314.

Blanco White, J.M. (1823). Retazos de la novela inglesa intitulada Ivanhoe . *Variedades; o, Mensagero de Londres*, 1(1), 31–38.

Blanco White, J.M. (1825). Literatura anglo-hispana. *Variedades; o, Mensagero de Londres*, 2(8), 251–253.

Braudel, F. (1984). *The Perspective of the World*. Trans. Siân Reynolds. Vol. 3 of *Civilization and Capitalism 15th–18th Century*. London: Collins.

Brea, J.A. (2003). Population Dynamics in Latin America. *Population Bulletin* 58(1), 3–36.

Buescu, H.C. (2013). *Experiência do incomum e boa vizinhança. Literatura Comparada e Literatura-Mundo*. Porto: Porto.

Casanova, P. (2004). *The World Republic of Letters*. Trans. M.B. DeBevoise. Cambridge, MA: Harvard UP.

Churchman, Ph.H. and Peers, E.A. (1922). A Survey of the Influence of Sir Walter Scott in Spain. *Revue Hispanique*, 55, 227–310.

Crystal, D. (2003). *English as a Global Language*. 2nd edn. Cambridge: Cambridge UP.

Damrosch, D. (2003). *What Is World Literature?* Princeton: Princeton UP.

Darnton, R. (1982). What Is the History of Books? *Daedalus*, 111(3), 65–83.

Domínguez, César (forthcoming). *1838: World Literature, International Authorship, Euro-centrism and Law*.

Durán López, F. (2015). *Versiones de un exilio. Los traductores españoles de la casa Ackermann (Londres, 1823–1830)*. Madrid: Escolar y Mayo.

Elías de Molins, A. (1889). *Diccionario biográfico y bibliográfico de escritores y artistas catalanes del siglo XIX (apuntes y datos)*. Vol. 1. Barcelona: Fidel Giró.

Francis, C.W. and Viau, R. (2013). La Littérature-monde: vers une dynamique repensée du centre et de la périphérie. Une introduction. In: Francis, C.W. and Viau, R. eds. *Trajectoires et dérives de la littérature-monde. Poétiques de la relation et du divers dans les espaces francophones*. Amsterdam: Rodopi, pp. 5–12.

Freire López, A.Ma. (1999). Juan Nicasio Gallego, traductor. In: Lafarga, F., ed. *La traducción en España (1750–1830). Lengua, Literatura, Cultura*. Lleida: Universitat de Lleida, pp. 521–528.

Freire López, A.Ma. (2005). Un negocio editorial romántico (Aribau y Walter Scott). *Anales de Literatura Española*, 18, 163–180.

Gabriel, N.de. (1997). Alfabetización, semialfabetización y analfabetismo en España (1860–1991). *Revista Complutense de Educación*, 8(1), 199–231.

Galí Boadella, M. (2002). *Historias del bello sexo: la introducción del Romanticismo en México*. México: Universidad Nacional Autónoma de México.

García-González, J.E. and Toda, F. (2006). The Reception of Sir Walter Scott in Spain. In: Pittock, M., ed. *The Reception of Sir Walter Scott in Europe*. London: Continuum, pp. 45–63.

Ianes, R. (1999). *De Cortés a la huérfana enclaustrada. La novela histórica del romanticismo hispanoamericano*. New York: Peter Lang.

Kachru, B.B. (1992). The Second Diaspora of English. In: Machan, T. and Scott, C., eds. *English in Its Social Contexts: Essays in Historical Sociolinguistics*. Oxford: Oxford University Press, pp. 230–252.

Le Bris, M.*et al.* (2014). For a World-Literature in French. Trans. Delia Ungureanu. In: Damrosch, D., ed. *World Literature in Theory*. Oxford: John Wiley & Sons, pp. 271–275.

Leiva, A.D. (2005). El rol de la librería internacional en la difusión de la literatura jurídica. El caso de Rosa & Bouret en el Río de la Plata. *Revista de Historia del Derecho*, 33, 159–171.

Lukács, G. (1962). *The Historical Novel*. Trans. Hannah and Stanley Mitchell. London: Merlin.

Maluquer de Motes, J. (2008). El crecimiento moderno de la población de España de 1850 a 2001: una serie homogénea anual. *Investigaciones de Historia Económica*, 10, 129–162.

Marrast, R. (1988). Ediciones perpiñanesas de Walter Scott en castellano (1824–1826). *Romanticismo*, 3–4, 69–81.

Morán Orti, M. (2011). *Editores, libreros e impresores en el umbral del Nuevo Régimen*. Madrid: Consejo Superior de Investigaciones Científica.

Moretti, F. (2000). Conjectures on World Literature. *New Left Review*, 1, 54–68.

Moretti, F. (2003). More Conjectures. *New Left Review*, 20, 73–81.

Parada, A.E. (1995). Introducción al mundo del libro a través de los avisos de La Gaceta Mercantil (1823–1828). *Investigación bibliotecológica*, 9(18), 4–16.

Peers, E.A. (1967). *Historia del movimiento romántico español*. Trans. José María Gimeno. 2nd edn. 2 vols. Madrid: Gredos.

Posnett, H.M. (1886). *Comparative Literature*. London: Kegan Paul, Trench & Co.

Roldán Vera, E. (2003). *The British Book Trade and Spanish American Independence. Education and Knowledge Transmission in Transcontinental Perspective*. Aldershot: Ashgate.

Rose, M. (2002). *Authors and Owners. The Invention of Copyright*. 3rd rpt. Cambridge, MA: Harvard University Press.

Rubio Cremades, E. (1995). *Periodismo y literatura: Ramón de Mesonero Romanos y el 'Semanario Pintoresco Español'*. Alacant: Institut de Cultura 'Juan Gil-Albert'.

Sánchez Baena, J.J. (2009). *El terror de los tiranos. La imprenta en la centuria que cambió Cuba (1763–1868)*. Castelló de la Plana: Universitat Jaume I.

Sarmiento, D.F. (2017). *Recuerdos de provincia*. Barcelona: Red.

Schöning, U. (2000). Die Internationalität nationaler Literaturen. Bemerkugen zur Problematik und ein Vorschlag. In: Schöning, U., ed. *Internationalität nationaler Literaturen. Beiträge zum ersten Symposion des Göttinger Sonderforschungsbereichs 529*. Göttingen: Wallstein, pp. 9–43.

Sommer, D. (1993). *Foundational Fictions. The National Romances of Latin America*. Berkeley: University of California Press.

Suárez de la Torre, L. (2011). Construir un Mercado, renovar las lecturas y hacer nuevos lectores. La Librería de Frédéric Rosa (1824–1850). *Bulletin Hispanique*, 113(1), 469–484.

Wallerstein, I. (1974). *Capitalist Agriculture and the Origins of the European World-Economy in the Sixteenth Century*. Vol. 1 of The Modern World-System. New York: Academic Press.

Walsh, R. (1828). *Narrative of a Journey from Constantinople to England*. 2nd ed. London: Frederick Westley & A.H. Davis.

German, translation, and the world
in Czernowitz

Sherry Simon

In the course of narrating her first encounter since childhood with her 90-year-old cousin Rosa in the city of Czernowitz, Marianne Hirsch takes a moment to describe the bookshelves that occupy a prominent space in the apartment. The visit to Rosa Roth Zuckermann comes at the beginning of a remarkable exploration of the history and myths of that central European city, and the content of the bookshelves will play a central role in the story that will unfold. The largely German-language contents of the shelves speak of the rich intermixture of Jewish and German cultural experience in the Bukovina, the easternmost possession of the Habsburg empire from 1774 to 1918 (Hirsch and Spitzer 2010, 14–19). And the books also speak of the idea of a German-language world literature that prevailed in Central Europe. This chapter will track the ways in which cousin Rosa's library leads from the small space of a somewhat dilapidated and antiquated apartment into the wide expanse of a literary universe—with special attention to the role of translation in the creation of 'the world.'

In *Ghosts of Home: Czernowitz in Jewish Memory* (2010), Marianne Hirsch and Leo Spitzer accompany Hirsch's parents on a return to the city they left at the end of the Second World War. Their return is a voyage into memory as well an attempt to reconstitute the historical evidence of the Holocaust in Romanian-occupied Bukovina. Along the way, they evoke the singular culture of a city known for its bookishness, for its historical identity as a colonial outpost and for its allegiance to an international literary culture. For Aharon Appelfeld, who spent his early years in Czernowitz, the city was just like its more famous sisters, the great cosmopolitan cities of the empire, only 'smaller and less distinguished' (Appelfeld 2001, 36).

> Linguistically and culturally, the Jews of my early childhood had remained Habsburgs, and for many years after the empire crumbled, I regarded the Habsburg Jews of Vienna, Prague and Budapest whom I met in Israel as though they were from my own city of Czernowitz.
>
> (Appelfeld 2001, 36)

In the many descriptions of the 'Vienna of the east' is echoed this same sense of participating—from a small corner at the edge of empire—in the greatness of a large universe.

Hirsch provides a detailed description of the contents of the bookcase, defining three broad categories of books. The first is by Czernowitz authors, the most famous among them Paul Celan, but including Rose Ausländer, Selma Meerbaum-Eisinger, Viktor Wittner, Alfred Kittner, Eliezer Shteynbarg and Itzik Manger. A second category is that of the German classics, the beloved volumes that could be found from one end to the other of the German-language lands, and were especially treasured by the German-Jewish bourgeoisie: 'Goethe, Schiller, Heine, Rilke, Mann, Hauptmann, Keller, Storm ...'

> 'Those volumes,' Rosa indicated, pointing to the classics, 'were the books of my youth. My mother knew poetry by Heine, Schiller, and Goethe by heart, and she and my father introduced me to their poems as a young girl. They only had four grades of formal schooling, but they were very well read.'
>
> (cited in Hirsch and Spitzer 2010, 16)

And the third category are mainly non-German writers: Romanian works by Mihai Eminescu and Ion Luca Caragiale, many Russian and Ukrainian titles—by Tolstoy, Dostoevsky, Gogol, Bakunin, Kobylianska—as well as late-twentieth-century German, English, American and French novels. The bookshelves also display writings on the wartime concentration camps—Viktor Frankl, Bruno Bettelheim, Primo Levi—as well as Israeli fiction in German translation (and also Zweig, Feutchtwanger, Marcel Reich Ranicki)[1] (Hirsch and Spitzer 2010, 17) Most of the books are in German, but there are also some English, French, Russian and Ukrainian translations of Czernowitz authors as well as translations into German (such as Itzik Manger, originally in Yiddish).

Hirsch presents this library as a striking representation of the 'Deutschtum' that she will go on to describe in a later chapter—an 'idea of Germanness' and a library of German classics for which Czernowitz Jews expressed an utter and enduring loyalty, even after the city had passed into Romanian hands in 1918. While Rosa's library stood for a world past, it also represents a literature in motion. It was remarkably local—highlighting the fertile offerings of a small city with an intense literary life. But local takes on a new meaning when it becomes clear that because of the dramatic historical events which the city had experienced—the fall of the Empire in 1918, the subsequent occupation by Romania, and then the events of World War II and the Holocaust—much of Czernowitz literature was written by writers in exile, creating an extensive diasporic body of works. The great promoter and anthologizer of Bukovinian literature, Alfred Margul-Sperber, kept Bukovina's writing alive in Bucharest; Paul Celan, after the tragic events of the Holocaust, moved from Czernowitz to Bucharest to Paris; Rose Ausländer spent parts of her life in the United States and then chose her final exile in Germany; Aharon Appelfeld, who lost the German language with the murder of his mother and his subsequent experience as a Jewish child in hiding during the war, became an Israeli writer in Hebrew. And the onward movement of Jewish history would include Holocaust testimonies as well as Israeli literature. Many of the works are themselves nourished by translational relationships—whether it be the self-translation of Manger from German into Yiddish or Manger's and Shteynbarg's Yiddish works translated into German, the translational nature of so many Czernowitz authors, or the work of Czernowitz authors translated from German into other European languages.

Cousin Rosa, in 1998, was one of the few German-language speakers still living in the Ukrainian city now called Chernivtsi, and as such she was something of a relic. She remained immobile, while the literature of her city had been thrust into movement, shifting around her. Like the character Hanemann in Stefan Chwin's novel, *Death in Danzig*, cousin Rosa and her library were vestiges of the German language in a city which now spoke other tongues (Chwin 2004).

It is the combination of immobility and mobility, local and worldly, which will be the focus of this exploration of translation and world literature. World literature will be understood here as a cipher, an open question, a 'focus of reflection in literary studies' (D'haen et al. 2012, xviii)— that interacts with attendant notions of globalization and transnationalism, refusing an easy separation between home and the world. Translation, as has often been said, is integral to the existence of world literature—whatever its definition (Bermann 2012; Bermann 2012). Translation is essential to the processes of diffusion and consecration by which locally produced authors, texts and literatures become globalized; it is the explicit or implicit means through which literature written with a global or transnational readership in mind is created and disseminated. But translation can also be part of the very production of literature itself—the processes of creation through which some Czernowitz writers (the Ukrainian Olha Kobylianska, the Yiddish writer Itzik Manger, the poet Rose Ausländer and the great Paul Celan) brought their works into the world. Before these works travelled the globe through diasporic connections, they were first the product of the conflictual language relations of a multilingual city. The perspective of the multilingual city complicates the definition of world literature as 'non-national' as the intermixing of 'local' and 'foreign' forms (Bermann 2012, 171). In what follows, the relationship between German, translation and 'the world' will be examined from the perspective of east central Europe, the lands once called 'Mitteleuropa.'[2]

What does 'German' mean?

Despite the fact that the German language provided the initial and still very current term *Weltliteratur*, German has been largely absent from discussions on the topic (Beebee 2014). If for Goethe, German was the prime candidate for the language of the newly emerging world literature,[3] this pretension has withered with the course of world history, as has the geographical reach of the language. German was once a language exercising influence right across eastern Europe, both as an administrative imperial language and as the language of German settlers who had immigrated to the east beginning in the Middle Ages—with waves of immigration continuing until the late seventeenth century (Stevenson and Carl 2010, 53–56). German was the lingua franca and *koine* of Central Europe for more than two centuries, from the eighteenth century to the First World War. The defeat of Nazism in 1945 saw the expulsion of some twelve million German language inhabitants of eastern Europe, forced to travel west. Overnight Danzig became Gdansk, Breslau became Wroclaw, as refugee populations moved into the houses that were forcibly abandoned (see Davies and Moorhouse 2003; Chwin 2004). As the Iron Curtain isolated the now Communist Eastern European countries from the West, this heritage became even more invisible.

A recent attempt to draw German into the discussion of world literature, *German Literature as World Literature* (Beebee 2014) seems divided in its depiction of German literature as a 'national' literature which is refracted internationally, 'defining itself over, against, and through their others' (p. 4) and a literature whose 'transnational moments' include 'the processes of rewriting, translation, dialogue that create worldwide links' (p. 8). The only suggestion that German literature might not be so unquestionably 'German' after all is left to one final essay in the collection, which refers to a *new* World Literature which recognizes the hybrid identities of many of Germany's most important contemporary authors of Turkish or Iranian descent (Beebee 2014, 18).

One might argue, however, that a powerful example of what World literature, or a form of transnationalism, in German represents might already be found in the German-language world of Eastern Central Europe.[4] The history of the past century has continually redefined what may be called 'the territory' of the Germanist (Valentin 2007, 3).[5] And this view of a trans-German literary network was perhaps only enabled with the fall of the Berlin Wall in 1989, allowing the German-language world of Eastern Central Europe to be revisited. But the terrain had already been prepared, so to speak, by the writings of a critic like Claudio Magris, whose many essays but most importantly his literary travelogue *Danubio* had recast the German heritage of the Habsburgs in the light of cultural mélange. The Triestine essayist has become the most eloquent exponent of the idea of Mitteleuropa as a mixture of cultures, centered around the Danube, a river whose identity is diametrically opposed to that of the Rhine as a 'a mythical custodian of the purity of the race' (Magris 1990, 32). 'The Danube is the river of Vienna, Bratislava, Budapest, Belgrade and of Dacia, symbolizing a German-Magyar-Slavic-Romanic-Jewish Central Europe, polemically opposed to the Germanic *Reich*' (p. 29). In his voyage along the Danube, from its source to the Black Sea, Magris is highly mindful of the perversions which Nazism inflicted on German culture, and yet he reminds us of the 'great chapter in history' which the pre-Nazi German presence in Central Europe brought about. 'Its eclipse is a great tragedy, which Nazism cannot make us forget' (p. 32). Magris' literary heroes, Singer, Roth, Kafka, Musil, Svevo, are all products of that great chapter of history, which involved the fertile interconnections between German and the many other languages of Eastern Europe.

Subsequent critics, like Jacques le Rider, have come to understand the presence of German in central Europe as a 'vector of cross-cultural relations at the crossroads of Northern Europe and Southern Europe' (2008, 156). This means understanding East European German-language literature not as an extension of *German* literature but as a network of activities of cultural transfer which resulted in original amalgams—Germano-Jewish, Germano-Slavic, Germano-Hungarian, Germano-Romanian, etc. The realm of the former Mitteleuropa does not, then, correspond to a geographical reality but to a representation of the role of German language countries in central Europe (Le Rider and Rinner 1998, 21), an intercultural space structured by the German *koine* (p. 47). A more specific formulation of this same idea is given by Cornis-Pope and Neubauer when they propose the notion of 'literary interfaces,' to investigate the specific reality of hybrid literary identities and cultural production. They investigate the cities of Central Europe as 'relays of literary modernization and pluralization' and of linguistic overlays (Cornis-Pope and Neubauer 2006, 9), whether provincial cities like Czernowitz and Bratislava or metropolitan centers like Prague or Budapest (Cornis-Pope and Neubauer 2006, 11). They make a claim for a 'genuinely German transnational culture … alive from the Baltic sea to the Danube delta, with centres in Prague, Lemberg, Budapest, Cernowitz, Vilnius, and elsewhere,' which produced the great literary works from Canetti and Roth to Musil, as well as hundreds of newspapers, journals, theaters and cultural societies. 'German, and especially German-Jewish culture acted as a glue, an integrating force, among the various ethnic groups' (Cornis-Pope and Neubauer 2002, 9).

This reassessment of German-language hybrids in the region does not come without risks, in particular a tendency to celebrate the multiplicity of an intercultural world without critical attention to the real barriers to intercultural communication.[6] To automatically interpret proximity of languages, literatures and cultures as dialogue is to misinterpret the historical situation (Le Rider and Rinner 1998, 38). Certain sites of pre-World War II German-language culture have been elevated, perhaps too quickly, to ideal sites of interconnection. Along with the most important sites of German language literary creation in Central Europe, Prague (Kafka) and Galicia (Joseph Roth), it is the Bucovina, and its capital Czernowitz, that has attracted the most attention in this respect.[7] Made famous by Paul Celan, Czernowitz, the capital of the former Crownland of Bukovina, has been the object of countless memoirs and articles. Nostalgic images allowed scholars, for example, to have Czernowitz stand as a site of pre-Nazi German pluralism, a safe haven in German historiography (Menninghaus 1999) on the basis of pronouncements for instance by Rose Ausländer on the four-languaged town she grew up in ('Viersprachig verbrüderte Lieder in entzweiter Zeit,' Ausländer 1977, 72) or Paul Celan's oft-quoted salute to his 'city of books' (Hirsch and Spitzer 2010, 32), or the many memoirs by former inhabitants of the interwar period that evoke a long period of relative harmony—even against the backdrop of rising Romanian nationalism and anti-Semitism in the 1920s and 1930s. These oft-quoted refrains promoted a rosy view of a perfect 'then' protected from the shadow of the violence which followed. In fact, not unsurprisingly, the historiography of Czernowitz and the Bukovina has been tethered to the ideological forces which swept through it, and to the languages which expressed these forces.

Troubled history produces troublesome historiography and this category seems to dominate in the case of Bukovina. Already afflicted by nationalist shouting matches during the Habsburg years, fascism and mainly communism thwarted objective historical research until the demise of the communist regimes between 1989 and 1991.

(van Drunen 2013, I, 3, 30)

It has only been in recent years—that is since the fall of the Berlin Wall—that scholarship on the city has been able to have access to a wide variety of sources, in all the languages of the city's past. And so work by a scholar like van Drunen, who attempts to write a Bukovinian history of Bukovina, accessing narratives from all of Czernowitz's languages and national pasts, is a remarkably original initiative. Looking for indicators of regional identity rather than adhering to the traditional lines of separatist national narratives, van Drunen concludes that Habsburg Bukovina indeed boasted a 'remarkable political and cultural vibrancy,' especially in its last years. It produced an astonishing number of periodicals in numerous languages, and had a wide circle of intellectuals, a dynamic university and a lively local political scene. Most importantly, nationalist agitation reached Bukovinian society relatively late, which further enhanced its peaceful image (Van Drunen 2013, x). For Colin and Rychlo too, there was a particular 'receptiveness' in Czernowitz, fostered by the efforts of 'writers, artists, journalists, representatives of different religions and a few political figures': 'Until the late 1920s, tolerance defeated intolerance in Bukovina, mutual recognition outweighed contempt for the Other' (Colin and Rychlo 2006, 70).

Translation and the multilingual city

Like so many other cities in Central Europe—large cities like Budapest and Prague (where German was the first, then the second language), or smaller cities like Vilnius, Lviv, Riga, Danzig, Bucharest, Timisoara, Plovdiv or Trieste—Czernowitz was emphatically multilingual. Of 87,113 inhabitants in 1910, 48.4% gave German as their customary language, followed by Ruthenian (17.9%), Polish (17.4%) and Romanian (15.7%) (Czaky 2010, 309). What is unusual about Czernowitz in the central European context is that though Ukrainians, Romanians and Poles were all a significant presence in the city, the fact that none was dominant left considerable autonomy to the Jewish, largely German-speaking, population[8] (Corbea-Hoisie cited in van Drunen 2013, I, 3: 34 and Czaky 2010, 312). And although there were competing communicational spaces in the microcosm of urban Czernowitz, and though this competition became increasingly violent, German was until the beginning of the 1940s the 'overarching linguistic and cultural metaspace' (Czaky 2010, 313–314). The notion of 'metaspace,' as introduced by Czaky in his extensive study of intercultural relations in the central European city, offers a promising avenue of exploration for understanding the exceptionality of Czernowitz and its literature. The idea of 'metaspace' will be interpreted for the literary sphere as constituted by the 'translational' dimensions of Czernowitz literature. This translational dimension is perhaps a more specific interpretation of what Colin and Rychlo have referred to as the most salient feature of Bukovinian works written in German during the early twentieth century and interwar period—their meditational quality, referring both to the reciprocal borrowing of literary motifs, as well as to an intense activity of translation (Colin and Rychlo 2006, 72).[9] This translational nature can perhaps shed light on what has been called the estranged or deterritorialized language of Czernowitz writers—as a consequence of distance from the great urban centers and to certain kinds of linguistic hypercorrection.[10] While this idea of a deterritorialized language has been interpreted as a reflection of a sometimes retrograde taste for nature poetry and rhyme (Colombat 2007), or as a projection of Nazi ideology (Colin 1997), it has also been understood as an esthetic choice taking on modernist overtones. For Corbea-Hoisie, the hypercorrection of the German language tended towards a kind of literary distancing which would become the esthetic foundation of Czernowitz writing. Rather than see the deterritorializing qualities of the poetry in a negative light, he sees a continuity between this posture and the very best writers: Celan, Weissglass, Meerbaum-Eisinger, confirming the modernity, originality and legitimacy of Bukovinian literature (Corbea-Hoisie 1998, 159–160).

In what follows, I argue for the prevalence of a translational esthetic—one which emerged out of the multilingual city and its history, and which took on a variety of esthetic forms—as an expression of the encounter of languages within the city and as a result of the translational encounters which came about as a result of forcible displacement and exile (see Simon 2016, 2017). The brief descriptions of the work of four writers identify as many modes of translational writing: Celan's disfiguring and dislocation of German, Ausländer's exile from and reshaping of German through English, Manger's adaptation of the German ballad form into Yiddish and Kobylianska's importing of philosophical sensibilities into Ukrainian.

Celan (1920–1970), Ausländer (1901–1988), Manger (1901–1969), Kobylianska (1863–1942)

The writer who is at once exceptional and yet who best exemplifies the culture of mediation which issued from the multilingual matrix of Czernowitz is Paul Celan. The translational nature of his writing—and the brilliant and innovative ways in which he used German in order to 'make it strange'—have been abundantly evoked by fine scholars (among them Colin, Felstiner and most recently Nouss 2010), and so it suffices here to mention that Celan's early development as a poet in multilingual Czernowitz was decisive for his work. Celan reacted against the lyrical nature poetry that prevailed among Czernowitz poets like Margul-Sperbe (Colombat 2007) but the kind of 'deterritorialized' German that prevailed in Bukovina may well have moved his work in the direction of the multiple 'displacements' that Nouss puts at the heart of the Celanian esthetic. Writing in the language of the murderers of his parents, Celan finds a violent, precise manner of signaling his distance from a language he cannot consider other than his.

The imaginative worlds of Paul Celan and Rose Ausländer are deeply embedded in the originary crucible of languages in Czernowitz and marked especially by one enormous fact: the sudden reversal of meaning attached to the German language. For this city, so tied to the myth of the 'imaginary West in the East,' German had been elevated to the status of a religion—an affiliation so intense as to remain strong even during the Romanianization of the interwar years. Raised in the adoration of Deutschtum, Czernowitz authors were forced to see German undergo a spectacular transvaluation of values—and therefore to revise their relationship to the language. For Ausländer, following Paul Celan, this meant a mediated relation to German, one which showed the 'home' language to be partially alien.

Ausländer grew up and began her literary career in Czernowitz, where she was an active member of the Jewish German-language literary community, but left in her twenties to travel to the US and again returned to the US after the war. She spent the war years back in Czernowitz in hiding with her mother (she was one of the five thousand survivors of the ghetto, while 55,000 were murdered, Krick-Aigner 2009) and after another almost two decades of wandering finally settled in Dusseldorf in the 1960s. It was in the US after the war that Ausländer began a period during which she wrote poetry only in English. During a period of eight years, from 1948 to 1956, Ausländer 'found herself' writing only in English. She was living in New York, a city where she had previously spent several years during the 1920s, and perhaps contemplating a conversion to an American existence. But this period turned out to be only a hiatus in her writing life, as she later returned to Europe and to the German language—and most of the English poems were discovered only after her death. Yet these years in English introduce a significant translational element into Ausländer's esthetic, a more precise materialization of the Czernowitz multilingualism, and one that gave greater heft to the name she seems to have chosen to keep as hers—the name which belonged to the husband of a short-lived marriage: Ausländer, or outsider. Rose Ausländer owned two suitcases that she carried through her lifelong wanderings, and identified fully with her Jewish identity as someone who has wandered for hundreds of years, 'from Word to Word' (Krick-Aigner 2009).

The interweaving of diaspora and home, the long wanderings of much of her life, are reflected not only in the themes of her writing but in the consequences of the to-and-fro between English and German. In particular, her exposure to American modernism resulted in shifts in her formal expression, from a German-inspired lyricism to an American-inspired modernism. Inspired by the modernist poets she read and admired, including Marianne Moore and e e cummings, Ausländer could return to poetry only through the oblique angle of another language—one which had not been part of her home existence.

Ausländer is one of the sources most often quoted in favor of the image of a peaceful multilingual Czernowitz before the war. Indeed, Ausländer continued to praise the city of her birth and upbringing, despite the horrors she experienced during the war. Perhaps because she was always able to keep a distance between fatherland and motherland—her fatherland 'buried,' her motherland become 'word' (quoted in Morris 1998, 49). When she began again to write in German, it was through a renewed belief in the mother tongue. But the poetry became more angular, less lyrical. She used fewer adjectives, shorter lines, no rhyme or punctuation, the isolated word taking on new meaning.

The sheer number of Ausländer's poems, which are normally only some twelve lines long, suggests an esthetic of incompletion, of relentless recommencing. Ausländer translated some of her English poems into German, just as she also translated at various times in her career the poems of others into German or English—Yiddish poems by Itzik Manger (1901–1969) into German and German poems by Else Lasker-Schüler and Adam Mickiewicz (1798–1855) into English. The fragmented nature of Ausländer's various exiles and returns points to a kind of permanent diasporic state, and her poetry was irrevocably marked by the wanderings which were a result of the destruction of Jewish life in Czernowitz.

Itzig Manger offers a distinctive example of the kind of linguistic and cultural transfers that came to constitute Czernowitz literature. Manger was born in Czernowitz and lived there, as well as in Bucharest and Iassy, until 1928 when he left for Warsaw, then France, England, the United States and finally Israel. As a young writer, he was entirely immersed in German language culture. In a notebook entry written when he was 17, he made a list of some 75 books to be read—and all were German. Yet the language he soon after chose was Yiddish. Yiddish was a relatively marginal literary language for Czernowitz Jews, yet when the journal *Shoybn* (Windows) was founded in 1924, Manger 'converted' to this language— mainly under the influence of Eliezar Shteynbarg (Gal-Ed 2016, 36). Manger was passionately interested in dramatic forms, in Yiddish theatre and in gypsy music. He was able to combine these interests by adapting the German ballad form and elements of his favorite German authors, including Goethe, Schiller, Heine, Rilke, Trakl and Hofmannsthal, into Yiddish (Starck-Adler 2007, 128).

The ballad corresponded to Manger's fascination with visionary poetry and themes of madness, wandering, silence. The Earl King was perhaps the most elemental of these dramas, and one that he would often cite. His 'seething, hallucinatory' prose combined elements from the Bible or folktales with the night-time imagination of the ballad, its dark silhouettes, hunchbacked beggars (Manger 2015, xxxv, intro) which approaches the rhythms of expressionism. The borrowings from Rilke are also clearly discernible in his poems, especially at the moment, in 1927, when Manger is reorienting his vision. 'In repeated oscillations between German and Yiddish, he found his way to his own poetry, gained assurance in the reinterpretation and reconfiguration of the motifs and materials of his diverse sources' (Gal-Ed 2016, 49). The interlingual and intertextual dialogues which are at the origin of his poetic work are clearly recognizable in the movement from German to Yiddish.

> The young Manger who read world literature in German and dreamed of being a German poet, asserted Yiddish as his poetic language only when he saw in it a European language of equal value, and trusted that Yiddish

poetry could be an equally productive, integral part of European and world literature.

(Gal-Ed 2016, 52)

One could refer to the Ukrainian novelist and poet Kobylianska's impressive output of novels and short stories in Ukrainian as translational writing in its ongoing dialogue with German. Born into a family who used German as their daily language (her father was a Ukrainian who worked for the Austrian administration and her mother was of Polish origin), Kobylianska began her writing in German and in fact continued to keep a diary in German for her entire life. She was born and brought up in a small town not far from Czernowitz, but moved to the city when she was in her twenties. After 'converting' to the Ukrainian national cause in her late teens (much as Manger did with Yiddish), she began to translate herself into Ukrainian—sometimes asking fellow authors to help her or receiving editorial help from her publishers.

Kobylianska's writing is difficult to categorize, with its sometimes incongruous mélange of feminism, intricate exploration of inner sentiments, portrayal of the cruelty of peasant life, and outbursts of nationalist rhetoric. Critics are divided as to the elements of her work that are ironic or parodic and those that convey her true sentiments. Among her works, 'Valse mélancolique' stands out as a truly radical portrait of women sharing a life together as artists. Like some of her other stories, this takes place in an urban setting, recounting the daily life and conversations of women who have chosen to devote themselves to art rather than to a conventional married life. This story marked a radical beginning for Ukrainian literature. Kobylianska's writings move between urban stories and rural depictions that are gothic in their intensity. In one story, a wife kills her husband and the children live in terror of being killed as well—though in the end the story shows sympathy for the woman browbeaten by the drunken husband. In fact Kobylianska knew both the urban and rural worlds; she helped set up the first Ukrainian women's organization in Czernowitz. Much of her writing associates 'German' with high literature and a genteel life style. Kobylianska was the first Ukrainian intellectual to introduce Nietzsche to Ukrainian readers, incorporating many of his philosophical concepts to her own philosophical system (Ladygina 2013, 85).

Some critics disparaged her use of 'German technique,' which in this case included a combination of elements such as intellectualism, mysticism and estheticism, while others praised an influence that 'transported you out into the broader world of ideas and art' (de Haan 2006, 249). In turn, Kobylianska translated Ukrainian literature into German, including the works of Pchilka, Kobrynska and Ukrainka (Franko 1998). In the case of Kobylianska as for the many other writers of Czernowitz, the multilingual milieu meant that writing occurred in the presence of other languages, in the consciousness of competing literary systems, and in this case with or against the power of German. Mediation does not mean a generalized multilingualism, but rather separate and parallel forms of interaction with German as the overarching 'metaspace.'

The library

The fact that Kobylianska sits on cousin Rosa's library shelves, alongside the mainly Jewish writers of the city, creates a link between the idea of translational writing and a shared sense of a literary community. A personal library is a kind of imagined community, as Hirsch and Spitzer present it in the context of Czernowitz, or as Amitav Ghosh describes it in his own home city, Calcutta. In 'The Testimony of my Grandfather's Bookcase,' Ghosh reflects on the collection of books that graced his grandfather's house—mostly novels, in Bengali and English, many of these translations which for Ghosh reflect not only the shared tastes of a home community but 'the emergence of a notion of a universal "literature", a form of artistic expression that embodies differences in place and culture, emotion and aspiration, but in such a way as to render them communicable' (Ghosh 1998). This perspective is consonant with the vision of Calcutta pursued so lyrically in his novel, *Sea of Poppies,* of the multiple intersections of language and culture that prevailed in the nineteenth century city. The cosmopolitanism of the bookshelves mimics the variety of the city itself, the world coming to Calcutta as a reflection of the spirit it finds there. Both the bookshelves in Czernowitz and Calcutta, from points very distant from one another, offer a snapshot of the world that highlights the role of multilingual cities in shaping the literary imagination.

Notes

1 Marcel Reich-Ranicki was a celebrated literary critic in Germany. A survivor of the Warsaw ghetto, he, exceptionally, never abandoned his devotion to the German language.
2 The problem of naming this region of the world, which has lived in the uneasy and often violent space between the German-language and the Russian empires, reflects the conflicted interpretations of the history it has been subjected to. (Le Rider 2008) *Mitteleuropa* has become a term of nostalgia for some, but is today rejected by scholars in favour of Central Europe or East Central Europe (Le Rider 2008; Cornis-Pope and Neubauer 2002).
3 It should not be forgotten that Goethe's favouring of German as the language of *Weltliteratur* rested on an appealing paradox. Other nations should learn German, Goethe suggested, not because of the inherent wealth of the language of its superior literature, but because German would be a cosmopolitan repository, a shortcut to all other literatures. The source of the language's strength was the wealth of translations it had accumulated, as a result of its openness to outside influences. Which other literature, he boasted, had more eminent translations of the best works? (cited in Berman 2012, p. 26) If German was the richest of languages, it was because of its capacity to assimilate, to 'devour,' what lay outside its borders (p. 26).
4 The critical reception of Herta Muller—a German-language writer from the Romanian Banat, an area populated by a German-speaking minority for centuries—is indicative of the tensions which continue to mark the legacy of the German language in the East (Haines 2015, 148).
5 'L'histoire du siècle passé n'a cessé de modifier l'étendue et la nature de ce que l'on appellera – au sens propre du terme – le 'territoire' du germaniste. La fin des Empires – ottoman, austro-hongrois, allemand –, puis la dissolution du bloc soviétique n'ont pas seulement changé le tracé des frontières et officialisé de nouvelles

identités institutionnelles. Elles ont aussi déplacé des populations, transformé les paysages, affecté profondément les mémoires' (Jean-Marie Valentin 2007, 3).

6 Le Rider also cautions against an idea of peaceful and interrelational multilingualism in central Europe. 'Cases of genuine multilingualism combining two or three languages of the Central European region prove to have been limited to a few contact zones, to a few *milieux* (for example, Yiddish-speaking Jews who master the language of the country where they live), to the descendants of mixed couples and the elites of some metropolises (Trieste, Prague, Bratislava, Czernowitz, Lemberg). Wasn't knowledge of a neighbouring country's language much less widespread than that of German, French or English, or even of Russian or Italian?' (Le Rider 2008, 38).

7 See for instance Winkler (1951); Bickel (1956); Drozdowski (1984); Rudel (1994); Friedjung (1995); Korber-Bercovici (1995); Glasberg Gold (1996); Bartfeld-Feller (1998); Coldewey (1999); Scha'ary (2004); Kehlmann (2004); Gross (2005); Yavetz (2007); Hirsch and Spitzer (2009) (from van Drunen 2013, p. 30)

8 As a means of protecting his territories from the Russian and Ottoman expansion, Joseph II had turned the eastern provinces of the Austro-Hungarian empire into buffer zones. He actively promoted the settlement of Germans from Austria and southwest Germany, as well as the Germanization of Ruthenians and Roumanians, the two largest ethnic groups in the Bukovina. In the period of liberalism (from 1848 on) many Jews settled in the major Bukovinian cities. By 1918, 47% of the population of Czernowitz was Jewish. Since Bukovinian Jews were particularly loyal to the Habsburg monarchy and instrumental in its expansion in that region, Austrian officials tended to consider them representatives of the Habsburg empire (Colin 1991, 7).

In a recently published memoir, Edith Silbermann describes the city in this way: 'In Czernowitz there lived among Romanians, Ukrainians, Austrians, Germans, Poles and Armenians so many Jews that one had the impression that it was a Jewish city. For centuries the German language and Austrian culture had shaped the life of my native city. In Czernowitz there were German newspapers, a German university, German-language highschools, theater, and much more. The middle class spoke and read exclusively in German, and even workers and merchants used German as the everyday language, mixed in with Yiddish and Ukrainian' (Silbermann 2015, 7).

Amidst this intensely German life, Edith Silbermann describes experiences in many other languages: the French she and Paul Celan were so fascinated with at school, the Romanian she learned at school, Ukrainian and Russian that she and her father immediately began learning when the Russians occupied Czernowitz in 1940, the Latin she was determined to excel in and that her father helped her with. Finally Edith became celebrated for her professional life in a language unmentioned until now: Yiddish. It was only when she moved to Bucharest after the war that she discovered the Yiddish theatre and began intensive language learning to become one of the most famous singers and reciters of Yiddish songs and poetry in Europe after the war. When she and her husband could not get work in Bucharest as they were ostracized for their plans to leave the country, they both turned to translation and published extensively.

9 In her 1991 introduction to a book on Paul Celan, Amy Colin details the myriad activities of translation which were undertaken by the participants in the active literary milieus of the city. These include Alfred Margul-Sperber's German translations of British (T.S. Eliot), French (Apollinaire and Gérard de Nerval) and American modernist poets (Robert Frost, Nicholas Vachel Lindsay, Wallace Stevens, Edna St. Vincent Millay and e.e. Cummings) as well as American Indian texts. Immanuel Weissglas translated Eminescu's famous poem 'The Morning Star' into German and Grillparzer, Stifter and parts of Goethe into Romanian. There was also indirect translation—with Romanian and Ukrainian poets influenced by German authors and inversely. 'Authors writing in German often used motifs from Romanian and Ukrainian folklore and translated important historical and literary texts from one language into the other' (Colin 1991, 11).

10 There are certainly links to be made between this use of the term 'deterritorialization' and the libraries of commentary on Kafka's writing in Prague.

Bibliography

Appelfeld, Aharon. 2001. 'The Kafka Connection.' *The New Yorker*, July 23, 37–41.

Ausländer, Rose. 1977. *Selected poems [of] Rose Ausländer*. Trans. E. Osers. London: London Magazine Editions.

Ausländer, Rose. 1984–1990. *Gesammelte Werke in sieben Bänden*. Ed. Helmut Braun. Frankfurt am Main: S. Fischer Verlag.

Ausländer, Rose. 1995. *Mother Tongue*. Trans. Jean Boase-Beier and Anthony Vivis. Todmorden: Arc Publications.

Bartfeld-Feller, Margit. 1998. *Dennoch Mensch geblieben. Von Czernowitz durch Siberien nach Israel 1923–1996*. Ed. Erhard Roy Wiehn. Konstanz: Hartung Gorre Verlag.

Beebee, Thomas O. ed. 2014. *German Literature as World Literature*. New York: Bloomsbury.

Berman, A. 1983. *L'Épreuve de l'étranger*. Paris: Ed. du Seuil.

Bermann, Sandra. 2012. 'World Literature and Comparative Literature.' In *The Routledge Companion to World Literature*, ed. Theo D'haen, David Damrosch and Djelal Kadir, pp. 169–179. London and New York: Routledge.

Bickel, Schlomo (also Shloyme Bikl). 1956. *Dray brider zaynen mir geven*. New York: Farlag Matones.

Chwin, Stephan. 2004. *Death in Danzig*. Trans. Philip Boehm. New York: Houghton Mifflin.

Colin, Amy. 1991. *Paul Celan. Holograms of Darkness*. Bloomington and Indianapolis: Indiana University Press.

Colin, Amy. 1997. 'Writings from the Margins: German-Jewish Women Poets from the Bukovina.' *Studies In 20th Century Literature* 21, 1: 9–40.

Colin, Amy and Peter Rychlo. 2006. 'Czernowitz: A Testing Ground for Pluralism.' In *History of the Literary Cultures of East-Central Europe. Junctures and Disjunctures in the 19th and 20th Centuries*, ed. Marcel Cornis-Pope and John Neubauer, pp. 57–76. Amsterdam: John Benjamins.

Coldewey, Gaby *et al.*1999. *'Czernowitz is gewen an alte, jidische Schtot…' Überlebende berichten*. Berlin: Heinrich-Böll-Stiftung.

Colombat, Rémy. 2007. 'La nature dans la poésie bucovinienne.' *Études Germaniques* 1, 245: 133–144.

Corbea-Hoisie, Andrei. 1998. 'Autour du méridien: Abrégé de la civilisation de Czernowitz, de Karl Emil Franzos à Paul Celan.' In *Les littératures de langue allemande en Europe central. Des Lumières à nos jours*, ed. Jacques le Rider and Fridrun Rinner, pp. 115–162. Paris: Presses universitaires de France.

Cornis-Pope, Marcel and John Neubauer, eds. 2002. *Towards a History of the Literary Cultures of East-Central Europe. Some Theoretical Reflections*. New York: American Council of Learned Societies.

Cornis-Pope, Marcel and John Neubauer, eds. 2006. *History of the Literary Cultures of East-Central Europe. Junctures and Disjunctures in the 19th and 20th Centuries*. Vol. 2. Amsterdam: John Benjamins.

Czaky, Moritz. 2010. *Das Gedachtnis der Stadte. Kulturelle Verflechtungen—Wien und die urbanen Milieus in Zentraleuropa*. Wien, Köln and Weimar: Böhlau Verlag.

Davies, Norman and Roger Moorhouse. 2003. *Microcosm. Portrait of a Central European City*. London: Pimlico.

de Haan, Francisca, Krassimira Daskalov, and Anna Loutfi, eds. 2006. *Biographical Dictionary of Women's Movements and Feminisms: Central, Eastern, and South Eastern Europe, 19th and 20th Centuries*. Entry 'Olha Kobylianska.' Budapest and New York: Central European University Press.

D'haen, Theo, David Damrosch and Djelal Kadir, eds. 2012. *The Routledge Companion to World Literature*. London and New York: Routledge.

Drozdowski, Georg, *Damals in Czernowitz und rundum, Erinnerungen eines Altösterreichers*, Verlag der Kleinen Zeitung Klagenfurt 1984

Feichtinger, Johannes, Ursula Prutsch and Moritz Csáky, eds. 2003. *Habsburg postcolonial. Machtstrukturen und kollektives Gedächtnis*. Innsbruck: Studienverlag.

Felstiner, John. 2001. *Paul Celan: Poet, Survivor, Jew*. New Haven: Yale University Press.

Franko, Roma. 1998. 'Women's Voices in Ukrainian Literature. Olha Kobylianska (1863–1942). Biographical Sketch.' Language Lantern Publications. Accessed May 8, 2014, www.languagelanterns.com/kobylian.htm

Friedjung, Prive. 1995. *Wir wollten nur das Paradies auf Erden: die Erinnerungen einer jüdischen Kommunistin aus der Bukowina*. Vienna: Böhlau.

Gal-Ed, Efrat. 2011. 'The Local and the European: Itzik Manger and his Autumn Landscape.' *Prooftexts* 31, 1–2: 31–59.

Gal-Ed, Efrat. 2016. *Niemandssprache. Itzik Manger – ein europäischer Dichter*. Berlin: Suhrkamp Verlag.

Ghosh, Amitav. 1998. 'My Grandfather's Bookcase.' *Kunapipi; A Journal of Post-Colonial Writing (U.K.)* 19, 3, www.amitavghosh.com/essays/bookcase.html.

Glasberg Gold, Ruth. 1996. *Ruth's Journey, A Survivor's Memoir*. Gainesville: University Press of Florida.

Gross, Sidi. 2005. *Zeitzeugin sein, Geschichten aus Czenowitz und Israel*. Konstanz: Hartung-Gorre Verlag.

Haines, Brigid. 2015. 'Introduction: The Eastern Turn In Contemporary German-Language Literature.' *German Life And Letters* 68, 2: 145–153.

Hirsch, Marianne and Leo Spitzer. 2010. *Ghosts of Home. The Afterlife of Czernowitz in Jewish Memory*. Berkeley: University of California Press.

Kehlmann, Heinz. 2004. *So weit nach Westen –von Czernowitz nach New York*. Aachen: Rimbaud.

Kobylianska, Olha. 1999. *But…The Lord is Silent: Selected Prose Fiction*. Trans. Roma Z. Franko and Sonia V. Morris. Saskatoon: Language Lanterns Publications.

Kobylianska, Olha. 2000. *Warm the Children, O Sun: Selected Prose Fiction*. Trans. Roma Z. Franko and Sonia V. Morris. Saskatoon: Language Lanterns Publications.

Korber-Bercovici, Miriam. 1995. *Jurnal de Ghetou, Djurin, Transnistria, 1941–1943*. Bucharest: Editura Kriterion.

Krick-Aigner, Kirsten. 2009. 'Rose Ausländer.' *Jewish Women: A Comprehensive Historical Encyclopedia*, March 1. Accessed 15 June 2016. http://jwa.org/encyclopedia/article/-rose.

Ladygina, Yuliya Volodymyrivna. 2013. *Narrating the Self in the Mass Age: Olha Kobylianska in the European Fin-de-Siècle and Its Aftermath, 1886–1936*. San Diego: ProQuest UMI Dissertations Publishing.

Le Rider, Jacques. 2008. 'Mitteleuropa, Zentraleuropa, Mittelosteuropa. A Mental Map Of Central Europe. '*European Journal Of Social Theory* 11, 2: 155–169.

Le Rider, Jacques and Fridrun Rinner. 1998. *Les Littératures de langue allemande en Europe Centrale*. Paris: Presses universitaires de France.

Magris, Claudio. 1990. *Danube. A Sentimental Journey from the Source to the Black Sea*. London: Collins Harvill.

Manger, Itzik. 2015. *The World According to Itzik: Selected Poetry and Prose*. Ed. Leonard Wolf. New Haven and London: Yale University Press.

Menninghaus, Winfried. 1999. 'Czernowitz/Bukowina Als Literarischer Topos Deutsch-Jüdischer Geschichte Und Literatur.' *Merkur Stuttgart*, Part 600, 53, 3–4: 345–347.

Meylaerts, Reine. 2004. 'La traduction dans la culture multilingue.' *Target* 16, 2: 289–317.

Morris, Leslie. 1998. 'Mutterland/Niemandsland: Diaspora and Displacement in the Poetry of Rose Ausländer.' *Religion and Literature* 30, 3: 47–65.

Nouss, Alexis. 2010. *Paul Celan. Les lieux d'un déplacement*. Paris: Le Bord de l'eau.

Romero, Aurora Belle. 2016. *Heute hat ein Gedicht mich wieder erschaffen: Origins of Poetic Identity in Rose Ausländer*. PhD, Vanderbilt University. http://etd.library.va nderbilt.edu/available/etd-03242016-002137/unrestricted/Romero.dissertation.ETD.pdf

Rudel, Josef Norbert. 1994. *Von Czernowitz bis Tel Aviv gab's immer was zum Lachen*. Tel Aviv: Papyrus Verlag.

Scha'ary, David. 2004. ‏דוד שערי / העולם מלחמות שתי בין ובינה‎ (*Jews in Bukovina between the Two World Wars*). Tel Aviv: Goldshṭain-Goren.

Shchyhlevska, Natalia. 2004. *Deutschsprachige Autoren aus der Bukowina*. Frankfurt: Peter Lang.

Silbermann, Edith. 2003. *Rose Ausländer. Die Sappho der östlichen Landschaft. Eine Anthologie (Bukowiner Literaturlandschaft Bd. 19)*. Aachen: Rimbaud Verlag.

Silbermann, Edith. 2015. *Czernowitz—Stadt der Dichter. Geschichte einer judischen Familie aus der Bukowina (1900–1948)*. Ed. Amy-Diana Colin. Paderborn: Wilhelm Fink.

Simon, Sherry. 2012. *Cities in Translation. Intersections of Language and Memory*. London: Routledge.

Simon, S. 2014. 'Postcolonial cities and the culture of translation.' In *Language and Translation in Postcolonial Literature: Multilingual Contexts, Translational Texts*, ed.Simona Bertacco, pp. 97–109. London: Routledge.

Simon, S. 2016. 'Language Edges: Reading the Habsburg Border City.' In *Speaking Memory. How Translation Shapes City Life*, ed. S. Simon, pp. 87–99. Montreal/Kingston: McGill-Queen's University Press.

Simon, S. 2017. 'Translating at the Edge of Empire: Olha Kobylianska and Rose Auslander.' *Translation. A Transdisciplinary Journal*, 5: 93–110.

Spector, S. 2000. *Prague Territories*. Berkeley: University of California Press.

Starck-Adler, Astrid. 2007. 'Multiculturalisme et multilinguisme à Czernowitz. L'exemple d'Itzik Manger.' *Études germaniques* 62, 1: 121–132.

Stenberg, Peter. 1991. *Journey to Oblivion. The End of the East European Yiddish and German Worlds in the Mirror of Literature*. Toronto: University of Toronto Press.

Stevenson, Patrick and Jenny Carl. 2010. *Language and Social Change in Central Europe: Discourses on Policy, Identity and the German language*. Edinburgh: Edinburgh University Press.

Valentin, Jean-Marie. 2007. 'Mémoire, lieux, diversité.' *Études germaniques* 1, 245: 3–4.

Van Drunen, H.F. 2013. *'A sanguine bunch.' Regional identification in Habsburg Bukovina, 1774–1919*. PhD, University of Amsterdam. http://dare.uva.nl/document/2/126251.

Venuti, Lawrence. 2012. 'World Literature and Translation Studies.' In *The Routledge Companion to World Literature*, ed. Theo D'haen, David Damrosch, Djelal Kadir, pp. 180–192. London and New York: Routledge.

Winkler, Max. 1951. *A Penny from Heaven*. New York: Apple-Century-Crafts Inc.

Yavetz, Zvi. 2007. *Erinnerungen an Czernowitz – Wo Menschen und Bücher lebten*. Munich: C.H. Beck.

7   Minor translations and the world literature of the masses in Latin America

Martín Gaspar

Popularity breeds discomfort in world literature studies. We can sense uneasiness with popular, conventional literature already in Goethe, the precursor most often invoked by contemporary scholars: 'What appeals to the multitude [*Megen*] will spread endlessly and, as we can already see now, will be well received in all parts of the world, while what is serious and truly substantial will be less successful' (Goethe [1830] 1986: 227).[1] An intellectual of his time, in 1830 Goethe valued literary commerce (an exchange 'of substance' between like-minded 'men of letters'), and distrusted the crass, incessant forces of commercialization (D'haen 2012: 8–9). Our twenty-first century approaches to world literature, while more inclusive, still follow suit. Despite gesturing at encompassing all of literature in some of their formulations, they tend to focus exclusively on certain impactful works: on how some masterpieces bring about a new aesthetic technique or generic change (Moretti 2000, 2003), for example, or manage to secure 'literary legitimacy' by innovating within a system of recognition (Casanova [1999] 2007), or enter a mode of transnational circulation through which they gain (avant-gardist) significance (Damrosch 2003).[2] Substance, then, over volume; aesthetic achievements over crowd pleasers. Look for a worldwide popular author like Rudyard Kipling in *The World Republic of Letters* or *What Is World Literature?* and you will find his name relegated to a footnote or a marginal quote (by, significantly, a 'world literature-worthy' author like T.S. Eliot).[3] If world literary history were a novel, scholars have been constructing one in which a few heroically meaningful works move the plot forward—casting aside those that are considered popular, conventional or basic, thus destined to remain unmentioned.

While more attentive to market needs and conservative tendencies than the world literature field, translation studies tend to ultimately zero in on texts that are aesthetically innovative or politically subversive. Even-Zohar, for example, acknowledges that translated literature can hold a position 'connected with [both] innovatory ("primary") or conservatory ("secondary") repertoires,' but ultimately states:

> It is clear that the very principles of selecting the works to be translated are determined by the situation governing the (home) polysystem: the texts are

chosen *according to their compatibility with the new approaches* and the supposedly *innovatory role* they may play within the target literature.

(Even-Zohar 1990: 46, 47, my emphases)

Translation here operates in a Goethian paradigm: it renews, makes more 'worldly' or modernizes the importing culture by facilitating aesthetic or political commerce. Granted, scholars have noted that in the periphery (in what Even-Zohar calls 'weak' or 'young' literary polysystems) translation also introduces other kinds of texts.[4] But even a postcolonialist with a culturalist approach like Sherry Simon still predicates the value of translation on novelty: 'translation no longer bridges a gap between two different cultures, but becomes a strategy of intervention through which *newness* comes into the world, where cultures are remixed' (Simon 2000: 21, my emphasis). Translation, for Simon as well as for many others, is defined as a process that brings a meaningfully original aesthetic or political voice to a given cultural landscape. The recent sociological, or more specifically 'activist' (Wolf 2014), turn also canonizes translations that subvert or challenge norms: they are the protagonists, and only they seem to matter.[5]

As a result of this shared emphasis on disruption and newness, some of the best selling conventional literature has been usually left outside the purview of both world literature and translation studies. Neither field has found much to say about novels like Jack London's *The Call of the Wild*, for example. London has been translated more extensively than any other American or English novelist of the twentieth century, his work being wildly popular from Russia to Chile, China to Poland (Harte 2016; Tavernier-Courbin 1994: 28; Dyer 1997: xxiii). But while London has been, according to Doctorow, 'the most widely read American author,' he is also considered 'a great gobbler-up of the world,' who was 'never an original thinker' (Doctorow 1993: 14, 12). And to world literature scholars, the latter matters more than the fact that his most popular novel has been representing foreign literature in translation to significantly more readers, especially young but also old ones, and all around the world, than Joyce's *Ulysses*. So they neglect London's writings in their models,[6] focusing instead on the modernist masterpiece (indeed, one might suspect that *modernism* itself is at the core of their critical projects.) Translation studies scholars, similarly, have set their sights on, say, the increasingly more erudite translations of Joyce's *Ulysses* into Spanish (Salas Subirats in 1945, Valverde in 1976, Tortosa and Venegas in 1999), which they have appraised, discussed, and close-read, time and again. No one has taken the time to analyze the many more translations of *The Call of the Wild* into Spanish.

Focusing on translations of towering masterpieces from *Gilgamesh* to *Ulysses*, on the arrival of magical realism to the world stage, and on activist translations or ideological encounters—all this creates a narrative of mastery, innovation, and renovation in which only heroes participate. Yet there must be something 'of substance' (of a *different* substance) in the many translations of *The Call of the Wild* read by the multitude. There must be something that these minor translations can tell us about how literature travels and translation functions. In other words, and to continue with the narrative analogy: If these minor translations can solicit a 'story' that is at odds with the dominant pattern of attention that focuses on major works—what story, not yet revealed to our untrained eyes, can they tell us?[7]

To answer this question, I will look in what follows at the margins of the margins: Latin American translations of classics for young readers. Among them, London's 1903 novel sits alongside a canon of nineteenth and twentieth century popular classics like *Cuore* (Edmondo d'Amicis, 1886), *Little Women* (Louisa M. Alcott, 1868), *Sandokan* (Emilio Salgari, 1896), *Around the World in Eighty Days* (Jules Verne, 1873), *Black Beauty* (Anna Sewell, 1877), and many others. As I will show, these very successful minor translations represented the first vision of Literature for generations of readers—one in which literature *is* literature in translation. They made a first, strong impression of what a book is, what a novel looks like, and even how it reads. And they configured for their impressionable readers a literary perception of the world and how it works: its geography, gender dynamics, power structures, and values. Of course, gauged by the gold standard of innovation, these fictions lack value; assessed by their level of aesthetic sophistication or political impact, their corresponding translations are apparently worthless. Yet, it is in this seemingly barren territory that generations of Latin American readers were formed—and with substantial consequences.

The world literature-as-innovation and the translation-as-agent-of-change paradigms focus on exceptions, not norms; major, not minor works. So our approach in this investigation of translated bestsellers for young readers will stand as a negative to the prevailing ones. Minor translations do not reveal a cultural project—such as a state trying to secularize or Westernize the nation, as in Turkey and China at the turn of the twentieth century (Seyhan 1998; Gürçaglar 1998; Pollard 1998)—or cultural agents with a manifest political agenda. So we will have to look at publishers mainly interested in selling for profit. We will not find through these works translators asserting their agency or distinguishing themselves. We will have to listen, instead, to rumors or representations about how they worked and some may still do. We will not find *the* authoritative and influential translation of *The Call of the Wild* by a well-reputed expert. So we will be looking at many versions by anonymous translators working for different publishers. We will not find 'mature' readers, but novice (literally minor) ones. We will, finally, not find an evident impact of these fictions on the commerce of aesthetics and new ideas. The impact will be elsewhere: in the way these novels presented Literature to generations of readers, and in their deep and rarely seen repercussions on politics and society.

Developing readers

When Joseph Dent thought of an 'every reader' as he founded *Everyman's Library* in 1906, he imagined this collective as a sum of several groups: 'the worker, the student, the cultured man, the child, the man and the woman'

('Everyman's Library' 2006). In the popular collection for this heterogeneous 'everyman,' translation, and in particular literary translation, was assigned an increasingly more prominent role according to the reader's maturity. By 1935, the category 'For Young People' of *Everyman's* included 103 volumes, mostly novels, of which twelve (such as an adaptation of *Don Quixote* and versions of Aesop's fables) were in translation (roughly 11%) (Rhys 1935).[8] Readers would encounter more translations, the majority from French and Russian, in the 'Fictions' and 'Romance' categories (65 of 278 titles, at a rate of 23%). As readers matured, according to this progression, they would grow to become acquainted with great foreign authors like Stendhal and Dostoyevsky.

Almost the opposite is true about the role of translation in the Latin American landscape at the time, and during most of the twentieth century. Outside and often within classrooms, young Latin Americans grew up reading a vast majority of translated novels, and it was usually not until later in life that they encountered vernacular ones.[9] The number of collections including foreign novels for young readers was, especially during mid-century, nothing short of remarkable. Between 1941 and 1998, Argentine *Colección Robin Hood* (Editorial Acme), roughly equivalent to the 'For Young People' section of *Everyman's* but dedicated exclusively to longer fiction, included a total of 237 titles, 220 of which were translations. The catalogue of a direct competitor, *Biblioteca Las Obras Famosas* (Editorial Tor), numbered sixty-three novels for young adults by 1945—and only four were not adapted translations. From the 1940s to the 1960s Editorial Sopena, a Spanish company with close ties to the Argentine market, issued its own collection of science-fiction works targeted to mass readers, all by Anglo Saxon authors. Editorial Kapelusz and Editorial Atlántida participated in the market from the 1960s to the early 1980s with two collections of, for the most part, translated fiction: *Iridium* and *Billiken*. Between 1948 and 1972 but in Brazil, *Coleção Saraiva* published 232 titles: of the 165 that can be considered for young adults, over a hundred were adapted translations. Beginning in 1920 and until the 1960s, also in Brazil, Companhia Editora Nacional published three collections targeted to young adults: *Terramarear* (adventures, almost all adapted translations of authors like Edgar Burroughs, André Armandy, and Mark Twain), *Série Negra* (detective fiction, by authors like Marten Cumberland, Edgar Wallace, and Dashiell Hammet), and *Biblioteca das Moças* (Young Ladies' Library, an extremely successful collection of romances targeted to young women with all of its 176 titles in translation.)[10] In mid-century Chile, Editora Zig-Zag published a series for young readers called *Serie Amarilla*, with an overwhelming majority of novels by authors like Stevenson, d'Amicis, and Dickens. In Mexico, most collections of this kind were imported from Spain. Local counterparts like Editorial Tomo, Editores Mexicanos Unidos, Editorial Valle de México, and more recently Perymat and *Colección Millenium* also published novels in translation, by popular authors like Salgari, Stevenson, Conan Doyle, and Verne. Given the data available, it is safe to estimate that translation was involved in well over 70% of the fiction read by Latin American young readers until the 1980s. It is important to mention the existence of two other types of collections in which translation also thrived: institutionally sponsored anthologies of world classics destined to form 'future citizens,' and privately published collections 'for the household,' both usually conceived and prologued by eminent intellectuals.[11] My focus here is, however, on the more chaotic and less prestigious publications of minor translations of popular novels for young readers.

What spurred this boom of translated novels? Two major local factors seem to have played a key role, at least initially. First, the rise in literacy in the first half of the century (from 51% to 88% in Argentina, 35% to 49% in Brazil, 24% to 60% in Mexico) brought to the market new customers, new and young readers (Roser 2016). Second, internal and international migrations made cities grow rapidly—urbanization in Latin America increased in fifty years (1925–1975) from 25.0% to 61.2% due to economic and other factors (Cerrutti 2003). As a result, more consumers were directly exposed to the main publishing markets and the prospect of prosperity. And, intent on promoting reading habits that would put their children on the path of upward mobility, many found in cheap novels in translation a form of access to cultural capital. In Argentina, where this phenomenon was particularly pronounced and the publishing industry had an unprecedented boom, translated novels could be bought at most bookstores and newspaper stands, or borrowed from libraries at suburban working-class neighborhood associations (Romero 1995).

Numbers were staggering. During its 'golden age' (between 1930 and 1959), Argentine Editorial Tor used to sell books of its *Biblioteca Las Obras Famosas* by weight, and could print up to 20,000 copies of any given book in a day, four different books in a single week (Abraham 2012: 214). The impact of this single publisher was massive and extended across Latin America, with the sole exception of Brazil and Cuba (Abraham 2012: 43). Such was the demand for popular literature that, beyond abridged and unabridged translations of novels, there were also imported adaptations (Kapelusz, for example, published Spanish translations of French adaptations of novels originally written in English, like *Ivanhoe* and *Robinson Crusoe*) and even original writing that appeared as pseudotranslation (Tor commissioned the production of apocryphal novels with protagonists like Tarzan and Sexton Blake; in 1956, Companhia Editora Nacional, in Brazil, published seven novels with titles like *Tarzan e os homens-formiga* [Tarzan and the Ant-Men] and *Tarzan no centro da terra* [Tarzan in the Center of the Earth]).

Up until the 1980s—when the publishing market changed, and fiction dedicated to young adults and children in Spanish and Portuguese[12] became more prevalent—translations of popular nineteenth century and early twentieth century novels were a habitual presence in households. The result was that, upon reaching adulthood, a young Latin American would have potentially encountered the works of Alcott and Verne, Dickens and Stewel, Conan Doyle and Jack London. Fictions that would leave and still leave an indelible mark on readers—quintessential postcolonial subjects, one might say—that were persistently exposed to a metropolitan worldview.

In a 2009 TED talk, Nigerian writer Chimamanda Adichie gives us a hint about the impact of these kinds of readings in the postcolony. She recalls that, when she began writing,

> All my characters were white and blue-eyed, they played in the snow, they ate apples, and they talked a lot about the weather [...] My characters also drank a lot of ginger beer, because the characters in the British books I read drank ginger beer. [...] And for many years afterwards, I would have a desperate desire to taste ginger beer.
>
> (Adichie 2009: 0:38–1:36)

(She would overcome this bias, she says, when she graduated into reading local literature written by Chinua Achebe and Camara Laye and 'realised that people like me, girls with skin the colour of chocolate, whose kinky hair could not form ponytails, could also exist in literature' (2:14).) A similar perception of what can exist in literature was instilled in Latin American readers. A Brazilian young woman would read a love story set in France or England, sensing perhaps an intrinsic relationship between 'romance,' sunny meadows, and protagonists with French names. An Argentine young man would learn to reminisce[13] about horses and muddy roads near English orphanages, not out in the pampas. A young man in Mexico City would read about class privilege in d'Amicis Turin, not in his neighborhood.

There is a significant difference, however, between these readers' experience and Adichie's: the Latin Americans were reading translations—and translations that at times sounded, for reasons I will soon explain, rather strange and distant. A case, then, of layered *ostranenie*: foreign are these fictions' characters and diegeses—Salgari's Malaysia; Alcott's Massachusetts; Armandy's Africa—and alien sounds the Spanish or Portuguese in which they are narrated. Considering that most of the literature available to her was in translation, a young reader could conclude that adventure, fantasy, and romance novels, or rather *literature in general*, could only take place in a foreign setting and sound foreign. As if 'the novel' had come full circle to its distant origins in translation.[14]

Minor translators, invisible styles, rewarding genres

Before looking at minor translators of literature for young readers, let us glance first at an exception that highlights the rule. We find it in Brazil, where Monteiro Lobato—a towering figure in the book industry in the first half of the twentieth century—sought to indoctrinate generations of young Brazilians through his translations. As John Milton put it in his essay 'The Political Adaptations of Monteiro Lobato'—a study firmly within the aforementioned translation-as-agent-of-change paradigm—Lobato 'used his adaptations of children's literature [such as his version of *Peter Pan*] in order to insert many of his political, economic and educational ideas' (Milton 2010: 211). He is an exception in the field: a publisher, intellectual, and diplomat with a recognizable name. Most publishers of translations for young readers were motivated by profit. And most of their translators were overworked and underpaid anonymous workers.

Rumor has it that Juan Carlos Torrendell, editor and owner of the powerful Editorial Tor, used to place newspaper ads looking for translators and ask novice respondents for different 'sample chapters' from the same novel—then he would collate them and, having a complete translation of the work available for free, publish it (Bertazza 2012). Anecdotes like this encapsulate the world of minor translation—where rights to translations were borrowed, stolen, and unacknowledged, and where the translation was treated like any another cost to keep down. In this environment, hurried mass production was not uncommon.

Argentine writer Rodolfo Walsh's 1967 short-story 'Nota al pie' ('Footnote') is based on the life of one of these workers: Alfredo de León, who translated for Editorial Sopena until his death in 1954. In Walsh's fiction the protagonist, renamed as León de Sanctis, commits suicide in great part because of alienating working conditions and lack of appreciation by his editor. The suffocating story consists mostly of a suicide note—a growing 'footnote' on the page—in which de Sanctis (a translator of Clark and Bradbury, among others) reveals an increasingly troubled relationship with his skills (he resolved 'every difficulty by omitting it altogether'), his dictionary ('Mr. Appleton looked at me sadly'), and his typewriter (Walsh 1981: 439, 441, my translation). By the end of the short story, the footnote takes over the page. The final lines read:

> In this time I have translated for the [publishing] House one hundred and thirty books of 80,000 words each, at 6 letters per word. That is sixty million taps on the keyboard. Now I understand why it is worn out, why every key is sunken, each letter erased. Sixty million taps are too many, even for a good Remington. I look at my fingers in awe.
>
> (Walsh 1981:446, my translation)

A worker like the protagonist of Walsh's story translates, first and foremost, to make a living. His idiosyncrasies and moments of rebellion are, much like the translator in Deszö Kosztolányi's 'Le Traducteur cleptomane,' minor and inconsequential (Kosztolányi 1994). Walsh's story exemplifies the internalization of a submissive behavior that, it has been argued, is at the root of the secondariness of translators (Simeoni 1998). In this respect, it is revealing that the translator in the story does not even engage the original text, or its author, but rather speaks humbly and posthumously to his *editor*—through a note that, the narrator tells us on the top part of the first page, the intended recipient will never read. Not merely a work of imaginative fiction, Walsh's story represents the working environment and *habitus* that surrounded the production of minor translations.

Partly as a result of this often exploitative employment, the style of some of these quickly translated and poorly revised Spanish versions of classics ends up being at times very homogeneous (every author reads the same), or, conversely, quite strange and unfamiliar sounding. Some translators would, like De Sanctis, resolve difficulties through omissions, or flatten metaphors with conventional turns of phrase to speed up the process. Some made their work sound rather strange because of certain stylemes: an abundance of archaic terms; hackneyed expressions; false cognates; purisms; and even a whimsical use of translator's footnotes. The Spanish vocabulary and expressions are stretched between two poles: some translators bleached regionalisms to construct a 'neutral' Spanish; others used local expressions freely, not expecting their work to be legally or illegally exported or reused by a foreign publisher.

Yet no matter how odd, simplified or foreign the prose is, the plot of these novels is seemingly immune to mistranslations. This is because unlike modernist fictions that revel in ambiguity and experimentation, adapted translations of popular novels for the young reader are positivistic, straightforward, and orderly. They are, then, ideal for inculcating certain values and belong to genres (adventure, romance, fantasy, *bildungsroman*) that, much like children's books, stand 'firmly within the domain of cultural practices which exist for the purpose of socializing their target audience' (Stephens 1992: 8). *Bildgunsromane* tend to embrace the value of perseverance and sacrifice, while other genres can serve as ideal compensatory fantasies for a class whose role is to sustain the systems in which heroes—the aristocrat, the detective, even the pirate, in any case, the well-off—can reach their goals.[15] These are all genres, significantly, in which progress is never questioned: every tap in the translator's typewriter is a penny earned; every page advances a plot that leads to a satisfying or meaningful ending. Every page, every novel bought and read brings the reader closer to becoming 'cultured.'

One of these novels was *The Call of the Wild*: an emblematic celebration of virtues that are expected from the young (male) reader: courage, determination, dignified action, and even good health habits.[16] Various conflicts in an unforgiving arctic setting, encounters with wicked antagonists, some mystery (the location of the 'Lost Cabin'), and the progressive maturation of a personality (from easy domestic life, to conflict with others, to love and loyalty, and finally to self-relying adulthood) complete the picture. The plot is conventional in its blend of adventure and *bildungsroman*. Conventional and minor are, too, the novel's many translations.

The Call of the Wild and its minor translations

What can we learn by reading comparatively translations of *The Call of the Wild*? Little, according to the paradigm of innovation we are revising. The original is neither experimental nor subversive of a genre or politics—it does not introduce 'newness' in the translating culture. Fittingly, it was translated and retranslated a large but nebulous number of times and sold as a well-known conventional commodity to generations of readers.[17] Because of that, however, these popular and cheap minor translations can reveal an all important aspect of translation and world literature: the manner in which generations of readers were presented Literature as an institution and encountered 'literary language' as a distinct form.

For the purpose of this brief case study, I will look at thirteen Spanish translations published between 1958 and 2012. For the sake of brevity, and to give a flavor of these different minor translations of *The Call of the Wild* and what we can read into them, I will focus on four textual elements: the various translations of the word 'wild'; the opening lines; the handling of a case of euthanasia in the novel; and the treatment of Manuel, the originator of the protagonist's troubles.

Taming the wild

Having finished the novel, the young reader would have found something odd in the title of the book, translated in many versions as *La llamada de la selva*. Because why does the translation refer to a *selva* (*jungle* or *rainforest*), if the novel is set in the frozen Arctic? The dreamy sequences in which Buck recalls the naked 'hairy man squatted by the fire' (37) might suggest the presence of a primordial jungle, but *selva* is clearly a mistranslation of the terms 'wilderness,' 'forest,' and 'the land of streams and timber' elsewhere (PY, OR).[18] Also, why *llamada* and not *llamado* (much more habitual in Latin America)? A Brazilian reader could have encountered, up until 1975, various options: *O grito da selva* [The Scream of the Jungle] (Lobato, 1935); *A voz da selva* [The Voice of the Jungle] (Eca Leal, no date); *O apelo da selva* [The Call of the Jungle] (Bagão e Silva, 1963); *Chamado selvagem* [The Wild/Savage Call] (Monteiro, 1972) (Daghlian 1975: 22). In Spanish, the title remained consistent. For most of the twentieth century, it was either *La llamada de la selva*—in imported peninsular Spanish editions (EC, GC, ED, PY, OR GV)— or *El llamado de la selva*—by Latin American translators (EA, GR, PD, AC). It was not until late in the century when other options started to appear: *El llamado de la naturaleza* (SP, in 1984), and *El llamado de lo salvaje* (PP, in 2000). The latter is seemingly a better alternative, as 'lo salvaje' captures the abstract notion of '*the* wild.' But most translators (or their editors) chose 'la selva' to follow early translations—or perhaps to suggestively echo Kipling's *El libro de la selva* [The Jungle Book].

For decades, readers must have concluded that the prominent word *selva* was either a poetic license or a vestige of some unfamiliar source. Unable to 'domesticate' the wild in the original, these translations make the translation process conspicuous. Not out of an ethical, purposeful resistance to the normalizing erasure of the source—we can hardly call this 'foreignization'— *El llamado de la selva* nonetheless foreignizes or, as Venuti puts it, 'signifies the difference of the foreign text, yet only by disrupting the cultural codes that prevail in the target language' (Venuti 1993: 61). An accidental disruption, surely absent in the translator's intentions but present in the text. Is this, a reader may wonder, a literary use of the word *selva*? Or is this place *selva* what other people identify with wilderness or the wild? Originating in these translations rather than in London's work, these questions in the readers' minds suggest to them that Literature may play a language game of its own.

A *matter of reading*

The opening clauses of the novel—'Buck did not read the newspapers, or he would have known that trouble was brewing...'—affirm the power of reading, which the second half of the sentence turns into something of a joke: 'not alone for himself, but for every tidewater dog, strong of muscle and with warm, long hair, from Puget Sound to San Diego' (London 1995: 3). Some minor translators decided to take advantage of this beginning to impart a lesson. One version opens with what reads like an admonition: 'Si Buck hubiera leído los periódicos' ['*Had Buck read* the newspapers...'] (ED, 3). Others point squarely at Buck's illiteracy, or even disability: 'Buck no leía los periódicos. De poder hacerlo se hubiera informado...' ['Buck did not read the newspapers. *If he had been able to*, he would have learned/informed himself...'] (PD, 3). These versions turn the humorous beginning into a teaching moment. Indeed, some of these translators felt they were educating, to the point that their role often overlaps with that of a teacher. Some versions preserve the humor of the original's beginning (AC, GC, GR, GV) but in many others ambiguities are hard to come by, smirks turn into laughter, puzzlement into certainty, and irony vanishes. *The Call of the Wild* can start off lightly, with tongue-in-cheek joke, or somberly. Different minor translations can make reading feel like a pleasure or a duty.

Linguistic and other laws

Beyond the oddities resulting from mistranslations or calques, minor translators usually play safe. Adjectives, like Homeric epithets, are paired with certain situations or nouns and can never appear near others. At the end of chapter four, we reach one of the saddest moments in the novel. The dog Dave, old and exhausted but dignified, needs to be euthanized. This happens, as it were, offstage: 'A revolver-shot rang out,' reads the original, 'The man came back hurriedly. The whips snapped, the bells tinkled merrily, the sleds churned along the trail; but Buck knew, and every dog knew, what had taken place behind the belt of river trees' (London 1995: 37). One translator found it objectionable that the man would come back 'hurriedly' under such a gloomy circumstance, and turned the adverb into 'tan lentamente como se había ido' ['as slowly as he had left'] (EC, 62). Others wondered why the bells would tinkle 'merrily' in such a sad scene. So they chose to omit the adjective (PY, EC). One of them went further, feeling compelled also to explain exactly why euthanasia is acceptable, expounding: 'Buck sabía, y los demás perros también, qué es lo que había sucedido detrás de ellos. Se había cumplido la ley del Norte: el débil debe morir para no ser un estorbo. Es una ley que todos acatan' ['Buck knew, and the other dogs knew, what had happened behind them. *The law of the North had been followed: the weak must die so as to not be hindrance. It is the law that everyone obeys*'] (PY 66). Again, as this instance suggests, depending on how the translator conceives of the reader's maturity, the same novel can be overtly instructive and provide explanations, standard phrases, commonsensical adjectives, and *the norm*. Or it can be more ambiguous, and expose the reader to exceptions and puzzling realities.

Manuel's help

In the first chapter we are introduced to Buck's aristocratic privileges in Judge Miller's Santa Clara mansion. Canine life is segregated across racial (or breeding) lines: there are kennel-dogs (fox terriers), house-dogs (both 'foreigners': Toots, a Japanese pug; Ysabel, a Mexican hairless, both 'strange creatures that rarely put nose out of doors or set foot to ground'), and there is Buck, who has inherited the mastery over the entire territory from his St. Bernard father Elmo (London 1995: 4). In the novel, humans are also somewhat organized in this manner. Every character with an English or French name is in a position of power: Miller early on; the ruthless Druther (a Southerner?) who teaches Buck that 'a man with a club was a lawgiver' in the middle; the ambitious Hans and Pete later; the loving John Thornton, 'the ideal master' towards the end; then there are two characters with names of French extraction (Perrault and François) who are, in turn, associated with calm administration of justice.

The Spanish reader is to identify with Buck (in OR 'Buck,' in quotation marks), another English sounding name. And she will notice, amidst this sea of foreign names, two in Spanish: Mercedes and Manuel. Their roles are limited but meaningful. Mercedes is the only woman in the text—and she represents the most chauvinistic gender stereotypes.[19] As to Manuel, he effectively ends the possibility of a civilized life for Buck. The only Spanish-named male in the novel, Manuel was 'an undesirable acquaintance': a gardener's helper who played Chinese lottery (London 1995: 4).[20] Manuel gambled with a system, which 'made his damnation certain. For to play a system requires money, while the wages of a gardener's helper do not lap over the needs of a wife and numerous progeny' (London 1995: 5). Seemingly driven by two vices (gambling and reproduction), Manuel kidnaps and sells Buck to work in the Klondike gold rush. At the end of the second chapter, and after Buck had set foot on snow for the first time, Manuel is mentioned again: '[Buck] came because men had found a yellow metal in the North, and because Manuel was a gardener's helper whose wages did not lap over the needs of his wife and divers small copies of himself' (London 1995: 19). From 'numerous progeny' in chapter one to 'copies of himself' here, Manuel's children were the source of trouble. But troubling is also the fact that he was not paid enough—and here London's socialist leanings seem to come into play. Notice, however, that while *Manuel's* greed is put into question, it seems unnecessary for the narrator to explain the (white) *men's*—taken as a mere fact of life.

How did minor translators negotiate this ideological minefield? One translator created more trouble, as he mistranslated Manuel's profession—correctly rendered as 'ayudante de jardinero' (*gardener's* helper) in chapter one—as 'ayudante de *cocinero*' (*chef's* assistant) in chapter two (EO, 4, 25). Among the other translators, some skipped over the landmines, dealing with the difficulty of translating 'copies of himself' by omitting it altogether and erasing the family from the equation: Manuel, a translator writes aseptically, 'recibía un salario que no bastaba a cubrir sus necesidades' ['earned a salary that was not enough to meet his needs'] (PY 36). Yet another decided to explain what this business of 'copies' meant: '[su] salario no cubría las necesidades de su mujer ni de las réplicas de sí mismo que eran sus hijos' ['his wages did not meet the needs of his wife nor those of the many copies of himself *that were his children*'] (VV 39). None of the translators reviewed cared to translate 'small' in '*small* copies of himself,' making Manuel's age indefinable. Then there is the matter of the wages. The original expresses poverty twice with an old fashioned expression: '[Manuel's] wages did not lap over the needs.' Translators simplified the matter by writing 'cubrir las necesidades' (an equivalent to 'meet the needs' in English.) But they disagreed on how to express this scarcity: to some translators the wages he was paid 'were not enough' ('no bastaba'; 'no cubría') (EA, GR, VV) to others they 'were barely enough' ('apenas lo necesario'; 'apenas lo suficiente'; 'escasamente cubría') (GV, GC, PY, EO). A small detail that nonetheless speaks to the degree of justification for Manuel's kidnapping of Buck.

We can only wonder how a Spanish reader (whose name could be Manuel) would react to finding this name associated with treacherous help, scarcity, gambling, excessive children, and (quite literally) the end of civilization. She may not recognize racial stereotyping at all. Because races, like breeds of dogs and disabilities, operate as shorthands to prefabricated roles in many nineteenth and early twentieth century novels. A Chihuahua dog could never be the protagonist in the same way as a blind human or dog would inevitably be associated with abnormal behavior. A Spanish-named character in this type of fiction can be either loyal or disloyal—but never a protagonist, and rarely a partner or worthy enemy.

The Call of the Wild is a novel about the recuperation of an ancestral voice: it begins with newspapers and ends with 'the song of the pack' (London 1995: 74). But in its trajectory, some readers of these translations may be admonished to read (read the newspapers, and keep on reading this novel, or else!) and others may picture for a second a funny image of a dog wearing spectacles. They would be exposed to an unusual use of language (why *selva*?), foreign-sounding phrases and words (llamad*a*?), and inconsistencies (gardener's helper or chef's assistant?) Depending on the version, a reader would have to imagine what happened to Dave behind the trees, and face the fact that sometimes bells tinkle 'merrily' in moments of sadness. Another would be instructed about the 'law of the North' (the North!). Some readers would empathies a little with Manuel (Manuel wasn't paid enough, so he had to gamble) or not (Manuel earned barely enough, but he wanted more.) The plot of *The Call of the Wild* might be simple, but ideology is in the details.

London's best-known novel still lacks a definitive Spanish version. Not even the matter of the title is quite settled.[21] In a sense, while many readers know the story, not everyone knows the same one—and this dilution of authority is a sign of strength and richness. Translators from below—well-trained some, unskilled others, commonsensical, faithful, pedagogical—all of them were formative to the young reader. Minor translations, like minor characters in the background, can be heard like an insidious cacophony of voices, each talking about a different kind of adventure, instructing, explaining and adapting, in a process akin to storytelling.[22]

A bookcase of literature in translation in Latin America is made of masterpieces on a high bookshelf, and a colorful set of minor translations for developing readers on a lower one. If we talk about cultural and political widespread impact, it may well be that the lower bookshelf takes the prize. We pick up a book from that shelf: it is *The Call of the Wild* or *White Fang*. Appended to the longer fiction, we notice 'other short stories'—surely added to make the book more voluminous. One of them is titled 'Encender una hoguera' (or 'Para encender una hoguera' or 'Encender un fuego,' depending on the version.) And a story born in the world literature for the masses slowly materializes.

Building a fire

In 1902, when Jack London was commissioned to write a short story by the weekly *The Youth's Companion*, he created the first version of 'To Build a Fire': a tale of a man who foolishly traveled alone with his dog in the Yukon, and ends up barely surviving death by hypothermia. Years later he revisited the story, creating the more famous version that came out in August 1908 in *The Century Magazine*. In this one the protagonist dies in the end, and his dog walks away from him to find new food and fire providers. The story was written for the masses: *The Youth's Companion* had a circulation of over half a million, and *The Century* was the leading American periodical at the time (Baer 2007). Relatively soon, Jack London's short stories and novels entered world circulation—the first translation of *White Fang* into Spanish possibly being the one published by Gustavo Gili in Barcelona in 1925. In Latin America, 'To Build a Fire' was not his best-known short story (that was 'The Concentric Deaths,' often anthologized as detective fiction), yet it was certainly available in the 1940s, along with *The Call of the Wild* or *White Fang*.

At the time, would-be revolutionary Ernesto Guevara was in his teens, fighting bouts of asthma and leading a life of relative privilege in Buenos Aires, while would-be cosmopolitan writer and youth icon Julio Cortázar was teaching in rural schools in the lazy pampas. They were both avid readers, and they certainly ran into minor translations of Jack London's work. Two decades later, in 1961, Che Guevara published *La sierra y el llano*, in which he recounts the guerrilla fights with Fulgencio Batista's forces prior to taking over the government. At one point during a fierce battle he is wounded, by the look of one of his comrades fatally:

> I saw in his eyes he considered me as good as dead. [...] I immediately began to think about the best way to die, since in that minute all seemed lost. *I remembered an old Jack London story in which the hero, aware that*

he is about to freeze to death in the Alaskan ice, leans against a tree and
prepares to die with dignity.

(Guevara 2006: 19, my emphasis)

When *La sierra y el llano* came out, Julio Cortázar was living in Paris, some-what aloof from political commitment and the revolutionary struggle. His jazzy masterpiece *Rayuela* (*Hopscotch*, 1963) must have been in the works. Guevara's memoir came to his hands and, somewhat displeased with its lack of literary value, decided to write a story called 'Reunión' [Meeting] (1964) inspired by the revolutionary's near-death experience.

The epigraph to the story is the italicized sentence above, in which 'old Jack London' is mentioned. The plot is a lightly veiled refraction of Guevara's memoir: an asthmatic doctor-turned-revolutionary and his comrades fight their way to a meeting with 'Luis' (Fidel Castro); he is wounded and, on the verge of death, lies against a tree and *sees* a quartet that contains his hopes and ideals. According to critics, this story signals Cortázar's attempt to reconcile his support for the Cuban revolution with his non-Sartrean views on aesthetics (Pérez-Abadín Barro, Standish, Orloff.) Read closely we notice the tentativeness of such attempt, since the short story reveals a poignant avoidance: Cortázar, by turning Jack London's *literature* (a source of inspiration to Guevara) into Mozart's *music* (a soothing hallucination for his protagonist), bypasses the question of the role of literature in the revolution.

Years later Cortázar refers to an episode involving 'Reunión' that took place in the mid 1970s in Chile. Pinochet had taken over the government, and cen-sorship was in full swing. Cortázar, in an imaginary dialogue with himself (this is an essay written as a 'self interview'), writes:

> And by the way, I guess you know that the Chilean Junta burnt a little pocket book that included 'Reunión' and other short stories, and that was going to be sold at newspaper stands for a few pennies, as part of a formidable effort by the [recently deposed] government to support popular culture. When I read that they were also throwing Jack London books into the bonfire I was shocked, but then I remembered that my story has an epigraph from *La sierra y el llano* in which Che thinks about a London character, and I inferred that between him and myself we had sent poor Jack to the flames—go figure, the atrocities that perfidious Marxist literature is capable of.

(Cortázar 1973: 45, my translation)

Cortázar's, Jack London's, and naturally Che Guevara's books, all burning together. The image suggests another path for world literature. A path that began in a minor translation. London's 'To Build a Fire' is both an indictment of the foolishness of a man who defies nature and a reaffirmation of the (con-ventional?) importance of dignity. We cannot, of course, affirm that Guevara internalized this value simply by reading translations of this story or of Jack London's works at large. But I think we can say that literature in translation was the place where many of the certainties that would guide his life were (re) presented to him. If we look at the constellation of values that Guevara praises in his writings time and again, we will find a correlative in minor translations: sacrifice (to the point of martyrdom), loyalty, dignity—D'Amicis *Cuore*; Sewell's *Black Beauty*; London's 'To Build a Fire'? It may all seem too commonplace, and perhaps it is and that is the point. There can be no *ironist* (to borrow Richard Rorty's term) in the revolution.[23]

One of the most lucid critics to explore the London-Guevara-Cortázar connection, Ricardo Piglia, traces the life of the revolutionary, who died in Bolivia eight years after the battle that brought 'To Build a Fire' to his mind. When Che Guevara died, Piglia writes, he did it 'with dignity, like the character in London's short story. Or, rather, he died with dignity, like a character in a *bildungsroman* lost in history [un personaje de una novela de educación perdido en la historia]' (Piglia 2006: 138, my translation). Guevara as a character in a *bildungsroman*. He may have thought of that himself, as a young reader enjoying the pleasures of a minor translation.

Notes

1 D'haen translates *Menge* as 'masses' (D'haen 2012: 8). Opposing the (presumably *loud*) masses, Goethe describes intellectuals discussing world literature as 'a silent, almost secret congregation [*eine stille, fast gedrückte Kirche*]' (Goethe 1972: 429).

2 These are three of the most frequently quoted voices in world literature studies. Moretti is concerned with genre, and the compromise between 'formal influence' (by masterpieces) and 'local materials' (Moretti 2000: 58). Casanova's book includes case studies on Kafka, Joyce, and Faulkner. Damrosch focuses on *Gilgamesh*, Kafka, and Menchú, among others. The emphasis on newness and impactfulness—a continuation, seemingly, of the 'great books' tradition, the comparatist project (following Auerbach and Spitzer), and even the 'canon debates' in the 1980s— is noticeable in the world literature debate (see Prendergast's 2004 collected volume *Debating World Literature*). Moretti's recent experiments with big data and distant reading—in *Graph, Maps, Trees: Abstract Models for a Literary History* (2005) and *Distant Reading* (2013)— are driven by a more comprehensive approach to world literature. However, 'lesser' classics widely read in the twentieth century, such as the ones I will refer to in this article, have not yet received attention.

3 In Casanova's book, Kipling is mentioned just as a 'recognised' author in London (Casanova 2007: 153). In Damrosch's, the quote by T.S. Eliot is, in turn, used to trace a genealogy that ends in Ishiguro, another anointed 'world literature,' modernist author (Damrosch 2003: 227).

4 Latin American translation scholars seeking to explore the role of literary translation in illustrated magazines, periodicals, low-priced collections, and weekly literary supplements have encountered conservative tendencies —both in content and style (Willson 2004, 2011). This article follows a similar preoccupation, more specifically with understanding the role of translation as 'background' rather than 'groundbreaking.'

5 Already in her 1996 article 'The Meek or the Mighty: Reappraising the Role of the Translator,' Bassnett states that the rise of Translation Studies is testament to the 'recognition of the role played by translation in shaping the literary polysystem. [...] Translation could be documented as having been at various moments *subversive, innovatory or radical*' (Bassnett 1996: 13, my emphasis). In many ways, her proposed reappraisal of the role of the translator has taken root, and much attention has been

paid to the 'might' of translation since then. My chapter is, so to speak, dedicated to meek translators and their work.

6 This absence is particularly glaring in the case of Damrosch's, in which world literature is defined *by* translation: 'literature stays within its national or regional tradition when it usually loses in translation, whereas works become world literature when they gain on balance in translation, stylistic losses offset by an expansion in depth as they increase their range, as is the case with such widely disparate works as *The Epic of Gilgamesh* and *Dictionary of the Khazars*.' (Damrosch 2003: 289).

   Jack London's writings, as well as those by Jules Verne, Emilio Salgari, and Louisa M. Alcott should, according to Damrosch's definition, be archetypical examples of 'rangy,' world literature texts that succeed in translation. The case of London is poignant because his world fame, it has been said, seemingly 'far outranks his fame in his native country' (Tavernier-Courbin 1994: 42).

7 The shape of this question is inspired by Alex Woloch's statement in *The One vs The Many*: 'narratives themselves allow and solicit us to construct a story—a distributed pattern of attention—that is at odds with, or divergent from, the formed pattern of attention in the discourse' (Woloch 2003: 41).

8 In his 'Introduction' to *The Readers' Guide*, editor Ernest Rhys mentions translation only in passing, ending with this curious statement: 'this Library ought, if it is worth anything, to be one of the safeguards of that superb instrument the English Tongue' (Rhys 1935: lxiv).

9 In the classroom, classics like *Platero y yo* by Spanish author Juan Ramón Jiménez were read for generations in Argentina, while in Mexico translations of Verne's *Le Château des Carpathes* and Salgari's *Il Corsaro Nero* were assigned regularly in schools. In the case of Brazil, young readers tended to be more exposed to national and even regionalist literature, as is evident in the *Coleção Saraiva* catalogue. The pleasure of reading a fiction independently 'for fun' rather than as an assigned task usually came from translated novels, printed in hard cover books with attractive illustrations and colorful covers.

10 In this collection of pink literature, the most popular author was M. Delli, whose *Magali* was reprinted ten times. A case study on the everyday life at a Florianópolis school from 1920 to 1960, a researcher found that the novels by M. Delli (pseudonym of the siblings Henri and Jeanne Marie Petitjean) were widely read and even sponsored by the school to instruct students on how to behave 'properly' (Santos Cunha 1999).

11 The most memorable state-sponsored collection was José de Vasconcelos' 1924 *Lecturas clásicas para niños*. As part of his 'civilizing mission' Vasconcelos, then Secretary of Public Education, along with towering intellectuals like Gabriela Mistral, anthologized this two-volume collection that traced classics form the Upanishads to Tolstoy and Wilde. In Argentina, newspaper *La Nación* published the very successful 'Biblioteca La Nación' (from 1910 to 1920, considered by Willson a 'project by the elite' to educate the masses) (Willson 2004, 47–55.) The London-Buenos Aires International Society (Sociedad Internacional), published in 1910 the *Biblioteca de Obras Famosas*, a 24 volume collection that included texts from the 'oldest short-story in the world' through Greece and Rome, and ending in Argentine contemporary fiction. After World War II, there were a series of collections were destined to 'the household': usually sold by door-to-door traveling salesmen, they enriched households culturally and served as 'decoration'—some even came with furniture to hold the volumes. Among these collections we find *Colección Jackson/Coleção Jackson* (Argentina and Brazil, 40 volumes, published during the 1950s and 1960s), and *Coleção Imortais da literatura universal* by the publisher Abril Cultural (Brazil, 50 volumes, published between 1970 and 1972).

12 A 1985 article about the new 'market tendencies' for children and young adult literature in Brazil states that from 1980 onwards (only *then*) the number of new books by Brazilian authors is larger than the number of translations (688 to 471 that year)

(Sandroni 1985: 110). In Spanish, the late 1980s marked the beginning of a radical transition in the publishing industry. Small publishers were bought out by large Spanish transnational corporations, creating a lack of 'bibliodiversity.' Small boutique publishers now satisfy particular niches, whereas transnational conglomerates like Planeta control much of the market, including young adult and children literature (Saferstein and Szpilbarg 2014).

13 Many of these fictions have a deeply nostalgic undertone. It was not until mid-twentieth century that novels for young adults (and by them, like S. E. Hinton's *The Outsiders*) depicted adolescent life, with its troubles, angst, and sense of urgency.

14 'Romance, [the etymological origin of French's *roman* (novel)] derives narrowly from the verbs *enromancier* and *romançar*, meaning "to translate into the vernacular" the product of which was *romanz, romant,* or *romanzo*' (Schellinger 1998: 942).

15 A children's books critic summarizes this Marxist reading thus: 'The success of adventure and sentimental novels has been attributed to the fact that their genres offer a condensed and digested compensation to sectors of the population [that] support the capitalist system of production. The romantic heroine and the gallant night have worked as safety valves for these sectors' (Alvarado 1993: 49).

16 Harte explains that London 'came into his own as a writer in an age when "manliness" was in vogue' (Harte 2016). Health, in this understanding of manliness, is essential. We read in *The Call of the Wild* that, 'Hunting and kindred outdoor delights had kept down the fat and hardened [Buck's] muscles; and to him, as to the cold-tubbing races, the love of water had been a tonic and a health preserver' (London 1995: 5).

17 On the one hand, these translations are not preserved in public or research libraries or catalogues; on the other, the rights to certain versions (and even their prologues) were (and are) bought, borrowed, or stolen from publisher to publisher, who very often do not indicate the translators' names.

18 PY refers to the 'Perymat Edition.' Refer to the key to each version in the Bibliography. Clear misuses of the word 'selva' (jungle/rainforest) appear in the PY edition when the word is used in these contexts: 'John Thornton [...] was unafraid of the *wild*'; 'With a handful of salt and a rifle he could plunge into the *wilderness*' (65); '*deep in the forest*' (62). '[T]wenty moose had crossed over from the land of streams and timber' (79) is translated, also in Perymat's edition, as 'Unos veinte alces habían cruzado la zona desde la *región de las selvas*' (119). The thought of moose crossing a rainforest can only strike a jarring note in the mind of the reader.

19 Buck first sees her in a scene of chaos: 'Buck saw a slipshod and slovenly affair, tent half stretched, dishes unwashed, everything in disorder; also, he saw a woman. "Mercedes" the men called her. She was Charles's wife and Hal's sister—nice family party' (London 1995: 62). And chaos is what she brings about. She 'continually fluttered in the way of her men and kept up an unbroken chattering of remonstrance and advice.' And when it is time to get rid of superfluous items, she turns into a hysterical 'tornado' (translated as 'huracán' in most Spanish versions.) Even when Mercedes shows some positive traits by pleading the men to not whip Buck and the other dogs, she is the *source* of the punishment: the dogs cannot make progress if they are to carry her belongings.

20 It has been argued that 'the comment that Manuel's faith in a system points not to his own sin but to a larger faith in a machinelike capitalist establishment that exists for the betterment of men like the Judge, based on the labor of poor workers like Manuel' (Reesman 2009: 80). This apologetic reading is both dubious and certainly unavailable to the young reader of this novel.

21 In the prologue to his own translation entitled *La llamada de la selva*, Colombian translator Javier Escobar Isaza proposes *Lo salvaje llama* (The Wild Calls) as a better alternative (Isaza 1991: 31).

22 According to Walter Benjamin, a storyteller concerns himself with what is useful to the community of listeners: 'The usefulness may, in one case, consist in a moral; in another, in some practical advice; in a third, in a proverb or maxim. In every case the storyteller is a man who has counsel for his readers' (Benjamin 1969: 101). Not unlike a storyteller, a minor translator of these fictions often imparts knowledge while holding the reader's hand.

23 In *Contingency, Irony, and Solidarity*, Rorty distinguishes two kinds of readers. 'Ironist' readers, addressed by modernist fictions, continually doubt their final vocabulary and are then open to exploring differing vocabularies. Commonsensical readers, on the other hand, expect solidity: 'To be commonsensical is to take for granted that statements formulated in [the final vocabulary to which the non-ironist is habituated], suffice to describe and judge the beliefs, actions and lives of those who employ alternative final vocabularies' (Rorty 1989: 74).

Bibliography

Abraham, Carlos (2012) *La editorial Tor: Medio siglo de libros populares*. Temperley, Tren en Movimiento.

Adichie, Chimamanda (2009). 'The Danger of a Single Story.' *TED. Ideas Worth Spreading*. Available from: www.ted.com/talks/chimamanda_adichie_the_danger_of_a_single_story/transcript?language=en [Accessed March 2017]

Alvardo, Maite and Massat, Elena (1993) *Incluso los niños. Apuntes para una estética de la infancia*. Buenos Aires, La Marca.

Baer, John W. (2007) *The Pledge of Allegiance. A Revised History and Analysis*. Annapolis, Free State Press.

Bassnet, Susan (1996) 'The Meek or the Mighty: Reappraising the Role of the Translator.' *Translation, Power, Subversion*. Ed. Román Álvarez and M. Carmen-África Vidal. Pennsylvania, Multilingual Matters. 10–24.

Benjamin, Walter (1969) 'The Storyteller.' *Illuminations*. Trans. Harry Zohn. Ed. Hannah Arendt. New York, Schocken Books. 83–109.

Bertazza, Juan Pablo (2012) 'Un tornado.' *Página/12. Radar libros*. August 20. Available from: www.pagina12.com.ar/diario/suplementos/libros/10-4767-2012-08-20.html [Accessed June 2016]

Casanova, Pascale. (2007) *The World Republic of Letters*. Trans. M. B. DeBevoise. Cambridge: Harvard University Press. Originally published in French in 1999 as *La République mondiale des lettres*. Paris, Éditions du Seuil.

Cerrutti, Marcela and Bertoncello, Rodolfo (2003) 'Urbanization and Internal Migration Patterns in Latin America.' *Centro de Estudios de Población. Ricardo Rojas Data bank*. June 2003. Available from: http://dr-muele.mak.ac.ug/pluginfile.php/170462/mod_resource/content/1/Urbanisation%20and%20internal%20migration%20patterns%20in%20Latin%20America.pdf [Accessed March 2017]

Cortázar, Julio (1973) 'Estamos como queremos, o los monstruos en acción.' *Buenos Aires, Crisis B.A.* Tomo 1. 40–49.

Cortázar, Julio (1994) 'Reunión.' *Cuentos Completos/1*. Buenos Aires, Alfaguara. 537–547.

Daghlian, Carlos (1975) 'Jack London in Brazil and Portugal.' *Jack London Newsletter* 8. 22–27.

Damrosch, David. (2003) *What is World Literature?* Princeton, Princeton University Press.

D'haen, Theo. (2012) *The Routledge Concise History of World Literature*. London, Routledge.

Doctorow, Edgar L. (1993) *Jack London, Hemingway and the Constitution. Selected Essays.* New York, Random House.

Dyer, Daniel. (1997) *Jack London: A Biography.* New Jersey, Scholastic.

Even-Zohar, Itamar (1990) 'The Position of Translated Literature within the Literary Polysystem.' *Poetics Today* 11, 1. Polysystem Studies. Spring. 45–51.

'Everyman's Library: A History.' (2006) Available from www.everymanslibrary.co.uk/history.aspx [Accessed March 2017]

Fusco, Richard (1987) 'On Primitivism in "The Call of the Wild".' *America Literary Realism, 1870–1910* 20, 1. Fall. 76–80.

Goethe, Johann Wolfgang (1886) 'On World Literature.' *Essays on Art and Literature.* vol 3. Ed. John Gearey. Trans. Ellen von Nardroff and Ernest H. von Nardroff. New York, Suhrkamp. 224–228.

Goethe, Johann Wolfgang (1972) *Berliner Ausgabe, vol. 18: Schriften zur Literatur II: Aufsatze zur Weltliteratur.* Ed. Siegfried Seidel. Berlin and Weimar, Aufbau-Verlag.

Guevara, Ernesto (2006) *Reminiscences of the Cuban Revolutionary War.* Trans. Aleida March. Melbourne, Ocean Press.

Gürçaglar, Şehnaz Tahir, Paker, Saliha and Milton, John (1998) 'Introduction.' *Tradition, Tension and Translation in Turkey.* Amsterdam, Benjamins. 1–25.

Harte, Tim (2016) 'Transforming Defeat into Victory': Jack London and Vladimir Nabokov's Glory,' *Nabokov Online Journal*, X–XI, 2016–2017.

Isaza, Javier Escobar (1991) 'Los ciclos de la vida y la crítica. Reflexiones sobre Jack London.' *La llamada de la selva.* Bogotá, Norma. 13–34.

Kosztolányi, Deszö (1994) *Le Traducteur cleptomane et autres histoires.* Trans. Ádám Péter and Maurice Regnaut. Paris, Viviane Hamy.

Labor, Earle, Leitz, III, Robert C., and Shepard, I. Milo (1993) 'Introduction.' *The Complete Short Stories of Jack London. Vol. 1.* Stanford, Stanford University Press.

London, Jack (1995) *The Call of the Wild. With an Illustrated Reader's Companion.* Oklahoma, University of Oklahoma Press. 3–80.

Milton, John (2010) 'The Resistant Political Translations of Monteiro Lobato.' *Translation, Resistance, Activism.* Ed. Maria Tymoczko. Boston, University of Massachusetts Press. 190–210.

Moretti, Franco (2000) 'Conjectures on World Literature.' *New Left Review.* Jan–Feb.54–68.

Moretti, Franco (2003) 'More Conjectures.' *New Left Review.* Mar–Apr. 73–81.

Moretti, Franco (2005) *Graph, Maps, Trees: Abstract Models for a Literary History.* New York, London, Verso.

Moretti, Franco (2013) *Distant Reading.* New York, London, Verso.

Orloff, Carolina (2014) *La construcción de lo político en Julio Cortázar.* Buenos Aires, Godot.

Pérez-Abadín Barro, Soledad (2010) 'Cortázar y Che Guevara. Lectura de "Reunión".' *Hispanic Studies: Culture and Ideas.* Oxford: Peter Lang. Vol. 29.

Piglia, Ricardo (2006) *El último lector.* Buenos Aires, Anagrama.

Pollard, David E. (1998) 'Introduction.' *Translation and Creation: Readings of Western Literature in Early Modern China, 1840–1918.* Amsterdam, Benjamins. 5–25.

Prendergast, Christopher (2004) *Debating World Literature.* London, Verso.

Reesman, Jeanne Campbell (2009) *Jack London's Racial Lives.* Athens, University of Georgia Press.

Rhys, Ernest (1935) 'Introduction.' *The Readers' Guide to Everyman's Library, being a catalog of the first 888 volumes.* London, J. M. Dent & Sons, Ltd. iii–li.

Romero, Luis Alberto (1995) 'Una empresa cultural: los libros baratos.' *Sectores populares, cultura y política*. Ed. Leandro Gutiérrez and L. A. Romero. Buenos Aires, Siglo XXI. 51–66.

Rorty, Richard (1989) *Contingency, Irony, and Solidarity*. London: Cambridge University Press.

Roser, Max (2016) 'Literacy.' *OurWorldInData.org*. Available from https://ourworldinda ta.org/literacy/ [Accessed March 2017]

Saferstein, Ezequiel and Szpilbarg, Daniela (2014) 'La industria editorial argentina, 1990–2010. Entre la concentración económica y la bibliodiversidad.' *alter/nativas latin american cultural studies journal*. Available from http://alternativas.osu.edu/es/issues/a utumn-2014/essays2/saferstein-szpilbarg.html [Accessed March 2017]

Sandroni, Laura Constância (1985) 'Panorama da Literatura Infantil e Juvenil Brasileira Hoje: Tendências do Mercado.' *Perspectiva*. Florianópolis 1(4). Jan./Dec.109–112.

Simeoni, Daniel (1998) 'The Pivotal Status of the Translator's Habitus.' *Target: International Journal of Translation Studies* 10: 1. 1–39.

Standish, Peter (2001) *Understanding Julio Cortázar*. Columbia: University of South Carolina Press.

Santos Cunha, Maria Teresa (1999) *Armadilhas da sedução. Os romances de M. Delly*. Belo Horizonte, Autêntica.

Schellinger, Paul (1998) 'Novel and Romance: Etymologies.' *Encyclopaedia of the Novel*. Vol 2. London, Routledge.

Seivach, Paulina (2005) *Las industrias culturales en la Ciudad de Buenos Aires*. Buenos Aires, CEDEM y Secretaría de Desarrollo Económico del Gobierno de la Ciudad de Buenos Aires.

Seyhan, Azade (1998) 'Saved by Translation: German Academic Culture in Turkish exile.' *Tradition, Tension and Translation in Turkey*. Amsterdam, Benjamins. 107–124.

Simon, Sherry (2000) 'Introduction.' *Changing the Terms: Translating in the Postcolonial Era*. New Delhi, Orient Longman. 9–31.

Stephens, John (1992) *Language and Ideology in Children's Fiction*. London, Longman.

Tavernier-Courbin, Jacqueline (1994) *The Call of the Wild. A Naturalistic Approach*. New York, Twayne.

Venuti, Lawrence (1993) 'Translation as Cultural Politics: Regimes of Domestication in English.' *Textual Practice* 7. 208–223.

Walsh, Rodolfo (1981) 'Nota al pie.' *Obra literaria completa*. Mexico, Siglo XXI. 419–446.

Willson, Patricia (2004) *La Constelación del Sur: traductores y traducciones en la literatura argentina del siglo XX*. Buenos Aires, Siglo XXI.

Willson, Patricia (2011) *Paraísos perdidos: la traducción en Caras y Caretas (1898–1908)*. Mexico City, UNAM.

Wolf, Michaela (2014) 'The Sociology of Translation and Its "Activist Turn".' *The Sociological Turn in Translation and Interpreting Studies*. Ed. Claudia V. Angelelli. Amsterdam, Benjamins. 7–22.

Woloch, Alex (2003) *The One vs. The Many: Minor Characters and the Space of the Protagonist in the Novel*. New Jersey, Princeton University Press.

Spanish translations of The Call of the Wild reviewed [with key]

El llamado de la naturaleza (1984) Trans. Jorge Barros. Santiago, Pehuén. [SP]

El llamado de la selva (1958) Trans. Cora Bosch. Buenos Aires, Atlántida (Colección Billiken). [EA]

El llamado de la selva (2002) Trans. Mariela Aquilano. Buenos Aires, Gárgola (Colección Modelo para armar). [GR]

El llamado de la selva (2003) Trans. not credited. Buenos Aires, Plaza Dorrego. [PD]

El llamado de la selva y otros cuentos (1970) Trans. not credited. Buenos Aires, ACME (Colección Robin Hood). [5th reprint] [AC]

El llamado de lo salvaje (2000) Trans. Esteban Magnani. Buenos Aires, Puerto de Palos (Colección del Mirador) [PP]

La llamada de la selva. (1997) Trans. Enrique Campbell. Barcelona, Edicomunicación. [EC]

La llamada de la selva (1972) Trans. Hugo A. Brown. Barcelona, La Gaya Ciencia [GC]

La llamada de la selva (2003) Trans. not credited. Madrid, Estudio Didáctico [ED]

La llamada de la selva (1984) Trans. not credited. México, Perymat (La punta del iceberg) [PY]

La llamada de la selva (1972) Trans. Orestes Llorens. Barcelona, Orbis [2nd reprint] [OR]

La llamada de la selva. Colmillo blanco (2001) Trans. Tradutex. Madrid, Gaviota [GV]

La llamada de lo salvaje (2012) Trans. José Ramón Insa and Gabriel Casas. Buenos Aires, Vicens Vives [VV]

8   Maxim Gorky and world literature
Challenging the maxims

Svetlana Page

Describing a phenomenon he terms 'the Russian Reading Revolution', Stephen Lovell acknowledges,

> Anyone who has spent much time with urban educated Russians over recent years can testify that they tend to get rather emotional about reading. One often hears (even from people with no great love of the Soviet system) that the Soviet people was the 'best-read' (*samyi chitaiushchii*) in the world.
>
> (Lovell 2000, 1)

He adds that in Russia 'the rhetoric of cultural crisis – with its particular reference to "the death of the book" – is heard with much greater insistence than in the West' (2000, 1) Written at the brink of the millennium, within the same decade that witnessed the breakup of the Soviet Union, his words resonate back to a hundred year old polemics in the Russian Empire. That discussion was also happening at a time of epic tectonic shifts in political, social and cultural systems in Russia and it also stressed the civilising power of the book, seeing literature as a way, sometimes *the* way, towards social progress.

One of the leading Russian writers of the time whose work stems from this belief is Maxim Gorky (1868–1936). His ideas found practical expression in the World Literature Publishing House (1918–1924), a project of an unprecedented breadth and depth which would make it 'the first and sole one in Europe' (Gorky 1919, 21). The legacy of this short-lived, state-sponsored yet uncharacteristically independent publishing house, founded in Petrograd soon after the October Revolution, has had a lasting influence on the Russian, and later on the Soviet and post-Soviet cultural and literary domain. In publishing, it helped shape both editing and reading practices, by offering translations catering for different audiences and setting high expectations for the 'main' or 'educated readership'. Its insistence on scholarly commentaries brought forth, in embryonic form, a discipline of *textology*, a practice of scholarly social and historic commentary which would accompany all the multi-volume editions, rare and ancient texts as well as numerous translations published in the USSR. In literary terms, its legacy is still traceable in Russian and post-Soviet critical theory, comparative literature, world literature and translation studies.

In effect, the World Literature Publishing House project was nothing short of revolutionary. Yet paradoxically, which is what this chapter is trying to question, did it also deserve its reputation as being Soviet or Bolshevik? What is offered here is a revisionist reading of Gorky's project, which is examined not via the conventional prism of 'Gorky-the-leading-Soviet-writer' or 'world literature in its Soviet guise' as has been contended, but as a large-scale evolution of '*prosveti-telski*' ('enlightenment' or 'educational') projects typical of Russian literati and intelligentsia of the late nineteenth and early twentieth centuries. In so doing, this chapter wishes to examine whether the project should not be regarded as a Soviet one by considering its precursors, the guiding principles of the publisher's Catalogue and its text selection. It also assesses its legacy in terms of its 'internal' influence (Russian, Soviet and post-Soviet critical theory, translation theory and practice) and 'external' role (world literature debates and translation studies).

Gorky in world literature discourse

Traditionally, Russian Studies, both Soviet and anti-Soviet in nature, have viewed Gorky as 'the father of socialist realism', the 'first proletarian writer' and a loyal supporter of the Bolsheviks. World literature scholarship, in the few existing publications which mention Gorky and World Literature Publishers, also follow this conventional trend. Thus, the only paragraph dedicated to Gorky's project (and, perhaps, by logical extension, to his input into world literature) in the seminal *The Routledge Companion to World Literature* (D'haen, Damrosch & Kadir, 2012) presents it as an early Soviet enterprise. The introduction to the *Companion* reads:

> Closer to Goethe's original ideas on Weltliteratur, yet inflected by their particular situations, were the views of Rabindranath Tagore and Maksim Gorky early in the twentieth century. [...] What mattered most for Gorky was to recuperate the idea of world literature for the ideology of the newly created Soviet state in the wake of the European cataclysm of the First World War. In Gorky's presentation, world literature provides a privileged means of access to other people's thoughts and experiences, fostering solidarity and harmony in the dual struggle for physical and social wellbeing
>
> (D'haen, Damrosch & Kadir 2012, xix)

This reading is developed in Theo D'haen's *The Routledge Concise History of World Literature* (D'haen 2012, 21–23), where he is also presented alongside Rabindranath Tagore, and in Maria Khotimsky's (2013) article tellingly titled 'World Literature, Soviet Style: a Forgotten Episode in the History of the Idea'. Khotimsky sees Gorky as 'a prominent Soviet writer and cultural leader' whose World Literature project was 'a curious crossover between Goethe's *Weltliteratur* and the Marxian commodity of universal literature [...] both Romantic and political' (120). She aims to offer 'a reading of a specific and overlooked episode in the history of 'world literature' as a cultural concept and editorial practice' (122). In this reading, World Literature's 'ambitious plan for the publishing house represented a 'new' socialist vision of internationalism, hailed as superior to the Western equivalents' (128). Challenging universalist tendencies in world literature debates (namely, Casanova and Pizer), Khotimsky uses the World Literature project to aid 'the notion of "world literature" as a time-specific, rather than universal, concept that is shaped by particular institutional, ideological, and historical contexts' (121). Read from an historical perspective, this 'Soviet vision of world literature' (136) becomes a curiosity, 'a forgotten episode in the history of the idea' barely more than 'a useful example of how institutional and ideological frameworks can define seemingly universal categories' (154).

In this sense, it is little wonder, therefore, that such a venture, defined by institutional and ideological frameworks of its time, came to its inevitable demise together with the system which created it:

> Gorky's name would later be given to an institute dedicated to the study and propagation of world literature along Soviet lines. It is under the auspices of this Institute that the multivolume *Istoriia vsemirnoĭ literatury v deviati tomakh* (History of World Literature in Nine Volumes) started appearing as of 1983 in Moscow. The project never reached its full nine volumes, as the Soviet Union imploded in the years after the fall of the Berlin Wall in 1989, and the work was discontinued after the eighth volume appeared in 1994: the history of world literature was overtaken by world events
>
> (D'haen, Damrosch & Kadir 2012, xix).

On the one hand, very little can be argued against this point of view, since the project was time and place specific and the publication of the *History* was discontinued. Khotimsky is right in her criticism of universalist tendencies in world literature and her article convincingly argues against the tendencies in world literature which Apter (2013, 8) would term 'too pluralistic, too ecumenical'.

In agreeing with Khotimsky here, this chapter nevertheless wishes to make two distinctions. Firstly, one may wonder if by nature *every* project is time-specific and contextual, rather than universal. In this sense, World Literature is not an exception: it was a specific project with its temporal and spatial limitations, the fact of existence of which was mentioned by Gorky himself in the World Literature Catalogue:

> Of course, Literature is not entirely free from what Ivan Tourgeniev [sic] called 'the pressure of time'; this is natural, for 'sufficient for the day is the evil thereof'; perhaps, this evil of the day – poisons these inspirations and prayers with the dust of the present day oftener than is really wanted by those free 'inspirations and prayers' which are raised to the Holy Spirit of beauty and research
>
> (Gorky 1919, 19)

Moreover, simply 'being of its time' can hardly be sufficient to be regarded as Soviet and in that sense it would be necessary to examine the foundations of this venture so casually written off within current world literature debates. After all, if translation is manipulation, as has been convincingly argued (Bassnett & Lefevere 1998, Hermans 1985, Lefevere 1992), then the question would be what kind of manipulation was carried out in the case of the World Literature translation project within the target literary system's constraints, both external (patronage and ideology) and internal (poetics and professionals). Did the World Literature publishers shape their production in line with their patrons' guidance? Was the core of the project Soviet or was it only loosely aligned with the dominant ideology and patrons' wishes? This chapter will examine the project's fit within Soviet ideology (external constraints) to which it has been conventionally assigned, by examining the project's internal constraints, such as the attitudes of the professionals involved. The conclusions will be based on the Catalogue programme, text selection principles contained therein, as well as newspaper articles and diary entries written by some of its participants at the time.

Secondly, it is important to examine whether the project was a product of its time, as is argued within world literature scholarship, or whether it would carry equal or similar validity, if it were reinstated in its original form today. Was the World Literature project an evolutionary, rather than a revolutionary project, within Russian publishing of the time? In attempting to answer this question, the chapter will consider the place of the project along a temporal axis, from finding its place within the dominant publishing trends of the late nineteenth and early twentieth century, to tracing its legacy within current Russian and post-Soviet literary fields and cultural institutions of today.

Precursors to the World Literature project

The 1880s–1900s were a time of intensive development of Russia's publishing system, a time of implementing daring innovative projects. Ivan Sytin, the leading Russian publisher of the age, wrote in his memoir, 'The more my publishing work developed, the stronger I became convinced that publishing in Russia is boundless and that there is no corner in people's lives where a Russian publisher would have absolutely nothing to do!'[1] (Sytin 1962, 91). Assessing Sytin's work for the fiftieth anniversary of his publishing career in 1916, one of the leading Russian educators Nikolai Tulupov declares,

> He brought the real book closer to the people. He turned the noble aspirations of the best minds of our intelligentsia – to give healthy spiritual food to people – into flesh and blood. This is the greatest merit of Sytin, which grants him the right to take a place of honour among the developers of Russian education [enlightenment].[2]
>
> (Tulupov 1916, 102)

This rhetoric of education, or as Gorky's precursors would term it, 'enlightenment' (*prosveschenie*), is characteristic of the leading publishing projects implemented in the wake of Alexander II's Great Reforms which led to the democratisation of numerous aspects of the country's social institutions, including the 1861 Emancipation of Serfdom. Paradoxically, literature became the platform on which a number of these reforms found their implementation: 'given the relative weakness of mediating civil institutions, literature acquired a significant role in nation-building and political debate; educated and socially active groups (the intelligentsia) inherited Enlightenment ideas concerning the socializing effect of literature and applied them dogmatically' (Lovell 2000, 10).

The breadth of material coverage and the production level for mass audiences of the 'educational' publishers was prolific. The case of Sytin would be a good example of these tendencies, and he was hardly an exception. Florentij Pavlenkov, for instance, published over 750 titles with 3.5 million copies in circulation and bequeathed the acquired capital to create 2000 free village libraries in Russian provinces which were nicknamed 'Pavlenkov's libraries'. For the first time in its history, Russia was rapidly developing mass culture which also included a new 'mass' reading public and unprecedented print runs (Sytin 1962).

Many of the publishers had a dedicated specialism to which they devoted their 'educational' efforts: Mir Iskusnikov ('World of Masters') worked with art, the Brothers Sabashnikov worked with science and, to a lesser extent, with fiction, while Belyaev's Publishers (M. P. Belaieff, Leipzig) and the Russian Music Publishers, or Editions Russes de Musique, founded by the conductor Sergi Kusevitsky and his wife, worked with music (Karajchentseva 2004). A number of them worked in close cooperation with Russian literati. Thus, Sytin famously collaborated with Chekhov at the *Russkoe Slovo* ('Russian Word'), one of the leading broadsheets he published. He was also in charge of distribution for Tolstoy's publishing house Posrednik ('Negotiator', 1884) which he described as 'not just work, but ministry' (Sytin 1962, 63) and collaborated with Gorky on several projects. The publishing projects of the 'Silver Age' simultaneously released, at both ends of the spectrum, the 'mass market paperback' and the 'elite' editions, the latter represented by the work of the Symbolists and Cubofuturists and organisations such as the Society of the Amateurs of Fine Publications (Karajchentseva 2004).

Alongside fiction, a number of fundamental encyclopedia projects were published (Brockhaus and Efron's, Granat's, Pavlenkov's encyclopedic dictionaries). The scale of the projects produced at the time is exemplified by Brockhaus and Efron's encyclopaedic dictionary in forty-one volumes (or eighty-two semi-volumes) published between 1890–1904, with a further four semi-volumes added in 1906–1907. While some of its articles were translated from the German edition, its contents were mainly written by leading Russian scholars. Its legacy has been such that it is still considered one of the two fundamental encyclopaedias in Russian (along with the Big Soviet Encyclopaedia).

Examined in the light of its precursors, the World Literature project can be seen as a natural evolution of the dominant 'enlightenment' tradition within Russian literary publishing of the time: as an educational large-scale project published for 'mass' audiences. The publishing house intended to produce translations of 1200 authors in its Western Series alone, beside Eastern Series texts, and intended to 'shortly [...] complete the above list by selected works of the Polish, Lithuanian, Bohemian, Serbian, Bulgarian, Greek and Hungarian Literature' (Catalogue 1919, 160). The series approach unites it with Sytin's editions, who preferred to publish series or 'libraries' of books, rather than 'single volumes', to market specific literary trends and boost their distribution (1962). The People's, or as the Catalogue's English translation terms it, 'Popular Series', were cheap editions for newly literate readers, a readership well familiar to Sytin. The link between the 'healthy spiritual food' and the masterpieces of world literature translated for wide audiences is another obvious link which unites the ethos of the project with its predecessors.

In terms of direct influences on the idea itself, there were a number of projects which might have helped Gorky evolve his publishing ideas. Khotimsky offers two possible sources: Valery Brusov's series of modernist poetry translations Biblioteka Novoi Poezii (Library of New Poetry) including 'detailed introductions and bibliography' (2013, 123) and Merezhkovsky's essays *Vechnye sputniki: Portrety iz vsemirnoi literatury* ('Eternal Companions: Portraits from World Literature', 1897). Her suggestions are based upon Brusov and Gorky's collaboration in Parus and Merezhkovsky's acquaintance with Gorky, 'even though Merezhkovsky did not participate in the World Literature project' (2013, 123–124). In fact, both Merezhkovsky and his wife *did* take part in the venture by editing translations as evidenced by Chukovsky (1991) and Merezhkovsky's open letter to H.G. Wells published in the émigré press. While this chapter does not disagree about the possible influences of the publications mentioned above, placing the project's prototypes exclusively within modernist framework could limit its aesthetic foundations. Hence the consideration of an earlier project with a similar title, which at one stage was running parallel to World Literature, would add further insight into the motivation behind the project.

In the late 1890s, Sabashnikovs, one of the leading 'educational' publishers of the time, decided to publish a series entitled 'Eternal Books' which subsequently became one of their best-known productions titled *Pamjatniki mirovoj literatury* (*The Milestones of World Literature*). It started as a series of the editor's selection of the 'best' works of world literature in the 'best' Russian translations which were published irregularly from 1913 to 1925 (Saidova 1998). The programme included the following sections: 'Writers of Antiquity', 'Creations of the East', 'Writers of the West', 'Folklore', 'Russian Folklore', 'Books of the Bible'. 'Milestones' included translations from the classics (Euripides, Sophocles, Thucydides, Marcus Aurelius) as well as oral epics, such as the *Edda*, the Russian *bylinas* and others. Sabashnikovs' programme stated:

> All outstanding works of world literature have to be at the disposal of the reader in his native language. In our age of the democratisation of education hardly anyone will raise objections [...] *Milestones of World literature*, unlike the existing *Libraries of the Classics* and traditional *Pantheons*, will

embrace the works selected not for their aesthetic and literary merits but for their value in terms of a more modern and a broader historical and literary point of view, whereby literature is considered as a section of the general history of human culture

(cited in Smirin 1967, 138–139)

Several crossover points can be observed between Gorky and Sabashnikovs' projects: a global approach to literary production ('world literature'); the thematic series approach with differentiating series within the project; similarities in text selection principles, e.g. geographical divisions (East vs West); the view of world literature as a current evolving process as well as the existence of scholarly commentary (Rossels 1964) and their emphasis on translation (Smirin 1967). A certain crossover of interest sometimes led to direct competition: Alexander Blok, for instance, originally gave his translation of Franz Grillparzer's Die Ahnfrau (*The Ancestress*, 1817) to Mikhail Sabashnikov but later asked for it to be returned for publication by World Literature (Belov 1987).

Thus, it is possible to see a direct link which unites World Literature with the breadth of the 'educational' projects of pre-revolutionary Russian literature. Rather than rejecting or revising the principles of its precursors, World Literature was continuing and expanding the prevalent ethos and traditions of the 'enlightenment' Russian publishers. It focused on a representation of world literature in Russian for mass audiences, propagated the view of world literature as an active process, insisted on scholarly commentary to translations, and was organised as a series on an unprecedented encyclopaedic scale which aimed to represent the manifoldness of human literary activities through time and space for the Russian-speaking reader.

These continuities are hardly surprising. By the time of World Literature's foundation, Gorky had already become an experienced editor with several publishing houses and journals to his name. As early as 1900, he was already in charge of Znaniye ('Knowledge', 1989–1913) whose profile changed under his guidance to publishing contemporary literary works written in the traditions of critical realism. After Znaniye, Gorky was in charge of another company, Parus ('Sail', 1915–1918) which published literature by the Russian Empire's ethnic minorities. Parus also produced *Letopis*, a literary and political journal (1915–1917). *Letopis* was co-published with Sytin, whom Gorky appreciated for his longstanding dedication to publishing and of whom he spoke highly in numerous letters (Sytin 1962).

A number of collaborators from Parus followed Gorky to World Literature. His authority as a writer and leading cultural figure with a wide portfolio of pre-established contacts in literature, politics and publishing, as well as his 'proletarian' biography was attractive to the new Bolshevik government which proclaimed it was giving power to the subalterns. Since both liberal and radical reformists believed in the power of the printed word, it is no surprise that 'when one group within the intelligentsia (the Bolsheviks) gained a monopoly on enlightenment' its victory 'brought the projects of the pre-revolutionary prosvetiteli (educators) into sharp focus' (Lovell 2000, 13) and created an opportunity for a state funding platform necessary for large scale project implementation, without which the scope of the World Literature initiative would not have been possible. Hence, World Literature was placed in a unique and privileged position: a state-funded enterprise, with its material selection entrusted to an individual.

'Untimely Thoughts' and untimely projects

Having established the continuity between World Literature and its literary pre-revolutionary precursors, let us consider its fit within the Soviet ideology and its acceptance, propagation or resistance in regards to Soviet values. Namely, the focus here will be on the adherence of the leading professionals involved in the project (Lefevere's internal constraints) to the external constraints implemented by its state patrons.

One of the main problems with defining the World Literature project as 'Soviet' is its time frame: the Soviet Union was only established in 1922, several years after the World Literature programme was formed in 1918 and already past its most productive initial three years. By 1922, the bulk of the translators, editors and associates with the publishing house, including Gorky himself, had left or were leaving the Soviet Union. It would be therefore factually incorrect to define it as 'Soviet'.

The next question arising is whether it can therefore be termed 'Bolshevik'. Given that 'Soviet' and 'Bolshevik' are a convenient shorthand used by modern literary historians, I would like to pre-empt quick re-definitions and examine whether the project can be regarded as 'Bolshevik'. In the first instance, the answer seems obvious: the publishing house was founded on 4 September 1918 under the auspices of Narkompros, the People's Commissariat for Education. Indeed, Gorky's reputation established from the 1930s onwards as the 'first pro-letarian writer', the 'founder of socialist realism' and the infamous pro-Soviet *Belomor* account of which Gorky was the editor, seem to further affirm this deduction. Hence it is the more surprising to find his position regarding the Bolsheviks openly expressed and published during 1917–1918 in the *Novaya Zhizn'* ('New Life') newspaper, which was eventually shut down on Lenin's direct orders in 1918. One of the biggest literary discoveries of the perestroika years, Gorky's *Untimely Thoughts* (1968), shows his uneasy relationship with the government and his mediation between the 'proletarian' state and the literati.

Both the Catalogue and *The Untimely Thoughts* contain a number of similar themes. In particular, they are both critical of the Revolution. Gorky compared it to the slaughter of World War I: 'after the bloody storms of wrath and hatred [...] in the midst of this festival of the Beast and Devil' (1919, 22). The Revolution, a proponent of which Gorky had been initially, rather than liberating the best, had freed the bestial, 'the animal element in man' (1919, 18), in his compatriots. Faced with a social restructuring of this magnitude, humankind was no longer 'a lord of facts, a free creator of life' (1919, 20) but was bound by 'the chains of humiliating reality' and 'feel[ing] himself [...] a slave' crushed by 'all that keeps back the free development of the spirit and gives man as a prey to his own animal instincts' (1919, 20) Gorky saw people as victims of the great social disaster: they are powerless and left at the mercy of 'the present social catastrophe' (1919, 19) with its 'cruel contradictions of life that excite the enmity and mutual hatred of nations, classes and individuals' (1919, 20). *Untimely Thoughts* contains numerous examples of social unrest, from public executions of pickpockets to the new government's arrests of its opposition members. For him, this much despised brutal and wild *aziatchina* (literally 'Asiatic substance' which means 'unculturedness, barbarism, rudeness' in Russian), a legacy of the Tatars' yoke, 'a prolonged rout of Mamay' (1968, 6) was rampant in post-revolutionary Russia, and Gorky hoped to offer a solution to its extirpation through culture.

There, the bestial could be countered by the intellectual, the brutal by the rational. For Gorky, there was nothing admirable in the bestial element, it was not what he regarded as true humanism and he did not see any advantage from it: 'men of coarse instincts are like each other everywhere, – but in the world of intellect the infinite fullness of variety is to be found' (1919, 18). For him, a Russian military call to arms, 'the Fatherland is in danger!' was not as urgent 'as the cry: "Citizens! Culture is in danger!"' (1968, 36).

The remedy for social ills lay for him within the power of the intellect and 'culture' passed down from generations before in the form of the written word, 'perhaps the greatest and most complex miracle of all the miracles wrought by man' (Gorky 1919, 19). In fact, 'books – ordinary, every-day books so familiar to us – are as a matter of fact one of the greatest and most wonderful mysteries of the earth' (19). Gorky was fascinated by the opportunities the printed word and, by extension, translation could bring to people alienated by spatial and linguistic differences, when:

> someone quite unknown to us, sometimes speaking in an incomprehensible tongue many thousand [sic] of miles away – traced certain combinations of some score or so of signs on paper – which are called letters and words; and we, utter strangers, having nothing in common with the author of the book, – we who look at these characters are brought in some magic way to understand the meaning of all the words, thoughts, feelings, images.
>
> (Gorky 1919, 19)

This optimistic view of translation was inherited from nineteenth century positivism, together with the 'educational' stance. Yet Gorky's humanism, expressed through the collective wisdom of humankind gained through history, as the main prerogative for intercultural communication, was a stance which still holds relevance within modern cross-cultural communication approaches.

Belief in science, in the rational, was also embodied within his construct. Thus, 'Literature rises high above life and, with the help of Science, illuminates those paths that lead all men to the attainment of their aims, to the development of their best innerself' (Gorky 1919, 19) This primary role of culture, particularly, the supremacy of cultural capital over political and economic prosperity for society's progress, is rooted in Gorky's earlier philosophical system called *god-building* (*bogostroitelstvo*) where enlightened humankind, enriched with strong feelings and new moral values, would be able to get rid of evil, suffering and even death, ideas which found expression in his novel *Confession* (1908).

By developing a revised world literature programme, Gorky hoped to provide a timely response to the participants of the 'festival of the Beast and Devil', to the people of the world, to those observing this social experiment carried out by Lenin (1968) and eventually to their offspring, by urging his readers to 'remember all the truly human, all that has been worshipped through bygone ages, all the world has been taught by Talent and by Genius' (Gorky 1919, 22).

Having described the revolution in no uncertain terms as a social catastrophe, the preface finishes on a somewhat discordant panegyric to the revolutionary government. Gorky claims that

> the honour of realising such a scheme belongs entirely to the creative powers of the Russian Revolution, that same Revolution which is considered by its enemies as an 'Outbreak of Barbarians'. By creating such an immense and responsible culture work in the very first year of their active life, under inexpressibly difficult circumstances – the Russian people is justified in saying that they are erecting a monument worthy of them
>
> (Gorky 1919, 21)

How sincere was Gorky in his praise of the government of 'Lenin, Trotsky, and their companions' whom he believed to 'have already become poisoned with the filthy venom of power', as evident from 'their shameful attitude toward freedom of speech, the individual, and the sum total of those rights for the triumph of which democracy struggled' (1968, 85). Moreover, how pervasive was the Bolshevik stance in terms of the core ethos of the project?

The mystery of that contradiction is revealed in Kornei Chukovsky's (1991, 109) diary:

> November 12 [1918]. [...] Yesterday a board meeting – with Gorky. Gorky was telling me about the preface he would write to our outline – and suddenly looked down, a smirk on his face, playing with his fingers. '*I will say* that such magnificent editions are supposedly possible only with the Workers and Peasants' Government. It is necessary to cajole. Yes, to cajole. So that they, you understand, won't carp. Because, after all, these devils are intriguers. It is necessary, you see, to cajole ...'

Chukovsky's diary entries of that time show Gorky's deepening rift with the Bolsheviks. He curses Bolsheviks (5 March, 8 November 1919), he never uses 'us', only 'they', as an attribute while referring to them (2 April), he complains that 'they' should let people go abroad (11 November). The state was equally suspicious of Gorky: when Chukovsky applied for permission for a new journal from Smolny, he was asked to send every issue for censorship because the state was very doubtful about Gorky's 'reliability' (7 June). He was warned by the Kremlin because of the talks held at the World Literature board meetings (5 November). He took an active mediating role, capitalising on his public reputation, to plead for the release of many of the imprisoned (2 April). At one stage, he was even seen crying and threatening to make a public exit from the Communist Party if one of the arrested were not released (4 September). A negotiator and diplomat, as described by colleagues (13 November) he took on a dual role of mediating between the state and the literati. In a reported phone conversation with Lenin, Gorky was 'jokingly' asked why he had not been arrested yet and there were hints of forthcoming arrests within his company (14 November).

Mediation was needed: World Literature had become a unifying platform for a number of literati across a wide-ranging spectrum of political views, with most of them being overtly anti-Bolshevik. With foreign languages having been traditionally taught as part of a classical education available mainly to the upper and middle classes, his collaborators could hardly have had 'workers and peasants' backgrounds. In fact, is difficult to find a single name of any literary importance amongst the Silver Age literati and literary scholars who was not engaged in the project in some capacity: translators alone comprised as many as 350 people, a significant number yet still deemed insufficient for the project's success. Describing his impressions of a visit to World Literature, H.G. Wells called it 'a grandiose scheme for the publication of a sort of Russian encyclopaedia of the literature of the world' (1921, 69) where 'the bulk of the writers and artists have found employment' (69). Having arrived at 'this strange Russia of conflict, cold, famine and pitiful privations', Wells was surprised to find a functioning 'literary task that would be inconceivable in the rich England and the rich America of to-day' (69).

That task would have been inconceivable without the input of the editors, authors, translators and scholars whose expertise was mostly formed within the confines of the pre-revolutionary dominant literary poetics, which yet again highlights the continuities of the project and its predecessors and which hardly makes the core attitudes and values of the professionals involved, Bolshevik.

Cataloguing the 'Russian Encyclopaedia of the Literature of the World'

The next step in evaluating World Literature's internal and external constraints in terms of Bolshevism tenets is to examine its cataloguing principles. Outlined briefly, they would be instrumental in further assessing the core values upheld by the project's participants. Since Gorky was officially entrusted with material selection, it may be assumed that the external pressures by patrons (apart from financial and provisional shortages) were less pervasive for the core of the project and thus it is its internal constraints (literary poetics, professional's views) that are primary for this case. By providing a brief overview of the World Literature catalogue, it is also possible to provide a brief, albeit still schematic – due to lack of space – answer to the question posed in the *Routledge Companion* on 'making sense' of Gorky's *mirnaya* [sic] *literatura* (D'haen, Damrosch & Kadir 2012, xix).

World Literature had a two-fold approach: it had two distinct products for different audiences depending on their reading backgrounds, which they termed 'the Main Series' and 'Popular' (a more literal translation would be 'People's'). The Popular Series were cheap brochures ('from 3 to 5 thousand pamphlets ... 32–64 numbered pages' each) (Gorky 1919, 21) with one or several short stories, 'the most available on the subject to understanding the widest layers of democracy' (CGA RSFSR, 73). The significantly titled Main Series would consist of 1500 'separate volumes' of approximately 320 pages and 'also a whole series of books devoted entirely to works by the greatest European writers, chosen so that they could create a small, but systematically selected library of European literary classics' (CGA RSFSR, 73). Both series would contain introductions, commentaries and bibliographical references. Thus, the guiding principles were two-fold: the Main Series was focused on 'educated' readers used to responding to literary works and who were already familiar with some of the works either in the original language or in translation, e.g. the Eastern Catalogue specifically mentions the existing Eurocentric bias of the Russian public. The Popular Series were publications specifically focused on the newly literate audience who was offered 'engaging' literature, yet, nevertheless, what the publishers considered 'healthy reading' as opposed to 'foul 'literature' of morbid and sadistic fabrications' published in the wake of the revolution (Gorky 1968, 20).

Gorky hoped the books would constitute:

> an immense historical and literary collection, enabling the reader to acquire close knowledge of the rise, development and decay of different literary schools, as well as of the perfectioning [sic] techniques of poetry and prose, of the mutual influence of the literature of various nations, and of the course of literary evolution in chronological order, from Voltaire to Anatole France, from Richardson to Wells, from Goethe to Hauptmann, etc.
>
> (Gorky 1919, 20)

Thus, all entries, which included poetry, prose, plays, memoirs, speeches and letters, were distributed according to their corresponding national literary corpora. The Western section of the Catalogue focused on major literary schools, e.g. the *Lake Poets, Les Poètes maudits,* and literary movements (Classicism, Romanticism, Realism, Naturalism, etc.) as reflected within French, English, German, Italian, Spanish, Portuguese, Swedish, Norwegian and Danish literatures from the late eighteenth to the early twentieth centuries. The selected period – from the French Revolution to the Russian Revolution – was well suited to both the funders' ideas and to the humanistic ethos of Gorky and the 'educationalists'. His plans were, however, much wider, and included publishing works from antiquity to current literary trends (Gorky 1919, 20). The breadth of the project is also evident in the fact that even within the selected time frame, its reach stretched beyond Europe and included its former colonies: the Catalogue contains literatures of the USA, Canada, Cuba, Mexico, India, San Domingo, Nicaragua, Venezuela, Colombia, Argentina, Peru and Brazil. Thus, the Western section of the Catalogue covered more than 1200 authors mostly unpublished in Russian.

The Eastern section's time frame was broader: it was guided by translation practicalities, the existing large gaps in the Russian representation of most literatures and the limited availability of specialist language expertise. Here the eighteenth–twentieth centuries periodisation accepted for the Western Section and agreed upon in the contract with the Narkompros funders, was not kept. This demonstrates the publishers' flexibility in terms of periodisation and 'uneven' stages of literary development in world literary processes which were fully endorsed by Gorky. The Catalogue lists a variety of literary works and folklore of the Middle East and the Far East, from Antiquity to the early twentieth century, including Egyptian, Assyrian, Phoenician, Persian, Arab, Indian, Hebrew, Chinese, Japanese and other literatures. It also contains a dedicated section of Russia's own Orient – the Caucasus – including old and new Georgian and Armenian literatures (Catalogue 1919).

When considering the duality of World Literature's production, in regards to its propagation of Bolshevist tenets, it is possible to claim that had World Literature's focus only been on fulfilling the requirements of the state, it would not have produced the obviously 'bourgeois' Main Series but focused its sole efforts on the Popular Series instead. As it was, the work done by the editors and translators mostly focused on the Main Series, which testifies to the inherent preferences and literary tastes of the professionals involved, many of which were inherited from the pre-revolutionary dominant poetics. The lists compiled by Gorky and the Board members, who had a fair degree of independence (Chukovsky 2003) were later taken as a foundation for the publishing programme of Academia Publishers which inherited many of the World Literature participants along with its guiding principles, translation ethos and emphasis on scholarly approach to translation.

World Literature and the 'Soviet Translation School'

Any assessment of the significance of the World Literature project would be incomplete without a consideration of its legacy both internally (Russian and Soviet literary influences) and externally (world literature and translation studies). Have the publishers, who only managed to produce 213 volumes and eleven issues of 'The East' and 'The Modern West' journals, had any lasting influence or was the project valid only for its own time?

'Internally', or at least as much as it is possible to define this as such, given the territorial expanses of the Soviet Union and the *lingua franca* status acquired by Russian within the Soviet and post-Soviet space, World Literature pioneered the establishment of professional translator training and research into translation theory in the USSR, the traditions of which are shared by the multiple countries of the post-Soviet region. Driven by the practical necessities in translation quality appraisal and collaborative translation on an unprecedented scale, the publishers were faced with both practical and theoretical gaps.

Chukovsky dates the beginning of the idea of what would later become 'Soviet translation theory' to November 12, 1918:

> At the meeting, I had a heated argument with Gumilev. This gifted crafts-man has taken into his head to compile Rules for translators. In my opinion, there are no such rules. What rules can there be in literature? One translator writes – and it comes out excellent; and another one conveys the rhythm and everything else – and yet it does not move you. What kind of rules? But he became angry and began to shout. However he is funny and I love him.
> (Chukovsky 1991, 109)

Chukovsky was eventually convinced by his protégé and in two months' time, on 12 January, 1919, delivered a paper 'The principles of literary translation'. Later that year World Literature published a brochure *The Principles of Literary Translation* co-written by Chukovsky (an article on 'Prose translations') and Gumilev ('Poetic translations'). In 1920, an expanded edition of the brochure appeared, with two articles by F.D. Batyushkov ('Aims of literary translations', 'Language and Style') published posthumously.

Simultaneously with theoretical investigations, a Studio of Literary Translation was founded in 1919. Its focus was on talented youth (337 students) who attended various clusters of lectures and seminars (e.g. a seminar on poetry led by Gumilev, on prose led by Zamiatin, on literary criticism led by Chukovsky). Mikhail Lozinsky led the poetic translation seminar. His students, 'lozinistki', as one of them recalls, were 'fifteen refined ladies, murmuring in French aged from thirty to forty' who 'in 1919 Petrograd, translated de Heredia's sonnets together. They spent many days over each line. And there were so many var-iants, delights, the subtlest observations, witty guesses, ardent exclamations, oohs and aahs, rustlings, crunchings and trepidations!' (Chukovsky 1989, 105).

The Studio was also the meeting place of the Serapion Brothers and OPOYAZ, with a number of famous Russian writers and internationally known Formalist scholars, including Viktor Shklovsky and, more importantly for translation studies, Roman Jacobson, whose categorisation of translation types is amongst one of the seminal publications in the field.

After the closure of the publishers, the translators associated with the World Literature Publishers formed the bulk of the Leningrad Translation branch at the All-Russian Writers' Union. They were joined by the young Andrei Fedorov who delivered his paper, 'The problem of poetic translation', in 1925, while still a student, and who began his rise to fame as one of the leading theorists of trans-lation studies in the Soviet Union by co-publishing an expanded version of the initial *Principles* brochure with Chukovsky. Fedorov became a proponent of the 'linguistic theory of translation' which gradually grew into a formal discipline taught to all Soviet and post-Soviet translators and interpreters. Chukovsky's work stayed within the 'literary' stream of translation theory: the paper from *Principles was* developed into a monograph *The Art of Translation/Iskusstvo perevoda* (1936) and later expanded into *The High Art/Vysokoye iskusstvo* (1941). The Leningrad section, with names such as Yury Levin (raised in the family of a staff member of World Literature) and Efim Etkind amongst its associates, still remains an active professional body and continues the traditions (including specialised seminars) begun by World Literature.

In conclusion, the legacy of Gorky's World Literature project can hardly be limited by strict 'Soviet' timeframes. It is better defined as a project which evolved not from Soviet or Bolshevik ideology tenets, but as a logical evolution of the pre-revolutionary 'educational' publishers' traditions and a foundation for new approaches to literary production and translation which lasted long after the demise of the Soviet system. Its influence maybe observed from the various aspects of its work: in editing, from the practices of scholarly commentary and textology, in translation theory, from development of translation theory, translation quality assessment and laying the foundations for professional translator training, in literary studies, in the perception of world literature as a current process and in the subsequent development of comparative literary studies by the Gorky Institute, in publishing, in its programme partly realised later by Academia Publishers and Khudozhestvennaya Literatura (Fiction Publishers), whose 200 volume translation project 'World Literature' was found in just about every household of the Soviet *intelligentsia*. While these 'internal' influences still resonate within the post-Soviet space, the World Literature' Project's 'external' or 'international' indirect effects include, among others, seminal publications in critical theory and translation studies by once-associated authors and scholars.

By offering a revisionist reading of the project, it is possible to see it not as a refraction, a historical obscurity within the Russian literary process affected by out-dated ideological constraints, nor merely as a Soviet or Bolshevik project destined to decline with the demise of the system which gave birth to it, as has been suggested by contemporary world literature scholarship. Rather, it should be seen as a viable part of the various functioning modes of literary production and translation currently discussed within world literature debates. The blend of evolution of literary philosophies and production modes canonised by its precursors and the revolution of these modes make it a project worthy of reassessment within World Literature studies and integral to our understanding of world literature translation production.

Notes

1 All translations from Russian sources are done by the author, SP.
2 The term used in the source text is the Russian word *prosveschenie* which could be translated both as 'enlightenment' or 'education'. In the quoted source it was used as 'education' whereas now it is generally used as 'enlightenment'. In Russia and, largely, in Eastern Slavonic contexts, enlightenment and education have been semantically tied. Lovell, quoted further, is using the Russian derivative *prosvetiteli* (educators) precisely for this reason.

Bibliography

Apter, E. (2013). *Against World Literature: On the Politics of Untranslatability*. New York: Verso.

Bassnett, S. and Lefevere, A. (1998). *Constructing Cultures*. Clevedon: Multilingual Matters.

Belov, S.V. (1987) 'Blok i pervye poslerevolyutsionnye izdatelstva (M.& S.Sabashnikovy, Alkonost)'. *Literaturnoye nasledstvo*, 92: 713–725.

Catalogue (1919) *Katalog izdatel'stva 'Vsemirnaja literatura'*. Petersbourg: Literatura Vostoka.

CGA RSFSR, F. (1918) 2306, op. 1, jed. khr. 3, l. 73.

Chukovsky, K. (1991). *Dnevnik (1901–1929)*. Moskva: Sovetskij pisatel'.

Chukovsky, N. (1989). *Literaturnye vospominanija*. Moskva: Sovetskij pisatel'.

D'haen, T. (2012). *The Routledge Concise History of World Literature*. London: Routledge.

D'haen, T., Damrosch, D. and Kadir, D. (2012). *The Routledge Companion to World Literature*. London: Routledge.

Gorky, M. (1919) *Katalog izdatel'stva 'Vsemirnaja literatura'*. Petersbourg: Vstupitelnaya stat'ja M. Gor'kogo.

Gorky, M. (1995). *Untimely Thoughts: Essays on Revolution, Culture and the Bolsheviks, 1917–1918*. 2nd ed. Translated by Herman Ermolaev. London and New Haven: Yale University Press.

Hermans, T. (1985). *The Manipulation of Literature*. London: Croom Helm.

Karajchentseva, S.A. (2004). *Knigovedenie: literaturno-hudozhestvennaja i detskaja kniga*. Moskva: MGUP.

Khotimsky, M. (2013). 'World Literature, Soviet Style: A Forgotten Episode in the History of the Idea'. *Ab Imperio*, 3: 119–154.

Lefevere, A. (1992). *Translation, Rewriting, and the Manipulation of Literary Fame*. London: Routledge.

Lovell, S. (2000). *Russian Reading Revolution*. London: Palgrave Macmillan.

Rossels Vladimir (1964). 'Radi shumiashchikh zelenykh vetvei' in *Masterstvo Perevoda 1964*, ed. K. N. Polonskaia. Moscow: Gosudarstvennoe izdatel'stvo, P. 12–33.

Saidova, L.Kh. (1998). *Literaturno-khudozhesvennaya kniga v izdatel'stve M. i S. Sabashnikovykh. Dissertatsiya na soiskaniye uchenoj stepeni kandidata filologicheskikh nauk. Spetsialnost 05.25.04 'Knigovedenie'*. Moscow: Moscow State University of Print (in manuscript).

SmirinV.M. (1967). 'Perevody literaturnyh pamjatnikov antichnosti v sovetskih izdanijah 1918–1933 gg'. *Vestnik drevnej istorii*, 4: 138.

Sytin, I.D. (1962). *Zhizn' dlja knigi. Stranicy perezhitogo. Sovremenniki o I. D. Sytine*. Moskva: Gosudarstvennoe izdatelstvo politicheskoj literatury.

Tulupov, N.V. (ed.) (1916). *Polveka dlia knigi, 1866–1916*. Moscow: Sytin Publishers.

Wells, H.G. (1921). *Russia in the Shadows*. New York: George H. Doran Co.

9 The proliferating paths of Jorge Luis Borges' work in translation and the resistance to an innovative trait[1]

Cecilia Alvstad

Jorge Luis Borges (1899–1986), one of the most critically acclaimed authors of the twentieth century, was himself a translator into Spanish of a list of much-admired authors that includes William Faulkner, Franz Kafka, James Joyce, Walt Whitman and Virginia Woolf (Willson 2004: 113, 169), as well as the author of two seminal essays on translation (Borges [1932] 1974, [1936] 1974). Borges was highly aware of the fact that a translation is never identical to its original, and he strongly objected to the idea that a translation is necessarily inferior to its source text (Borges [1932] 1974: 280).

This chapter will focus on a few selected translations of Borges' literary prose, showing that Borges' translators have chosen different paths, and that these are not always reconcilable one with the other. Although only a few examples are offered, all of which will hail from English and Swedish translations, the aim is that they will suffice to indicate that 'Borges in translation' is highly reminiscent of the labyrinth from one of his most well-known short-stories, 'El jardín de senderos que se bifurcan' (Borges 1944, 'The Garden of Forking Paths'; a synopsis is given further on).[2]

This approach will draw upon two strands of research: translation studies, with its strong tradition of paying attention to how texts are modified in translation as well as to what they add to translating cultures (see, for example, Bassnett 1980, 2014; Hermans 1999; Pym 1998; Toury 1995), and world literature studies, with its emphasis on change and transnational literary circulation (se, for example, Damrosch 2003). I will also draw attention to the fact that scholars who refer to Borges sometimes seem to base their interpretations on translations rather than on Borges' original texts in Spanish, so that what they argue, and at times demonstrate by their close readings of the translated Borges, may in fact hold true for a specific translation but not for Borges' work in Spanish (or for other translations). The way Borges is 'made' in translation differs between different target cultures, hence he has various author profiles that can be said to make up the transnational Borges. I do not claim that all scholars who comment on Borges (or on the work of any other authors, for that matter) must do so by reading the original. But I do argue for a greater awareness of how translation contributes not only to making an author present in other languages but also potentially to the proliferation of an author's work, in which one translation may very well contradict another.

Scholarly readings of Borges

Scholars from a wide range of disciplines have explored Borges' aforementioned story about the garden of forking paths – French philosopher Gilles Deleuze (1968: 153), for example, used the story in his discussion of difference and repetition. Another scholar who has turned to this story is Patricia Waugh (1984) when discussing 'textual contradiction' as a strategy of metafictional writing. According to Waugh, contradiction is a part of what she calls 'radical metafiction':

> [Such novels] function through forms of radical decontextualization. They deny the reader access to a centre of orientation such as a narrator or point of view, or a stable tension between 'fiction', 'dream', 'reality', 'vision', 'hallucination', 'truth', 'lies', etc. Naturalized or totalizing interpretation becomes impossible. The logic of the everyday world is replaced by forms of contradiction and discontinuity, radical shifts of context which suggest that 'reality' as well as 'fiction' is merely one more game with words.
>
> (Waugh 1984: 136–137)

Differently from realist or modernist writing, Waugh argues that textual contradiction in metafictional writing is never resolved, and that Borges' short story about the garden of forking paths both discusses and exemplifies this:

> It is a story of a maze which is a maze of a story. A fourth dimension is posited where numerous possibilities of time and space coexist: 'in some you exist and not I: in others I and not you: in others both of us' (p. 53). The theory is made explicit in the story: 'in all fictional works, each time a man is confronted with several alternatives, he chooses one and eliminates the others: in the fictions of Ts'ui Pên, he chooses – simultaneously – all of them' (p. 51). Readers of the French New Novel will immediately recognize the form this strategy takes in the novels of Alain Robbe-Grillet, for example. The obsessive repetition of incidents within new contexts, slightly shifted, mutually contradictory, occurs throughout *The Voyeur* (1955) or *In the Labyrinth* (1959).
>
> (Waugh 1984: 137–138)[3]

Translation studies scholar Edwin Gentzler turns to the same story and passage, but instead of emphasising contradiction and irresolvability he reads it as an analogy of the work of the translator:

> Whereas fiction in the West is generally governed by linear time and characters making choices that eliminate other possibilities, in Ts'ui Pên's fiction characters can simultaneously choose all the alternatives. The result is chaotic: each decision results in multiple forkings and possibilities, all of which are followed [...]. The analogy to translation is clear: so too does translation involve forking paths, opening up often infinite creative opportunities based upon initial decision. If one decides to translate a word or a

sentence in one fashion, that decision sets up a paradigm for the rest of the text; however, if that same word took an even slightly different turn, the resulting text would be correspondingly different.

(Gentzler 2008: 117)

In a similar vein, media studies scholars Noah Wardrip-Fruin and Nick Montfort discuss the same story from within their field, including a full text translation of it in their *The New Media Reader*, with the following introduction by Montfort:

Borges was no hacker; nor did he specify the hypertext novel in perfect detail. But computers do not function as they do today *only* because of the playful labor of hackers or because of planned-out projects to program, develop, and reconfigure systems. Our use of computers is also based on the visions of those who, like Borges – pronouncing this story from the growing dark of his blindness – saw those courses that future artists, scientists, and hackers might take.

(Montfort 2003: 29–30)

It may be noted in passing that Montfort here seems to suggest that Borges predicted the future, rather than addressing an age-old philosophical topic, in my view a more credible explanation for the analogies between Borges' story and the way computers work. However, by doing this Montfort manages to present hypertext novels and computers as something fundamentally new.

The above quotes illustrate how scholars from a variety of disciplines use the same short story to exemplify a point in their different fields. This is, of course, entirely commonplace, but it is worth noting that while doing so they are all making partial interpretations of the story. But as Borges himself has suggested with reference to Bertrand Russell, a reference that incidentally may also come across as partial, this is in fact an inherent condition of the verbal:

Bertrand Russell define un objeto externo como un sistema circular, irradiante, de impresiones posibles; lo mismo puede aseverarse de un texto, dadas las repercusiones incalculables de lo verbal. Un parcial y precioso documento de las vicisitudes que sufre queda en sus traducciones. ['Bertrand Russell defines an external object as a circular system from which possible expressions emanate. The same may be said of a text, given the untold repercussions the verbal may have. A partial and precious document of the changing fortunes it suffers remains in its translations.']

(Borges [1932] 1974: 280, my translation)

Borges here pursues the idea that translations are 'possible expressions' of a text. In other words, translations are not copies of their originals (see Hermans 1999: 95): they do not present the same text word by word, and even if they were to do so, it would not be the same text. This has been shown vividly by Borges (1944) in another of his most frequently discussed short stories, 'Pierre

Menard, autor del *Quijote*' ('Pierre Menard, Author of the *Quixote*'). This is a story about an author who decides to write *Don Quixote* anew, but nevertheless exactly as Cervantes wrote it, and who, after many drafts and much painstaking work, succeeds in writing two chapters and a fragment of a third that repeat Cervantes' text word for word. But, as the narrator of the text makes clear, his version nonetheless differs from it, since the new text was written by somebody else in a different time and place.

Returning now to the garden of forking paths, if indeed we ever left it, Borges' foreword to his anthology *Ficciones* (1944) presents the tale as a detective story. And it does in fact borrow many traits from the detective genre, but as always with Borges, this is of course not all there is to it. In the story, a Chinese agent working for the Germans in World War I is about to kill a random British citizen named Albert. It does not matter to the agent who Albert is: it is just that Albert is also the secret name of the place that the Germans wished to attack. Killing a person named Albert is thus a way of conveying a message to his German employers, assuming that he would be arrested and that the news thereof would spread. This intrigue, however, does not become clear until the end of the text. When the agent arrives at the house where the character Albert lives, it turns out that Albert is an expert on a labyrinth-novel created by Ts'ui Pên, an ancestor of the agent. Albert has discovered that the labyrinth-novel is at the same time a novel and a physical labyrinth, that is a real maze, and that this labyrinth-novel therefore works in a different way as compared to other fictional work.

One of the sentences most frequently discussed from this short story, incidentally the one that Deleuze, Waugh, Gentzler and Montfort all referred to above, reads in Donald A. Yates' translation into English:

> In all fictional works, each time a man is confronted with several alternatives, he chooses one and eliminates the others; in the fiction of Ts'ui Pên, he chooses – simultaneously – all of them. He *creates*, in this way, diverse futures, diverse times which themselves also proliferate and fork.
>
> (Borges [1958] 1972: 51, translated by Yates)

That precisely these two sentences are so widely referred to by scholars in diverse disciplines may not be surprising because, as Waugh suggests (see above), it makes the 'theory' of the story explicit. Considering that this is a key passage, it is very interesting to compare what different scholars make of it. In order to delve more deeply into this matter, let us compare two Borges scholars' readings of the sentence given below, where marked in bold are the different 'paths' their readings take at one of crossroads of this sentence:

> 'The Garden of Forking Paths' is undoubtedly one of Borges' most discussed and critically elaborated stories. Its central conceit of a literally 'labyrinthine' novel, in which, instead of choosing between various narrative alternatives, **the author chooses all of them**, has been tremendously

influential, not only on the future development of the novel but also on cinema and philosophy.

(Butler 2010: 18–19, my bold)

Albert realizes that when **characters** are faced with a dilemma, **the novel chooses** not just the one option of traditional fiction, but all the options, simultaneously: '*He creates,* thereby 'several futures', several *times,* which themselves proliferate and fork.'

(Boldy 2009: 103, my bold)

Butler and Boldy are clearly discussing the same story and the same sentences here, but the difference between their two readings is striking. According to Butler, it is the author who chooses, whereas Boldy claims it is the novel. At first sight it may therefore seem that Butler's reading could be part of an author-centred paradigm, whereas Boldy's would be more text-oriented. Alternatively, Butler's reading seems to expect Borges (given, for example, the time and or place in which he wrote the story, previous readings of or about his work, and so forth) to be more author-centred than is the case in Boldy's reading. This might have led them to have different expectations to what the text actually says. Readers might recall, however, that Gentzler (see above) referred neither to the 'author' nor to the 'novel' but to 'characters making choices that eliminate other possibilities' (Gentzler 2008: 117). The reasons to why they differ may be more complex.

Bearing all this in mind, let us now go back to the text itself. To make my argument readily available for readers who do not understand Spanish, I will refer to Donald A. Yates' translation of the sentences in question (see above). His translation will suffice for the comparison between Butler, Boldy and Gentzler because it closely reproduces Borges' way of formulating the same sentences. Moreover, although some hints are given in their respective lists of references, we do not know in what language(s), or in what translation(s), Butler, Boldy and Gentzler actually read the story.

In Donald A. Yates' translation the words 'author', 'novel' and 'characters' – that is, the meanings that Butler, Boldy and Gentzler infer from the passage – are not explicitly spelled out. The choosing agent in Yates is simply 'a man', and the sentences work with a repetition of two instance of 'he chooses' and then 'he creates'. Although all these three instances of 'he' must syntactically refer back to 'a man' at the beginning of the first sentence, the mention of the fictional author Ts'ui Pên, right before the second instance of 'he', may make it far from crystal clear who is actually the agent here. It is therefore possible that some readers would intuitively take the second instance of 'he' as referring to Ts'ui Pên, so that the subsequent points would refer to the fictitious author Ts'ui Pên's actions, or even take the rather vague formulation 'a man' as referring to authors in general and the choices they make when writing.

The leap from Yates' 'man' to Boldy's and Gentzler's 'characters' is bigger. This is partly due to the change from the singular to the plural, but above all there is nothing in this passage of the text that hints at characters. Whereas the fictional author Ts'ui Pên appears very close in the passage to 'he chooses' and 'he creates', in these syntactically intricate sentences there are no indices in the text that could point toward characters. Another explanation for why these scholars differ in their word choices (i.e., between 'author', 'novel' and 'characters') may therefore be that they have read other versions of the text, either Borges' Spanish original and/or another translation or even other translations. With this in mind, I will now turn to Borges' text in Spanish, comparing it to Yates' translation as well as to two other translations into English. But let me remind the reader that I am not making a complete translation archaeology of Borges' translations here (for the concept of translation archaeology, see Pym 1998: 5), I am only quoting a few translations in order to illustrate my argument. The above quoted scholars might of course also have read and thus been influenced by other translations, either into English or into other languages.[4]

Borges in Spanish and in two other translations into English

I have referred to Donald A. Yates' translation as a near-verbatim translation of Borges' Spanish text. In a close comparison of the two texts it may, nevertheless, be noted that Yates' translation drops the Spanish adjective *inextricable*, which means something like 'impenetrable, hopelessly complicated' or, borrowing from Andrew Hurley's translation given below, 'impossible-to-disentangle'. Somewhat paradoxically, the effect of this is that these sentences in English therefore become a bit less impossible-to-disentangle than in Spanish. Borges' Spanish text reads:

> En todas las ficciones, cada vez que un hombre se enfrenta con diversas alternativas, **opta** por una y elimina las otras; en la del casi inextricable de Ts'ui Pên, **opta** – simultáneamente – por todas. *Crea*, así, diversos porvenires, diversos tiempos, que también proliferan y se bifurcan.
>
> (Borges 1944: 121, my bold)

Another difference between Yates' text and Borges' original is that a structural difference between English and Spanish more or less forces the translator to spell out the personal pronoun 'he' before 'chooses' and 'creates'. Spanish does not usually spell out the subject pronoun, unless it is needed for disambiguation, and *opta* and *crea*, the Spanish counterparts of 'he chooses' and 'he creates', are hence third-person singular forms of the verb, which when used without a subject pronoun, as is the case here, may refer to either 'he', 'she' or 'it' depending on the context. As argued above in relation to Yates' translation, it would not be strictly syntactically correct in Borges' Spanish original to connect *crea* and the second *opta* to Ts'ui Pên rather than to *hombre* ('man'), but there are pragmatic reasons for which it may be tempting to do so. In two other translations into English the sentences read as follows:

In all fiction, when **a man** is faced with alternatives **he chooses** one at the expense of the others. In the almost unfathomable Ts'ui Pên, **he chooses** – simultaneously – all of them. **He** thus *creates* various futures, various times which start others that will in their turn branch out and bifurcate in other times.

(Borges 1993: 75, translated by Temple and Todd, my bold)

In all fictions, each time a man meets diverse alternatives, he chooses one and eliminates the others; in the work of the virtually impossible-to-disentangle Ts'ui Pen, **the character chooses** – simultaneously – all of them. *He creates*, thereby, 'several futures,' several *times*, which themselves proliferate and fork.

(Borges 2000: 83, translated by Hurley, my bold)

Both these translations use the same verb sequence 'chooses', 'chooses' and then 'creates', and according to the rules of English they spell out the subject. But whereas Temple and Todd (just like Yates) spell out all these third person singulars as 'he', Hurley changes one of them into 'character', thus making the translated text more determined than Borges' Spanish text and the other two English translations cited here. As already noted in relation to the Gentzler quote above, the word choice 'character' is a bit surprising here. It might be added that, just like 'man', *hombre* is not a typical way of speaking about a character in a story. Gentzler's way of formulating himself is thus more congenial with Hurley's text than with Borges' Spanish text or the other quoted translations. This seems to indicate that Gentzler was influenced by Hurley's formulation when creating his analogy between the story and the work of the translator, an analogy, it should nevertheless be noted, that works well also with Borges' Spanish text and the other translations.[5]

As for Temple and Todd, they translate *en la del casi inextricable de Ts'ui Pên* metaphorically as 'In the almost unfathomable Ts'ui Pên' rather than as the more literal 'In the fiction of the almost unfathomable Ts'ui Pên'. This conflation of Ts'ui Pên and his works possibly contributes to making the leap between 'he' and 'Ts'ui Pên' even smaller than in Yates. It should nonetheless be noted that Temple and Todd do not explicitly spell out that it is 'the author' who is doing the choosing in Borges' text.

The Swedish context and the resistance to an innovative trait

A translation that even more clearly suggests that it is 'the author' who chooses and creates is Sun Axelsson's 1963 translation into Swedish. In this translation the agents connected to the verb series 'chooses', 'chooses' and then 'creates' are not translated into a series of three 'he', as in Yates translation, but gets a different rendering in each case. The first is translated into *hon* ('she'), the second into a passive construction (no agent) and the third into *han* ('he').

I alla berättelser där **en människa** står inför olika alternativ, väljer **hon** ett och utesluter de övriga. I **Ts'ui Pên** nästan outgrundliga verk **väljs** alla samtidigt. **Han** skapar på så sätt olika framtider, olika tidsåldrar vilka också förökas och förgrenas. ['In all stories where a **human being** faces several alternatives, **she** chooses one and excludes the others. In the almost unfathomable works of **Ts'ui Pên**, all **are chosen** at the same time. **He** creates in this way different futures, different eras which also multiply and branch out.']

(Borges 1963: 59, translated by Axelsson in collaboration with Marina Torres, my translation into English, my bold)

Though the word 'author' is not spelled out, the pronoun *han* ('he') could not refer to anyone other than Ts'ui Pên here.[6] This is because Axelsson translates *hombre* into *människa*, which unlike *hombre*, or the English 'man' for that matter, can only refer to the ungendered 'human being'. *Människa* furthermore is one of few ungendered nouns in Swedish that take the feminine pronoun *hon*. The link between the three verbs referring back to *hombre* is broken as they cannot be linked to one and the same agent in this text.

As we have seen earlier, Axelsson is not the only one to interpret this passage in an author-centred way, as Butler did as well in his book on Borges. Temple and Todd also made a translation where this interpretative possibility is readily at hand. It is of course possible to read Borges' text in this way, but it is worth noting that Axelsson's translation offers more restrictive possibilities of interpretation than Borges' text. The change transforms the metafiction of Borges' story. It is shifted into a more traditional author-centred form. Borges' text also opens up other possibilities that are not transferred into Swedish. On the basis of this translation alone, and not on other versions of the text, it would therefore, for example, have been difficult for Gentzler to draw the analogy to translation in the way he does.

The transformation of metafiction into more traditional forms transgresses this individual translator. Innovative metafiction was also changed into more traditional forms in other Swedish translations of the work of Latin American writers in the 1960s. Julio Cortázar's story 'La continuidad de los parques' (Continuity of the parks), translated by Jan Sjögren in 1969 is another example (Alvstad and Johnsen 2013). The change of the innovative metafiction into a more traditional form can thus be considered as typical of the time, and considering that Scholes (1970) had yet to coin the concept of metafiction, that Iser (1976) had still to launch his reader-oriented aesthetics of reception and that postmodernist scholarship had yet to discover these traits in Borges' texts (e.g. Waugh 1984), it is unsurprising that these traits at that time would be modified into more traditional forms.

What is remarkable, though, is that Axelsson's 1963 translation is still the only translation into Swedish of Borges' story about the garden of forking paths. Moreover, it was republished in a new edition as recently as in 2007; the same goes for Cortázar's story, which has also been republished recently (see

Alvstad and Johnsen 2013). Both these volumes, published by two different publishers, Bonnier and Modernista, draw together old translations of Borges and Cortázar texts, respectively. These old translations were carried out by a large number of translators from the 1960s and onwards, and had been published in anthologies of selected stories. The Borges volume *Fiktioner* that appeared in 2007 (Borges 2007) is therefore a patchwork of translations previously published in other contexts and now drawn together as a new whole. The same was done to *El Aleph*, published for the first time as *Alefen* in Swedish in 2011 (Borges 2011). Much could be said about this publishing practice as a less expensive alternative to having one translator retranslate the whole volume. What is most relevant to note here, however, is that old translations in this way enter a completely different reception context than the one they were originally intended to cater for.

Swedish readers who read Borges in the new reception context today will be directly or indirectly influenced by postmodern scholarship, either because they have read such criticism themselves or because they have read literary authors who have incorporated postmodern features in their work. But when the story about the garden with the forking paths was first published in Swedish in 1963, the emphasis was on Borges as a metaphysical writer concerned with time, not on Borges as a writer concerned with the conditions of fiction. The 1963 volume, which was the first full-length book by Borges in Swedish, was a collection of selected stories from *Ficciones* and *El Aleph* (Borges 1963). In that introduction, written by Artur Lundkvist, an important introducer of Latin American literature into Swedish, the main emphasis was not on Borges as an author concerned with books, readings, authors and so on, but on Borges as an author concerned with metaphysics (Lundkvist 1963; for Lundkvist as an introducer of Latin American literature, see Alvstad 2011, 2012 and Alvstad and Lundahl 2010).

Even more noteworthy is that three of Borges' most metafictional stories, 'Pierre Menard, autor del *Quijote*' ('Pierre Menard, Author of the *Quixote*'), 'Examen de la obra de Herbert Quain' ('An Examination of the Work of Herbert Quain') and 'Tlön, Uqbar, Orbus Tertius' ('Tlön, Uqbar, Orbus Tertius') were not included in the 1963 volume. It would, in fact, take until 1991 these stories to be published for the first time in Swedish (Borges 1991).[7] Borges' concern with writers, libraries and the conditions of fiction, widely conceived of as Borges' trademark (e.g. Macherey 1966; Scholes 1977) was thus not only left undiscussed in the early 1960s, it was resisted through both selection, paratextual presentation and through translation solutions that would cast Borges' writing in a more traditional form. In other words, this seems to be a case of what Mattelart and Mattelart (1998: 119), in a discussion of Jauss' (1970) horizons of expectation, refers to as a 'resistance to innovative initiatives of the writer'.

When Borges is mentioned in Sweden in the twenty-first century, he is generally characterised as a writer concerned with metafiction. *Ord & bild*, one of the most well-established Swedish cultural magazines, dedicated a special issue to new Latin American literature in 2009 (Elensky 2009: 2–3), and the introduction of the issue argues that two major trends have dominated what the rest of the world expects of Latin American literature: magical realism à la Gabriel García Márquez and metafiction à la Jorge Luis Borges. Likewise, when a major Swedish newspaper dedicated a page of its cultural supplement to six books written about books, the number one recommendation was the Swedish translation of Borges' collection *Ficciones* (Olsson 2010). A third example is the very introduction to the first full-length Swedish edition of *Ficciones* from 2007, titled *Fiktioner*. Borges is here introduced as a writer who writes about fiction in the following manner:

> Borges gör vad ingen annan författare tidigare gjort. Han sätter boken själv i centrum för sitt berättande. Hans noveller är en närmast religiös hyllning till boklärdomen, till den extra och mystiska dimensionen som skriftspråket skänker oss i form av fiktionen. ['Borges does what nobody had done earlier. He places the book itself in the centre of his narrative. His short stories are almost a religious tribute to book learning, to the additional and mystic dimension the written language provides us in the form of fiction.']
>
> (Håkansson 2007: 7, my translation)

This means that in the 2007 volume, there is a considerable mismatch between the way in which the text is translated and the way it is paratextually presented. The context of reception has changed, and reprinted versions of Swedish Borges translations from the 1960s may actually not be well suited for the new job. That they in any case were published in this form signals that Bonnier, perhaps the most prestigious publishing house in Sweden, was not aware that translation changes the text and that this translation in particular might have become dated.

Some books only exist in translation

Thus, the first, almost complete translation of *Ficciones* into Swedish was not published until 2007. This means that the stories had not been published together before and that this was the first time that Swedish readers had the opportunity to appreciate the connections between the different stories in the volume. The first Swedish Borges book from 1963 included selected stories from both *Ficciones* and *El Aleph*, so that some of the original connections between the stories of each of these volumes were already put out of play, in other words, instead of being part of a whole designed by Borges, they were turned into a number of short stories published jointly. In a way they did, of course, become part of a new whole; readers might therefore in any case discover or establish points of connections and contradictions, but this whole, it should be noted, was never designed by Borges.

The idea of publishing selected stories is certainly not a Swedish invention. In fact, there is a long history of publishing foreign literature in anthologies, often joining together a number of authors from a certain country or continent.[8] Books that only exist in translation, be they anthologies bringing together different authors, or compilations that bring together work by only one author but in creative ways, clearly take the authors' works along new paths. New relations are created with the surrounding texts, at the same time as relations that were in the original format of publication are put out of play.

In turn, such restructurings of the work of an author generally have as a consequence that new chronologies are created. Literary authors typically create and publish in what we may call an organic way. One book follows another, and over time there may be one or several changes of direction in an author's career. When an author begins to be translated into another language, a new logic of growth is set in motion, since selection for translation seldom repeats the chronology of the organic publication process of an author's original oeuvre: any book from an author's body of work could be the first one to be translated, older books by the same author can be translated after more recent ones, and, importantly, not all the writings by a given author may be translated at all. Borges' essays on translation have for example not been translated into Swedish. New logics of growths that take place in different languages will contribute to the author profile of a specific author in the target culture, and to different profiles in different languages. A similar process is set in motion when the translation of some works from a previous whole are delayed, as in the Swedish case of the most metafictional stories from *Ficciones*. These stories, by the way, were the ones that later appeared in the Swedish anthology *Labyrinter* (Borges 1991), which included only four short stories. The volume therefore differs considerably from the English and Norwegian volumes titled *Labyrinths* (Borges [1958] 1972) and *Labyrinter* (Borges 1964). The same title can in other words masquerade in quite different contents, and it may be noted in passing that although Borges did publish a poem called 'Laberintos', no Borges book in Spanish was ever published with that title. The point again being that some books only exist in translation.

Concluding remarks

Although a full translation archaeology of all of Borges' translations, or of all scholars who have ever written about 'The Garden of Forking Paths', has not been attempted here, it should nevertheless have become clear that translators and scholars have taken Borges along many different paths, some of which are irreconcilable with one another. The result is a Borgesian universe reminiscent of the forking paths of Borges' short story that have served as the main example throughout this essay.

I have first drawn attention to the fact that scholarly interpretations and translators' decisions bear many similarities. This may be due to the fact that the interpretative processes of these two activities also bear many similarities. But some of the congeniality between what scholars write and the way translations are formulated also seems to be due to the fact that scholars might have been influenced by published translations. The opposite – that professionals who produce translated books are influenced by what scholars write – also takes place. In my examples this is evident from the way that *Fiktioner* is presented to the Swedish readers in the twenty-first century as compared to in the 1960s.

With the textual examples cited in this chapter, the aim has been to show that both scholars and translators sometimes spell out, at times in different ways, something that was not explicit in the original, thus, they choose one path and close others. Borges' original formulation in Spanish can therefore be read as much more up-to-date with later developments in literary theory, going from author-centred to reader-centred, but then again this might not be how Borges himself would have read it. Translations are, as Borges himself had it, 'possible expressions' of a text (see above). More specifically, I have shown that when grammar necessitated the inclusion of a pronoun that was not in the Spanish original, the Swedish translator's choice of 'she' over 'he' changed the possible interpretations of the text completely, while editorial decisions concerning which stories to include in (or exclude from) translated anthologies may have had very similar effects on the possibilities of interpretation.

I myself first read Borges in Spanish some twenty-five years ago, but to that initial reading I have added readings of Borges in several English translations, two Norwegian ones, one Danish, one Swedish, one French and one German, not to mention many re-readings. All these versions, along with scholarly studies on Borges, talks with friends and colleagues, and research visits to the Centro Cultural Borges and the Museo Borges in Buenos Aires are sure to have influenced my present idea of Borges' literary heritage. No doubt, Boldy, Butler and Gentzler have had similar (though different) experiences that have informed their readings, as have the different translations of 'The Garden of Forking Paths' they seem to have read. This is how literature works. To borrow from Borges, translations are thus not only partial documents of their sources, but also precious ones.

A conclusion to be drawn from the observations put forward here is that it is crucial to retranslate key literary texts, not primarily because the language of translations quickly becomes dated (a popular idea I am a suspicious of), but because interpretations become dated. It is also important to retranslate because all translators will choose their own path, and when doing so they will eliminate others. Crucially, in contrast to what happens in Ts'ui Pên's work, translators cannot choose several paths at the same time. But different translators can, and do choose different paths, and precisely because of this we need many translations of the same texts, translations that in turn can proliferate and fork into new interpretations.

Notes

1 Research for this article was carried out under the auspices of the *Voices of Translation: Rewriting Literary Texts in a Scandinavian Context* project, which was supported by the Research Council of Norway (project no. 213246) and the Faculty of Humanities at the University of Oslo. I wish to thank Signe Kårstad for her assistance.
2 The story was first published in Borges (1941) in a volume called *El jardín de senderos que se bifurcan*. In 1944 this volume was integrated to *Ficciones*.
3 Waugh quotes Borges in Donald Yates' translation.
4 Also the translators may have been influenced by other translators (and scholarly readings). It would certainly be interesting to dig deeper into the translation archaeology of Borges' translations, analysing possible influences from earlier translations on later translations in a transnational perspective, in other words to make a combined use of theory and methodology developed for the study of retranslations (see e.

g. Alvstad and Assis Rosa 2015) and indirect translations (see e.g. Assis Rosa, Pièta and Bueno Maia 2016). See also Solberg (2016) on complex combinations of direct translation and unacknowledged influence from translations into other languages in the first Scandinavian translations of Simone de Beauvoir's *Le deuxième sexe*. In order to get a complete picture of the transnational Borges, it would, as should have become clear by the examples above, also be necessary to include scholarly work on Borges, who may not only be influenced by, but also exercise influence on, translations.

5   The congeniality between Hurley and Gentzler may alternatively be explained by an example further on in Borges' story that indeed refers to the choices of a hypothetical character named Fang.

6   Still, it ought to be noted that the association between *han* ('he') and 'Ts'ui Pên' is pragmatic rather than syntactic.

7   See Svensson 2008 for a thorough bibliography of what was published by or about Borges in Sweden 1944–2008. Svensson also details the titles in Swedish and Spanish of the poems and stories that have been published in the various volumes.

8   In passing it might be observed that it was in such an anthology that the very first Borges story appeared in Swedish in 1954 (Rogberg 1954; see Alvstad 2012).

Bibliography

Alvstad, Cecilia (2011) 'Är det bara vita, heterosexuella män som skriver skönlitteratur i Latinamerika? Om att undersöka skandinaviska konstruktioner av en fjärran kontinents litteratur' [Are all Latin American writers white, heterosexual men? On examining Scandinavian constructions of the literature from a continent far away]. In E. Bladh & C. Kullberg (eds), *Litteratur i Gränszonen: Transnationella litteraturer i ett nordiskt perspektiv* [Literature in the border zone: Transnational literatures in a Nordic perspective]. Falun: Högskolan Dalarna, 159–173.

Alvstad, Cecilia (2012) 'Anthologizing Latin-American Literature: Swedish Translative Reimaginings of Latin America 1954–1998 and Links to Travel Writing'. *Anglo-Saxónica* 3, 39–68.

Alvstad, Cecilia & Assis Rosa, Alexandra (2015) Special issue of *Target* on Voice in Retranslation, *Target* 27.

Alvstad, Cecilia & Johnsen, Åse (2013) 'Continuidad de los textos: La metaficción en un cuento de Cortázar y su traducción sueca'. *Meta: Journal des traducteurs* 57, 592–604.

Alvstad, Cecilia & Lundahl, Mikela (2010) 'Den mörke brodern: Svensk negrifiering av svart poesi, 1957' [The dark brother: Swedish negrofication of black poetry in 1957]. *TFL Tidskrift för litteraturvetenskap* 40, 39–53.

Assis Rosa, Alexandra, Hanna Pièta & Rita Bueno Maia (eds) (2016). *Indirect Translation: Theoretical, Methodological and Terminological Issues*. Special issue of *Translation Studies* 10(2).

Bassnett, Susan (1980) *Translation Studies*. London: Methuen.

Bassnett, Susan (2014) *Translation*. London: Routledge.

Boldy, Steven. (2009) *A companion to Jorge Luis Borges*. Woodbridge: Tamesis.

Borges, Jorge Luis ([1932] 1974) 'Las versiones homéricas'. In Jorge Luis Borges (1974), *Obras completas 1: 1923–1949*, Buenos Aires: Emecé, 280–285. Originally published in *Discusión*, Buenos Aires: Manuel Gleizer.

Borges, Jorge Luis ([1936] 1974) 'Los traductores de las mil y una noches'. In Jorge Luis Borges (1974), *Obras completas 1: 1923–1949*, Buenos Aires: Emecé, 473–494. Originally published in *Historia de la eternidad*. Buenos Aires: Viau y Zona. A shorter version was published in 1934.

Borges, Jorge Luis (1941) *El jardín de senderos que se bifurcan*. Buenos Aires: Sur.

Borges, Jorge Luis (1944) *Ficciones (1935–1944)*. Buenos Aires: Sur.

Borges, Jorge Luis (1963) *Biblioteket i Babel: En antologi sammanställd ur novellsamlingarna Ficciones och El Aleph* [*The library in Babel: An anthology collected from the short-story collections Ficciones and El Aleph*]. Helsinki: Söderström. Translated by Sun Axelsson in collaboration with Marina Torres.

Borges, Jorge Luis (1964) *Labyrinter*Oslo: J.W. Cappelens forlag. Translated by Finn Aasen.

Borges, Jorge Luis ([1958] 1972) *Labyrinths. Selected Stories and Other Writings*. Harmondsworth: Penguin. Translated by Donald A. Yates, James E. Irby, John M Fein, Harriet de Onís, Julian Palley, Dudle Fitts, Anthony Kerrigan.

Borges, Jorge Luis (1991) *Labyrinter* [*Labyrinths*]. Lund: Umbra Solis. Translated by Johan Laserna.

Borges, Jorge Luis (1993) *Ficciones*. New York: Alfred A. Knopf. Translated by Anthony Kerrigan and Helen Temple & Ruthven Todd.

Borges, Jorge Luis (2000) *Fictions*. London: Penguin. Translated by Andrew Hurley.

Borges, Jorge Luis (2007) *Fiktioner* [*Fictions*]. Stockholm: Bonnier. Translated by Sun Axelsson, Marina Torres, Johan Laserna & Ingegerd Wiking.

Borges, Jorge Luis (2011) *Alefen* [*The Aleph*]. Stockholm: Bonnier. Translated by Sun Axelsson, Lars Bjurman, Artur Lundkvist & Ingegerd Wiking.

Butler, Rex (2010) *Borges' Short Stories: A Reader's Guide*. London: A&C Black.

Damrosch, David (2003) *What is World Literature?*Princeton, NJ: Princeton University Press.

Deleuze, Gilles (1968) *Différence et répétition*. Paris: Presses Universitaires de France.

Elensky, Torbjörn (2009) 'Introduktion' (introduction to a thematic issue on Latin America). *Ord & Bild* 2009(4), 2–5

Gentzler, Edwin (2008) *Translation and Identity in the Americas: New Directions in Translation Theory*. New York: Routledge.

Hermans, Theo (1999) *Translation in Systems: Descriptive and Systemic Approaches Explained*. Manchester: St Jerome.

Håkansson, Gabriella (2007) 'Förord' [Preface]. In Borges (2007), 5–14.

Iser, Wolfgang (1976) *Der Akt des Lesens: Theorie ästhetischer Wirkung*. Munich: Wilhelm Fink.

Jauss, Hans Robert (1970) *Literaturgeschichte als Provokation*. Frankfurt am Main: Suhrkamp.

Lundkvist, Artur (1963) 'Inledning' [Introduction]. In Borges (1963), 7–10.

Macherey, Pierre (1966) 'Borges et le récit fictif'. *Les Temps Modernes* 21(236), 1309–1316.

Mattelart, Armand & Mattelart, Michèle (1998) *Theories of Communication: A Short Introduction*. London: Sage. Translated by Susan Gruenheck Taponier & James A. Cohen.

Montfort, Nick (2003) 'The Garden of Forking Paths'. In Noah Wardrip-Fruin & Nick Montfort (eds) *The New Media Reader*. Cambridge, MA: MIT Press, 29–30.

Olsson, Lotta (2010) 'Sex bokböcker för vuxna' [Six book-books for adults]. *Dagens nyheter*, 1 August. www.dn.se/arkiv/sondag/sex-bokbocker-for-vuxna/, accessed 6 October 2016.

Pym, Anthony (1998) *Method in Translation History*. Manchester: St Jerome.

Rogberg, Martin (ed.) (1954) *Rosen från Cernobbio och andra latinamerikanska noveller* [*The Rose from Cernobbio and other Latin American short stories*]. Sigtuna: Sigtuna bokhandel. Translated by Martin Rogberg & Carl Lindberg.

Scholes, Robert (1970) 'Metafiction'. *Iowa Review*1, 100–115.

Scholes, Robert (1977) 'The Reality of Borges'. *Iowa Review* 8(3), 12–25.

Solberg, Ida (2016) 'Finding the X Factor: Support Translation and the Case of Le deuxième sexe in Scandinavia' In Turo Rautaoja, Tamara Mikolič Južnič & Kaisa Koskinen (eds), *New Horizons in Translation Research and Education* 4, 86–114.

Svensson, Anna (2008) 'Bibliografi över texter av och om Borges utgivna i Sverige 1944–2008' [Bibliography of texts by and about Borges published in Sweden 1944–2008]. Supplement to 'Borges en Gotemburgo: sobre su conferencia 'La Literatura Fantástica' y sus contactos con el Instituto Iberoamericano', *Anales N. E.* 11, 25–47, https://gupea.ub.gu.se/handle/2077/10436.

Toury, Gideon (1995) *Descriptive Translation Studies and Beyond*. Amsterdam: John Benjamins.

Waugh, Patricia (1984) *Metafiction: The Theory and Practice of Self-conscious Fiction*. London: Methuen.

Willson, Patricia (2004) *La constelación del sur: Traductores y traducciones en la literatura argentina del siglo XX*. Buenos Aires: Siglo veintiuno editores Argentina.

10 Two ages of world literature

Karin Littau

This chapter explores how media play a constitutive role in the worlding of literature. In particular, it seeks to demonstrate how the concept of world literature around 1800, in Goethe's era, was just as medium-dependent as the concept of world literature is today. Goethe coined the term *Weltliteratur* at a time when print was proliferating and more books were flooding the literary marketplace than ever before. His own work was caught up in this print-fever. In particular, his *Werther* came to epitomize this excess of print, of novels, of reading and translation. Similarly, the renewed interest in world literature that has developed over the last two decades is articulated against the backdrop of an accelerated and increasingly rich mediasphere. There is, however, a crucial difference between conceptions of world literature then and now. While Goethe's notion was importantly imbued with a sense of futurity, much contemporary debate about world literature seems to bear the sense of an ending. Similarly, while there is a sense in which Goethe considered translation as key to literary exchange and to opening up the world, translation now is threatened with disappearance by the rise of English as *lingua franca* and by the 'pan-translatability' (Apter 2006: 232) of machine translation. This chapter will set these *two ages of world literature* off one against each other to show that what is truly *worldly* about literature is neither literariness nor its untranslatability, but the various media in which the literary arts live on and find their transfiguration.

World literature now

The contemporary notion of world literature is a defensive measure taken in the face of a fast changing mediascape. That it appeared with such vigour after the 1993 ACLA report is not surprising. Charles Bernheimer's suggestion there that literature's horizon be expanded by placing it firmly in a 'multicultural, multimedia world' (1995: 15), and his recommendation that 'comparative literature should include comparisons between media, from early manuscripts to television, hypertext, and virtual realities' (1995: 45), were, despite his claim to the contrary, repeatedly read as a move to diminish literature's importance. Peter Brooks' insistence on literariness and on the study and teaching of 'literature as literature and not as something else' (1995: 102) as core to the project of comparative literature is a case in point. World literature proved an attractive alternative, with the promise of a truly international multiculturalism and the long-overdue re-balancing of a Eurocentric canon that had excluded swathes of literatures around the globe. In the decade following Bernheimer's report, world literature 'exploded in scope', as David Damrosch notes in the 2003 ACLA report (2006: 43), seemingly rescuing the literary from the datafication and 'Disneyfication' (Damrosch 2014: 1) of our 'postliterary age' (Damrosch 2013). Thus rather than countenance literature's expanded horizon in a multimedial world, as Bernheimer had proposed, the point was to raise its scale to the global and from there to the planetary (Spivak 2003) and interplanetary (Saussy 2011): literature was not going to be made smaller by other media or dwarfed by data bytes, it had to grow into a fully blown programme of world literature. But as world literature expanded as a disciplinary challenge to comparative literature, it was always already marked by a retreat into itself. The 'comparisons *with* literature' that have been so central to the project of comparative literature gave way to a renewed attention, albeit through a wider lens, to the 'comparison *of* literatures' (Saussy 2006: 23). Literature became bigger not smaller, both institutionally and spatio-temporally.

In the process world literature had to jettison a key component of comparative literature: the study of literatures in the original. The sheer scale of reading and teaching literatures from across the globe necessitated that one would need to rely on translations, since expertise in all the languages of the world is clearly not a viable option. Although it is undoubtedly a good thing to read a given text in translation than not to read it at all, critics like Gayatri Spivak pointed to the 'arrogance' of assimilating the local diversities of literature from around the world into an English-language canon of world literature (2003: 73); and Emily Apter called attention to the pitfalls of a 'global culture industry' that glosses over untranslatability, alterity and incomparability to serve up pan-translated literary products to the US classroom (2013: 326). In such critiques the project of world literature is viewed as something akin to *literary tourism*, a flattening of the foreign linguistically and culturally and a concomitant diminishing of the scope of translation insofar as the task at hand is merely to 'triangulate' some virtual original from translated versions (Damrosch 2003: 300).

Bernheimer, by contrast, expanded the remit of translation from a strictly linguistic matter when he proposed it as a paradigm for understanding media change as well as different discursive traditions, including 'what is lost and what is gained in translations between the distinct value systems of different cultures, media, disciplines and institutions' (1995: 44). At the basis of his report was an acknowledgement that the medium of the book was in 'the process of being transformed through computer technology and the communication revolution', and that since this was going to change the object of our studies, the discipline of comparative literature should therefore additionally be concerned with 'the material possibilities of cultural expression' (45). Rey Chow in the same report went so far as to recommend reinventing comparative literature as 'comparative media', stressing the importance of thinking about literature in terms of the media that make its storage, retrieval and transmission possible (1995: 116). Attention to matters of mediality gives renewed and altered focus to translation precisely because the afterlives of literatures are unthinkable without mediations (editions, rewritings, refractions, adaptations, transmedia, etc.) or without media (human memory, the scroll, the codex, the book, cinema, the computer, etc.). After all, books are media that are translated intramedially between editions and intermedially from one book-form to another, say from volumina into codices, handwritten codices into printed books, or now books into hypermedia. Insofar as it is not only the linguistic text but also the medial carrier that is subject to translation when works cross into other languages and cultures, this makes translation *de facto* part of the larger circuit of media history (Littau 2011: 277).

If we acknowledge that literature's *circulation* is dependent on a host of mediators such as scribes, editors, translators, booksellers, publishers, literary agents, readers, etc., and media technologies from mnemotechnics in oral culture to digital technologies, and that the *proliferation* of literature across a wide mediascape is not, nor has ever been, just book-bound or exclusively word-based,[1] then we must also acknowledge that literature is necessarily imbricated in a broader media history, which includes the visual arts, the performance arts and modern screen media. In such a conception it is not sufficient merely to read literary works in a greater geographical orbit with other literary works, as Haun Saussy's 'comparison *of* literatures' suggests, but we need 'comparisons *with* literatures'. It is for these reasons that a properly 'worldly' account of the place of literature requires, perhaps more than ever, that translation be recast as not reducibly inter-lingual, but additionally inter- and trans-medial.

To keep literary studies apart from media studies would be tantamount, especially in this day and age, to turning our backs on what is 'their shared past and necessarily entwined future' (Pressman 2014: 3). Andrew Piper's figure of the 'translatologist' (2009: 239) is suggestive here since it re-envisages the humanist scholar in the age of translation and the age of media, or in an age where mediality inflects what is required of translation. Instead of compartmentalizing disciplines according to specific media and instead of 'either separating or effacing the communicative difference between media', Piper's

> humanist as translatologist studies the losses, breaks, ruptures, discoveries, additions, negotiations, and doublings that occur in moving from one medium to another. In this vision of the humanist, the study of literature is reconceived as a linguistic performance across multiple media channels, requiring something akin to Alan Liu's notion of a new 'transliteracy'.
>
> (Piper 2009: 239)

Transliteracy as the ability to read across an array of media platforms[2] is the kind of worldly literacy that is prerequisite for understanding the changing role of literature and translation given prolific media changes. Piper's description of the work of the translatologist chimes not only with Bernheimer's comparatist but also with many of the concerns expressed in the most recent, the 2014–2015

ACLA report under the editorship of Ursula Heise. Although this current report does not include a programmatic statement on the state of the discipline of comparative literature, the report's contributions feature a great many essays that address questions of technology and media head-on.

Rebecca Walkowitz, for instance, clearly takes it as a given that 'we will have to approach literary works as if they exist in several languages, media, and formats' and that future modes of reading will therefore necessarily be comparative and entail that we 'read more versions of works, whether editions, translations, adaptations, or rewritings' (2014/15). Similarly, Gail Finney points to a 'growing interdisciplinarity' by drawing attention to 'the ability of comparative literature to assimilate and nurture itself from other media, such as film and television' and additional, related fields (2014/15); and Jessica Pressman, writing in reference to electronic literature with its high density multimediality and multimodality, comes to the conclusion that 'We can no longer just compare texts. We must now compare textual media' (2014/15). Here, the mediascape is the burgeoning of something new for literature and literary study rather than a threat to its existence.

That world literature as a prominent field of study emerged in the decades between Bernheimer's and Heise's reports as a kind of redemptive undertaking to counter precisely these expansions of translation and comparative media is all too apparent when Damrosch articulates his fear that, owing to new and disruptive elements in this expanded cultural ecology, literature is becoming an 'endangered species' (2013: 159). He writes: 'Long novels have lost ground for years to novellas and shorter fiction, and with so many electronic attractions competing for our students' time, we may wonder whether the modern literatures are fated to disappear beneath the new-media flood' (160). Put differently, contemporary conjectures on world literature are inseparable from a perceived sense of literature coming to an end, (hence also of course Damrosch's reference to the post-literary age in several of his articles).

By contrast, Goethe's conjectures on *Weltliteratur* are tied to a modern construction of literature, at the cusp of a distinction between *Schrifttum* (all kinds of writing) and *belles-lettres* (works of the imagination) as well as an emergent consumer literature, namely the novel. And yet, what both epochs share is that the notion of a world literature paradigm emerges at a specific media-historical juncture. In Goethe's case it was the abundance of print media (books, periodicals, etc.) and in Damrosch's case it appears to be the abundance of non-print media (internet, gaming, etc.). If print around 1800 effected a shift from 'intensive' to 'extensive reading' as historians of the book such as Rolf Engelsing (1974) have shown with the concomitant fear that the populus reads too much, in the twenty-first century, the fear is that we read too little and that there is, as Damrosch sees it, a 'broad cultural shift away from books – particularly long and serious books – towards new modes of reading and newer media' (2012: 71). In both instances, the shifts in practices of reading, and indeed translating, must be explained in reference to the mediascape of the time and in both instances literature is in the process of being remade.

World literature then

Goethe's age spans the period when translation was taken as a marker of civilization and a constitutive element in the shaping of a German national literature. It is also the period in which translation, writing and reading came under scrutiny more than ever. Take Johann Adam Bergk, for instance, a writer, translator and Kant disciple from Leipzig. In 1799 he complained that '[n]ever before has so much been read in Germany than right now. The majority of readers devour the poorest and most tasteless novels with such voracious appetite, in such a way that they debase head and heart' (411–12). His outcry was directed not only at excessive reading and the genre of the novel with which, in his mind, these intemperate tendencies were indissolubly associated, but at its underlying cause: the print medium. Several decades later, the Scottish novelist and travel writer Alexander Innes Shand pinpointed the beginnings of the malaise in these same terms:

> With printing and the promiscuous circulation of books the mischief that had broken out in Germany was spread everywhere by insidious contagion, like the Black Death of the fourteenth century. But unlike that subtle and deadly plague, it has gone on running its course ever since, and diffusing itself gradually through all classes of the community. The ferment of thought, the restless craving for intellectual excitement of some kind, have been stimulated; till now, in the last quarter of the nineteenth century, we are being driven along at high-pressure pace; and it is impossible for any one who is recalcitrant to stop himself.
>
> (Shand 1879: 238–9)

This remark is among countless during this period, stretching back to the eighteenth century, that regarded the technology of print as the devil's invention. If Gutenberg was held responsible for rotting minds, as Shand did, and for a host of reading-related illnesses with medical symptoms ranging from constipation, flabby stomachs, eye and brain disorders, to nerve complaints and mental disease, it is because the quantitative increase in book production clearly had qualitative cultural-aesthetic effects: overload in material and sensory terms (Littau 2006: 39–45). The speed of production fed the rate of consumption.

In turn, the mania for books seemingly also spurred readers into becoming writers themselves. Goethe speaks of the calamity, reports Johann Peter Eckermann, 'that nobody will enjoy what has been produced, but every one wants to reproduce on his own account' (Eckermann 2006: Wednesday 20 April 1825), echoing Samuel Johnson, who half a century before had noted that '*The Age of Authors*' was firmly on the horizon: 'there was never a time when men of all degrees of ability, of every education, of very profession and employment were posting with ardour so general to the press' (1753: 343). If Johnson's epitaph 'All dare to write, who can or cannot read' addressed a mania for writing (a refrain which echoes contemporary critiques of the twitter and blogosphere), Alexander Pope expressed distaste for another mania and singled out for critique another kind of writer, the translator, especially the kind who would translate anything for anybody: 'they'll swear they understand all the languages of the universe' (qtd. McMurran 2010: 55). The German terms most readily used in the eighteenth and nineteenth centuries to describe this array of conditions are 'reading-fever' (*Lesesucht*) and 'writing rage' (*Schreibwut*) (von König 1977: 89–124), and their correlate, the so-called 'translation-addiction' (Gottsched 1741: 516) or 'translation-mania' (Engel 1879).[3]

Translation here is a cog in the larger machinery industrializing writing and novel-translation, part and parcel of the broader commercialization of the literary market place. In this context it is hardly surprising that the reader should be likened to a 'machine' (Butterworth 1870: 501) or 'animated bookcase' (Murray 1886: 517) and that the translator should be conceived as an animated object. In reference to the translation factories[4] that had first sprung up in German lands in the late eighteenth century, Karl Gutzkow referred to translators as 'translator-machines' (1839: 59) and Friedrich Nicolai to translation as 'factory ware' (1799: 112). Indeed, translation had become so integrated in processes of print mechanization that a 'translation machine' had become entirely imaginable. All that was needed, the novelist and Walter-Scott-translator Wilhelm Hauff wrote satirically in 1827 was a 'steam machine that understands French, English and German. Then, there is no need for humans anymore'. The idea that steam drives literary translation is also picked up by Theodor Mundt in a review article on the Italian translation of Goethe's *Iphigenia in Tauris* (1832: 505–7). Here, translation and the steam engine are equated, since both make travel and transport possible, literally and metaphorically. More positively than critiques of the translation factory, Mundt saw steam and translation as the twin engines of cultural communication. Both can overcome the space-time continuum and both make possible the traffic between nations, cultures and languages. This '*Uebersetzungs-Verkehr*' (505), as he calls it, is something utterly new and peculiar in literary history.

What I have been describing up until now is, of course, part and parcel of Goethe's modernity, part of *Werther-mania*, and part of the media context in which Goethe first articulated the concept of world literature in 1827. Albeit scattered and inchoate, the concept is linked, as John Pizer explains, to 'the technological and communicative infrastructure that enabled the rapid exchange of ideas and texts' and which 'Goethe saw as the precondition for the world-literary dialogue' (2007: 11). It was prompted by reading translations from Chinese and Serbian, as well as translations of his own work into French, and it is indissociable from the movements and travels of material and symbolic goods. Here the word *Verkehr*, which repeatedly crops up in Goethe's writings including in the composite *Weltverkehr* ([1827] 1840: 190), does considerable work. In German the word denotes: (a) traffic, transport; (b) contact, communication, company, (sexual) intercourse; (c) trade, service, circulation (Collins Dictionary). *Verkehr* thus not only refers to the 'railways, quick mails, steamships, and every possible kind of facility in the way of communication' (Goethe [1825] 1887: 246) that shrink the world, it also encompasses personal contact and interconnectivity through letters and visits to fellow authors, impersonal modes of communication delivered through the periodical press, newsprint and books, commerce, trade, exchange and circulation of goods and ideas.

When Goethe wrote in 1829,

> But if such a world literature develops in the near future – as appears inevitable with the ever-increasing ease of communication [Schnelligkeit des Verkehrs] – we must expect no more and no less than what it can and in fact will accomplish.
>
> (Goethe 1994: 227)

It was clear that world literature was inevitable precisely because of *Verkehr* in all these permutations. This is to say, the German *Verkehr* condensed in a single word[5] a sense of modernity: fast, commercial, global. English waters this down when it has to opt for just one of the several meanings of this term. The sense of modernity is at the root of the concept of world literature, and Goethean world literature as Antoine Berman notes, is 'contemporaneous with the appearance of a *Weltmarkt*'.[6] That translation plays a key role in this *Weltverkehr* and *Weltmarkt* is evident in this statement by Goethe from 1828:

> And this is how we should see the translator, as one who strives to be a mediator in this universal, intellectual trade, and makes it his business to promote exchange. For whatever one may say about the shortcomings of translations, they are and will remain most important and worthy under-takings in world communication [Weltverkehr].
>
> (Goethe 1994: 207).

If world-literary relations were enabled on the one hand then by a concatena-tion of translation, the logistics of increased and faster transport links and improving communication networks, and the 'untrammeled intercourse among contemporaries' (Goethe, qtd. Strich 1949: 35), those relations were also made possible, Goethe tells us, through the greater 'efficiency of today's book trade' which makes 'any work [...] readily obtainable' (1994: 226). That the book trade and other print media play as significant a role as translation for Goethe in the circulation of literature, including his own work, is apparent in Goethe's short piece 'Bezüge nach Aussen' [foreign relations]. Piper summarizes these relations and their intricacies as follows:

> Goethe translated for his journal, *Ueber Kunst und Alterthum*, a portion of an article from the French journal, *Le Globe*, on the new 'commerce intel-lectual' which was itself a translation of an article from the British *Foreign Quarterly Review* on Swedish literature and which had been published as a direct response to Goethe's own initial appeal for a new 'world literature', we can begin to see the high degree of circularity that such cultural circu-lation had assumed.
>
> (Piper 2009: 14)

The print media, including the 'newspapers', 'critical journals', 'reviews', 'dailies' and 'literary magazines', all of which Goethe cites, are important vehicles for keeping readers informed about the latest literary news from abroad (1994: 225–6), they are also outlets for generating publicity. Media-savvy as he was, Goethe used the available channels of print culture to advertise his own work, announcing prequels, sequels, reprints, etc. of his novel *Wilhelm Meister's Travels*. Piper shows in sparkling detail just how highly evolved and 'self-referential' Goethe's 'publishing practices' were (Piper 2009: 30). Here is a glimpse Piper gives us of some of these machinations:

> the 'prepublications' of the *Travels* that stretched over the course of almost fifteen years and that uniformly appeared in the format of the miscellany consisted of a translation, an incomplete 'book' from the novel, half of a novella, half a novella with an original preface, an incomplete novella, and then the concluding half of a novella that had appeared three years earlier in print and that had been omitted in Goethe's autobiography published even earlier.
>
> (Piper 2009: 29–30)

The publication history of the novel is so complex and convoluted that Piper provides his reader with a map to help visualize the extent of the dispersions (35). What is at stake here is the undoing of the 'boundaries' (30) of this particular work as well as its repetitions across a range of print formats, all of which demonstrates, Piper shows, 'a constitutive feature of the modern literary market place' (31).

If the boundaries of what is ostensibly a single work are being undone here, *The Sorrows of Young Werther* – both a bestseller and world literature – is a novel that provides us with another type of undoing. Written in 1774, translated almost immediately into dozens of European languages, often more than once, and reprinted again and again, including in unauthorized versions as early as 1775, the novel's characters migrate from one media platform to another, and were transfigured for rewrites in prose and poetry, spin-offs and parodies, for stage adaptations and the visual arts. Sometimes Werther kills himself and other times he lives happily ever after with Lotte. Much of this happened even before Goethe had a chance to publish his own revised edition. Werther-fever was part of a full-blown reading epidemic, with some readers reduced to uncontrollable fits of weeping for weeks on end, others – if Napoleon is to be believed – devouring the novel no less than seven times, others still prompted to emulate Werther and take their own lives. Werther thus became a cult, which is why the town council of Leipzig made it a punishable offense to sell the novel, and dress up in Werther's garb – a ban first enforced in 1775 and only lifted half a century later (Swales 1987: 97). That the book had reached cult status during Goethe's lifetime and had become eminently merchandisable is summarized by Peter Watson in *The German Genius*: 'In Vienna there was a Werther fireworks display and in London there was Werther wallpaper. Meissen porcelain was designed, showing Werther scenes, and in Paris perfumieres sold *Eau de Werther*' (2010: 115–16). In this we see two aspects of the worldliness attaching to literature. The first is the frank concern with commerce both insofar as this facilitates the transportation and therefore accessibility of literature amongst other goods. The second, not in Goethe's gift, concerns the commercial potential of his novel identified and exploited by everyone from tailors to potters to perfumiers. These emphasize the worldly, i.e. non-literary context in which literatures emerge and circulate, a logistical fact that Goethe's conception of world literature celebrates as the material possibility of a genuine worldly literature.

Does this make *Werther* a forerunner of *Star Wars* with merchandise and tie-in paraphernalia? And relatedly, did Goethe 'predict [...]' the kind of global modernity 'we now inhabit', as Damrosch credits to him? (2003: 1). This depends on whether the futurity Goethe attached to his account of world literature is reducible to prediction. In other words, did Goethe predict a time when futurity would have arrived? Famously, Goethe stated in 1827 that 'National literature does not amount to much these days; the era of *Weltliteratur* is imminent, and it is incumbent upon everyone to work towards hastening its advent' (qtd. and trans. Frank 2007: 1511). For all Goethe's concern with logistics and commerce as the media of what he noted may constitute an emergent world literature, it was tempered by his demand that the latter's advent be hastened. We might then describe Goethean world literature – or literature's worldliness – as the intercourse of commerce and futurity.

Literature's worldliness

Literature is worldly in the material sense. That is, Goethe is not incidentally but essentially concerned with commerce, logistics and communications as the *sine qua non* of any world literature. This is not only in the trivial sense that there cannot be a *world* literature without large print runs and massive distribution,[7] but also in the sense that the same technologies that facilitate accelerated communications additionally supply the *material* of which literature is the expression.

Just as the world-literary formation of Goethe's age depended on *Verkehr* in all its permutations, so changes in the nature of *Verkehr* over the last two centuries make ours a 'second age' of world literature. This is confirmed when Joseph Tabbi, noting 'the electronic ... and social networks' (2010: 26) underpinning them, suggests that recent digital literary arts 'might in fact *be* an emerging world literature' (20). This is not to say that the second age is the future orientation of the first age realized in the second, but rather to draw attention to the agency of the *Verkehr* proper to each age in the realization of its own worldly literatures. If Goethe was right, and the worldliness of world literatures entails a future orientation, this will remain equally true of Tabbi's 'emerging world literature' as it was of Goethe's own. The futurity is not to be cashed in, in other words, in a future present, but to be translated into a futurity proper to a future age. With this caveat in mind, let us turn to exemplars of these new literary arts Tabbi might suggest are candidates for world literature.

The electronic online works, for instance, of the artist collective Young-Hae Chang Heavy Industries (YHCHI)[8] have been addressed in the context of an emerging world literature. Critics such Pressman and Walkowitz have shown the extent to which YHCHI's e-literatures comment on and enact translation in a technologized mediasphere where the Internet is a means of global circulation. These works 'seem to suggest', Walkowitz notes, 'that differences in geography and culture are irrelevant in an age of electronic literature' (2013: 176). Using *flashing* techniques derived from film and film-related media (e.g. photographic or tachistoscopic media), YHCHI's multilingual translation-works make visible the translation process on the screen. This makes translation not only the content of such work, but also its means of production, since translation operates not just at the level of languages (the artist duo Young-Hae Chang and Marc Voge utilize linguistic competences in English, Spanish, German, French, Korean, Chinese and Japanese), but also at the level of media, by drawing on them, whether textual, filmic or digital, in order to make translation itself variously visible. But visibility is no guarantee of legibility. Initiating a procedure of 'auto-translation', whereby a prose extract is continuously and instantaneously translated between one language and the next, both versions being presented simultaneously on a split screen, 'even a reader fluent in both languages', as Pressman points out with reference to their work *Nippøn*, 'is unable to read both texts simultaneously' (2014: 153). YHCHI's translations-in-motion fulfil *and* resist the dream of instant translation insofar as instantaneity is impossible to apperceive: we may perceive that a translation occurs but cannot apperceive the translation as translation. The temporal difference necessary to compare source with translation on an animated screen, unlike in printed parallel text editions, is eliminated by instantaneity. As such, their works are comments on translation as much as onscreen depictions of it in a computer age that promises that everything – including the translation process itself – can happen in an instant.

Automatic translation is also key to Warren Sack and Sawad Brooks's *Translation Map* (2003),[9] a project that was exhibited by the Walker Art Center in Minneapolis. It critiques machine translation's supposed pan-translatability and puts forward an 'alternative computer technology for translation' (Sack 2005: 10). As Sack explains: 'computers and networks should be used to facilitate collaborative work between people, rather than as a magic black box that [Warren] Weaver's translation-as-decoding problem implies'. The model of 'translation-as-collaboration' as an alternative to automatic translation thus uses a computer prototype system to locate human translators on the Internet, facilitating 'worldwide, cross-border, multi-lingual conversations'[10] and collaborative rewriting. Sack and Brooks' *Translation Map* is therefore part of an avant-garde genealogy of experimental writing practices, in particular the 'Surrealists' *exquisite corps* writing games'.[11] A computer programme tracks the circulation of a sent message and a map visualizes the translations taking place from language to language across the globe so as to make its movement through cyberspace geographically locatable. If a message does not reach its addressee, which is a real possibility given patchy internet access across the globe, the sender is encouraged to print out the message, fold it in a pre-described way, and relay it the old-fashioned way, through the postal system.

If the *Translation Map* uses the Internet and the postal service for crowd-sourced, collaborative translation, the project of the *Spectacular Translation Machine* uses the forum of the 2013 London Literature Festival[12] for face-to-face collaboration. In this way it de-digitizes online 'translation factories' and translates them into a pre- and/or post-electronic village. For one weekend, the public was invited to collectively translate a book from French into English. More scriptorium than online forum, this project demonstrates the worldly community on the threshold of a realized global village. Similarly, *Translation Games* [13] – a project first organized in 2013 and still ongoing – draws together artists, designers and translators through a host of public events in London to engage in multi-medial translations. Modelled on the game of Chinese Whispers, a specially commissioned creative work was translated for the 2013 game into several languages and across different media: 'from text to performance, from performance to video, from video to sculpture, from sculpture to painting, etc.' and 'at each stage of the language chain', the text was also translated into textiles. *Translation Games* has thus resulted in a range of artworks, and among other things, materialized into an 'interactive flip-book catalogue'. What projects of this kind demonstrate is that our traditional notions of writing, translation, making art, etc. are transforming in an age of large-scale connect-ability between people and interconnectivity between media platforms. Such projects are also, however, testament to translation's expanded remit in a broader media history.

If the digital sphere has prompted us to rethink writing and translation, it has also prompted us to rethink the book medium. Take *Nox*, first published by New Directions in 2010, which is a work of poetry and a book in a box, written by the classicist and translator of Aeschylus, Euripides, Sophocles and Sappho, Anne Carson. *Nox* is an *objet d'art*, designed in collaboration with Robert Currie, and a meditation on Carson's brother's death, based on a scrapbook she made in his memory. It is also a translation-work of Catullus's poem 101, itself an elegy to a lost brother, which Carson, we are told, has struggled to translate.

Nox is an exercise in translation as well as an exercise in media translation. The book opens with Catullus's original poem, followed by lexical entries on each Latin word together with Carson's commentaries, so as to provide us with a range of meanings for each word and crucially the means to create our own translation. It ends with an illegible English translation on a crumpled, stained, and smudged piece of yellow paper. The translation, on the left-hand side of the page, remains as ungraspable as the brother's life Carson tries to stitch together from fragments and memories on the right-hand side of the page. Presenting *Nox* in a concertina-folded book-form arguably 'marks an intermediate stage between the scroll and the codex' (Brillenburg Wurth 2013: 23). It further translates several media into one: handwritten and typed notes and letters appear alongside Xeroxed and scanned pages, photographs and drawings. By referencing ancient book-forms alongside contemporary forms of digital repro-duction, the work as a whole resists reduction to a mediatic 'Now'. As Kiene Brillenburg Wurth has shown, while 'the foregrounded presence of photo-ima-ging in *Nox* makes the connection with the digital screen all too evident', there is also 'resistance to the digital' (27), insofar as Carson herself is all too aware that *Nox*, produced in the Kindle age, is materially 'un-Kindle-isable' (Carson qtd. Brillenburg Wurth 2013: 27). If bookishness is understood here as a resis-tance to the digital, it is paradoxically the digital that has in effect made the bookishness possible in two senses: fear of the death of the book in a digital age has produced a host of books of late that revel in bookish materiality, and bookishness in *Nox* is achieved through distinctly digital means. Carson's *Nox*, then, is a work that thinks about books and about translation, and that demonstrates how books and translations are shaped by the media of today. Finally, it is a book that is contained in a box, but it is also a book without borders, forming part not only of an art installation at the Hampden Gallery in Amherst in December 2011 by Alexis Fedorjaczenko, but also part of a dance performance at the O, Miami Poetry Festival in April 2011 (Plate 2015: 106).

The worldliness of these works is immediately apparent in that they each in their own way articulate their material conditions of production while variously incorporated in or resisting incorporation into globalized communications infrastructures. For this reason, they all address translation and media transla-tion. If worldliness in this sense is evident in these examples, so too is their implicit futurity. That is, these practices are futurable in their own terms and so neither cancel their own futurability, nor that of some communications revolu-tion to come (the futurity proper to a coming age). New media will always change the modes of literary production and the requirements placed therefore on translation. Perhaps we will *remember* our fictions in the future, rather than witness them unfolding in a present?

When Damrosch suggests in *What* is *World Literature?* (emphasis added) that it is 'not an infinite ungraspable canon of works but rather a mode of circulation and of reading' (2003: 5), the 'what *is*' that frames this question jars with Goethe's futurity, because futurity by its very nature *is* not. Neither a canon nor graspable, world literature is emerging. And, just as literature is inexhaustible, so is the world. World literature is not graspable not *just* because there is too much of it (the sheer quantity Franco Moretti addresses), but because it is part of the function of literature to reimagine the world of which it is part. That is both the worldliness of literature and its futurity. How literature reimagines the world of which it is part is dependent upon the media, that is, the technical, logistical, communicative means that the world sets at its disposal. Viewed in this light, *worldly literature* is necessarily futural, because there is in principle no limit to the number of ways in which the world – an enormous engine for reimagining itself – can so reimagine itself. For example, if world literature were reduced to a *mode of reading*, what if literature were no longer read or seen? What if narrative were felt or partly recal-led, as Pat Cadigan imagines in *Fools* (1992)? Finally then, the present tense in 'what *is* world literature?' negates that literature perpetually reimagines itself and the world of which it is part.

Notes

1 I am thinking here of Christian Morgenstern's phonetic poems.
2 Liu's notion of transliteracy project is predominantly concerned with online reading, see website: http://liu.english.ucsb.edu/transliteracies-research-in-the-technologica l-social-and-cultural-practices-of-online-reading/; I am using Thomas's definition (2008: 101).
3 See Littau (2016).
4 See Bachleitner (1989: 1–49).
5 Arac makes this point, in the main, with reference to Marx and Engel's use of the word *Verkehr* in their conception of world literature (2007: 21).
6 Berman (1992: 55) is echoing a point made by Fritz Strich.
7 In this context, see Mani's concept of 'bibliomigrancy' (2011).
8 Their work can be read/seen online at: www.yhchang.com
9 See https://people.ucsc.edu/~wsack/TranslationMap/UsersManual/ for a User's Manual.
10 See http://translationmap.walkerart.org/index.html
11 See http://translationmap.walkerart.org/how.html
12 See www.southbankcentre.co.uk/whatson/the-spectacular-translation-ma chine-1000392
13 See http://translationgames.net

Bibliography

Arac, Jonathan (2007) 'Global and Babel: Language and Planet', *Shades of the Planet*, ed. Wai Chee Dimock and Lawrence Buell. Princeton NJ: Princeton University Press, pp. 19–38.

Apter, Emily (2006) *The Translation Zone. A New Comparative Literature*. Princeton NJ: Princeton University Press.

Apter, Emily (2013) *Against World Literature. On the Politics of Untranslatability*. London: Verso.

Bachleitner, Nobert (1989) 'Übersetzungsfabriken'. Das deutsche Übersetzungswesen in der ersten Hälfte des 19. Jahrhunderts, *Internationales Archiv für Sozialgeschichte der deutschen Literatur (IASL)* 14. 1, 1–49.

Bergk, Johann Adam (1799) *Die Kunst, Bücher zu lesen. Nebst Bemerkungen über Schriften und Schriftsteller*. Jena: In der Hempelschen Buchhandlung, rpt. 1966.

Berman, Antoine (1992) *The Experience of the Foreign: Culture and Translation in Romantic Germany*, trans. S. Heyvaert. New York: State University of New York Press.

Bernheimer, Charles (1995) 'Introduction: The Anxieties of Comparison' and 'The Bernheimer Report, 1993', *Comparative Literature in the Age of Multiculturalism*, ed. Charles Bernheimer. Baltimore: The Johns Hopkins University Press, pp. 1–17, pp. 39–48.

Brillenburg Wurth, Kiene (2013) 'Re-vision as Remediation: Hypermediacy and Translation in Anne Carson's Nox', *Image and Narrative* 14. 4, 20–33.

Brooks, Peter (1995) 'Must We Apologize', *Comparative Literature in the Age of Multiculturalism*, ed. Charles Bernheimer. Baltimore: The Johns Hopkins University Press, pp. 97–106.

Butterworth, C. H. (1870) 'Overfeeding', *Victoria Magazine* 14 (November to April), 500–504.

Cadigan, Pat (1992) *Fools*. New York: Bantam Spectra.

Chow, Rey (1995) 'In the Name of Comparative literature', *Comparative Literature in the Age of Multiculturalism*, ed. Charles Bernheimer Baltimore: The Johns Hopkins University Press, pp. 107–116.

Damrosch, David (2003) *What is World Literature*. Princeton NJ: Princeton University Press.

Damrosch, David (2006) 'World Literature in a Postcanonical, Hypercanonical Age', *Comparative Literature in the Age of Globilization*, ed. Haun Saussy Baltimore: The Johns Hopkins University Press, pp. 43–53.

Damrosch, David (2012) 'The End of the Book? Literary Studies in a Post-Literary Age, 1960/2010/2060', *Rethinking the Humanities: Paths and Challenges*, ed. Ricardo Gil Soeiro and Sofia Tavares Cambridge: Cambridge Scholars, pp. 67–86.

Damrosch, David (2013) 'World Literature in a Postliterary Age', *Modern Language Quarterly* 74. 2, 151–170

Damrosch, David (2014) 'Introduction: World Literature in Theory and Practice', *World Literature in Theory*. Oxford: Wiley Blackwell, pp. 1–12.

Eckermann, Johann Peter (2006) *Conversations of Goethe*, trans. John Oxenford (Digital Production, Harrison Ainsworth), online at: www.hxa.name/books/ecog/Eckerma nn-ConversationsOfGoethe.html#contents

Engel, Eduard (1879) 'Die Uebersetzungsmanie in Deutschland', *Magazin für die Literatur des Auslandes* 43/44, 461–464, 677–680.

Engelsing, Rolf (1974) *Der Bürger als Leser: Lesergeschichte in Deutschland 1500–1800*. Stuttgart: Metzler.

Finney, Gail (2014/15) 'The Reign of the Amoeba: Further Thoughts about the Future of Comparative Literature' (published online 3 July 2014), *ACLA Report on the State of the Discipline 2014–2015*, ed. Ursula Heise.

Frank, Armin Paul (2007) 'Translation and Historical Change in Post-Renaissance Europe', *Übersetzung, Translation Traduction: An International Encyclopedia of Translation Studies*, Volume 2, ed. by Harald Kittel, Juliane House and Brigitte Schultze Berlin: Walter de Gruyter, pp. 1460–1520.

Goethe, Johann Wolfgangvon (1840) *Goethe's Sämmtliche Werke in Vierzig Bänden*. Dreiunddreizigster Band Stuttgart und Tübingen: Cotta.

Goethe, Johann Wolfgang von (1887) 'Goethe to Zelter (Weimar 6 June 1825)', *Goethe's Letters to Zelter*, selected, trans. and annotated A.D. Coleridge London: George Bell and Sons, p. 246.

Goethe, Johann Wolfgang von (1994) 'On Carlyle's German Romance (1828)', 'On World Literature', *Goethe, The Collected Works*, Volume 3: *Essays on Art and Literature*, ed. John Gearey, trans. Ellen von Nardoff and Ernest H. von Nardoff Princeton University Press, pp. 206–208, 224–228.

Gottsched, Johann Christoph (1741) 'Nachricht über von neuen hieher gehörigen Sachen', *Beyträge zur critischen Historie der deutschen Sprache, Poesie und Beredsamkeit*. Band 7. Stück 27 Leipzig: Breitkopf, pp. 512–519.

Gutzkow, Karl (1839) 'Die Deutschen Uebersetzungsfabriken', *Telegraph für Deutschland* 7/8, 49–52, 57–59, retrieved from Gutzkow Editionsprojekt: https://projects. exeter.ac.uk/gutzkow/Gutzneu/gesamtausgabe/Abtei1/DDtUebe.htm1839

Hauff, Wilhelm (1827) *Die Bücher und die Leserwelt*. Wuppertal: Gerettete Schriften Verlag, Kindle 2013.

Heise, Ursula (2014/15) (ed.) *ACLA Report on the State of the Discipline 2014–2015*, online at: http://stateofthediscipline.acla.org

Johnson, Samuel (1753) 'All dare to write, who can or cannot read', *The Adventurer* No. 115 (Tuesday 11 December), 343.

König, Dominikvon (1977) 'Lesesucht und Lesewut', *Buch und Leser: Vorträge des 1. Jahrtreffens des Wolfenbütteler Arbeitskreises für Geschichte des Buchswesen, 13. und 14. May 1976*, ed. Herbert G. Göpfert Hamburg: Hauswedell Verlag, pp. 89–124.

Littau, Karin (2006) *Theories of Reading. Books Bodies and Bibliomania* Cambridge: Polity Press.

Littau, Karin (2011) 'First Steps towards a Media History of Translation', *Translation Studies* 4. 3, 261–281.

Littau, Karin (2016) 'Translation's Histories and Digital Futures', Special Section on 'Babel and Globalization: Translating in the 21st Century', ed. Paolo Sigismondi, *International Journal of Communication* 10, 907–928, online at: http://ijoc.org/index.php/ijoc/article/view/3508/1571

Mani, Venkat (2011) 'Bibliomigrancy: Book Series and the Making of World Literature', *The Routledge Companion to World Literature*, ed. Theo D'haen, David Damrosch and Djelal Kadir London: Routledge, pp. 283–296.

McMurran, Mary Helen (2010) *The Spread of Novels. Translation and Prose Fiction in the Eighteenth Century.* (Princeton, NJ: Princeton University Press).

Mundt, Theodor (1832) 'Deutsche Literatur im Auslande. Goethe in Italiänischem Gewande. – Bürger', *Magazin für die Literatur des Auslandes* 127 (Montag 19 November), 505–507.

Murray, J. (1886) 'Books and Reading', *Quarterly Review* 162. 324 (April), 501–518.

Nicolai, Friedrich (1799) *Leben und Meinungen des Herrn Magisters Sebaldus Nothanker.* Band I. Vierte verbesserte Auflage (4th improved edition) Berlin: Friedrich Nicolai.

Piper, Andrew (2009) *Dreaming in Books. The Making of the Bibliographic Imagination in the Romantic Age.* Chicago: The University of Chicago Press.

Pizer, John (2007) 'Towards a Productive Interdisciplinary Relationship: Between Comparative Literature and World Literature', *The Comparatist* 31 (May), 6–28.

Plate, Liedeke (2015) 'How to Do Things with Literature in the Digital Age: Anne Carson's Nox, Multimodality, and the Ethics of Bookishness', *Contemporary Women's Writing* 9. 1 (March), 93–111.

Pressman, Jessica (2014) *Digital Modernism. Making it New in New Media.* Oxford: Oxford University Press.

Pressman, Jessica (2014/15) 'Electronic Literature as Comparative Literature' (published online 28 June 2014), *ACLA Report on the State of the Discipline 2014–2015*, ed. Ursula Heise.

Sack, Warren (2005) 'Public Space, Public Discussion and Social Computing', Working Papers Series, Center on Organizational Innovation, Columbia University, online at www.coi.columbia.edu/pdf/sack_pspdsc.pdf,

Saussy, Haun (2006) 'Exquisite Cadavers Stitched from Fresh Nightmares: Of Memes, Hives, and Selfish Genes', *Comparative Literature in the Age of Globalization*, ed. H. Saussy Baltimore: The Johns Hopkins University Press, pp. 3–42.

Saussy, Haun (2011) 'Interplanetary Literature', *Comparative Literature* 63. 4, 438–447.

Shand, Alexander Innes (1879) 'Contemporary Literature, VII: Readers', *Blackwood's Magazine* 126 (August), 235–256.

Spivak, Gayatri (2003) *Death of a Discipline.* New York: Columbia University Press.

Strich, Fritz (1949) *Goethe and World Literature*, trans. C.A.M. Sym London: Routledge.

Swales, Martin (1987) *Goethe: The Sorrows of Young Werther*. Cambridge: Cambridge University Press.

Tabbi, Joseph (2010) 'Electronic Literature as World Literature; or, The Universality of Writing under Constraint', *Poetics Today* 31. 1, 17–50.

Thomas, Sue (2008) 'Transliteracy and New Media', *Transdisciplinary Digital Art: Sound, Vision and the New Screen*, ed. Randy Adams, Steve Gibson and Stefan Müller Arisona Berlin: Springer, pp. 101–109.

Walkowitz, Rebecca (2013) 'Close Reading in an Age of Global Writing', *MLQ* 74. 2, 171–195.

Walkowitz, Rebecca (2014/15) 'Future Reading' (published online 30 January 2015), *ACLA Report on the State of the Discipline 2014–2015*, ed. Ursula Heise.

Watson, Peter (2010) *The German Genius*. London: HarperCollins.

11 Seeing the Mediterranean again (in and out of translation)

Stephanos Stephanides

The man who finds his homeland sweet is still a tender beginner; he to whom every soil is as his native one is already strong; but he is perfect to whom the whole world is a foreign land

(Hugo of St. Victor quoted in Said 1977: 259)

I would suggest with Djelal Kadir (2010) that the 'world' in 'world literature' cannot be taken as given, since it is the performative outcome of our own interventions that makes a world. The performance, I would add, is enabled by claims on our embodied memory and by the multiple mediations of the imagination. Translation is one such performative intervention whose outcome may be random and unexpected in transcultural dialogue and through its readership. This chapter will seek to explore transcultural and translational interaction through fractures in space and time, to see how such interconnections might inject literature with a new energy through the unpredictable movements and affective allegiances that can come about through translation.

In thinking about my own writing and translation practice, I have found it valuable to reflect on Deleuze and Guattari's (1986) essay on *Kafka: Toward a Minor Literature*. They argue that the path of the minor is radical indeterminacy with a fractured consciousness whose perspective is vibrant yet uncertain as the writer (and by extension the translator) resists the symbolic powers of one single language. Writing and translation therefore become experimental. This suggests a kind of apophatic theoria, or *via negativa* in literary practice best expressed in the mantra from the *Upanishads* 'neti neti' 'neither this nor this'. Franz Kafka also spoke of the predicament of having to choose a language finding it equally impossible to write in Czech, Yiddish or German. In a letter to Max Brod of June 1921 he refers to the impossibility of not writing, the impossibility of writing in German, the impossibility of writing otherwise, and the impossibility of writing itself (Casanova 1999: 347, 370). Kafka seems to be a stranger in the language in which he writes and it is this sense of estrangement that makes him a paradigm of 'minor' literature.

In Deleuze and Guattari's discussion of the 'minor', the tetra-lingual model has been especially useful for understanding the spatiotemporal categories of language: vernacular (here), vehicular (everywhere), referential (over there) and mythical (beyond), and how these work in terms of territorialisation, de-territorialisation and reterritorialisation (Deleuze and Guattari 1986: 23). The distribution of these four functions of language and their interplay will change through time and among different groups and communities. In the cramped space of an island such as Cyprus, this interplay is more salient. For example, languages of territorialisation would be Cypriot variations of Greek and Turkish, the vernacular rural and maternal languages; the language of the island's various colonisers would be vehicular and de-territorialising, languages of the 'world' that are found 'every where': French during the Lusignan Dynasty, and Italian at the time of Venetian rule. And, of course, English, the language of the island's most recent colonisers, and the language of globalisation. Referential and reterritorialising languages of sense and culture in the postcolonial nation-state would be Modern Greek and Modern Turkish, the two official languages of the State. Also reterritorialising are the languages of the past, of myth, spirituality and religion, such as Classical and Byzantine Greek, and Ottoman Turkish. Writing and translation fracture and redistribute these functions of language, shift their centres of power and blur their borders, deterritorialising one terrain to map another. One might be here, elsewhere, everywhere and beyond all at the same place or perhaps nowhere at all.

World Literature, as conceived and developed by David Damrosch (2003), has moved from a canonical body to emphasising the cycle of production, circulation and reception of texts. This requires a reading and writing strategy that is a constant negotiation between the intimate and the strange as a means of exploring where we are in the world and how we construct that world imaginatively. Inevitably, in a field so vast and heterogeneous, contemporary theorisation of world literature raises apparently irreconcilable differences, which often emerge around the issue of combining global reach with textual closeness, transcultural humanism with power inequalities. Emily Apter (2003) broaches this issue in discussing the idea of 'global *translatio*' when she critiques Franco Moretti for his approach to 'distant reading' and for emphasising narrative over linguistic difference. However, we need both close and distant reading for a new poetics of the imaginary and the imagined, seeing them as social facts, as political and ethical ways of renegotiating the tensions between incorporation and dispersion in the re-formation of what we may call World Literature.

Translation is as fundamental to an understanding of world literature as ethnographic practice is to anthropology. However, Franco Moretti's world systems approach and Pascale Casanova's notion of the world republic of letters begin with the premise that the economies of linguistic and literary exchange are not the same everywhere. Moretti (2000: 61) draws on the polysystems theory of translation to discuss world literature as a system of variations, in which the least stable variant is the local narrative voice. Casanova (1999: 25–40) gives recognition to the importance of translators as mediators and as actors in the creation of literariness. In this chapter, I focus on fractures as geological and cultural gateways that give rise to creative moments so as to probe the thresholds of translatability and how they relate to the *poesis* of imagined forms of communities and ways of being in the world. We experience translation and literature across distance, mediation and dispersion.

On the island of Cyprus from which I write, the literature has been shaped across a spectrum of languages and trans-cultural relations, which may range from confrontation, indifference or mutual exclusion, to creative engagement depending on the social and cultural processes and historical moments. In post-colonial Cyprus literary studies have reflected the tenacity of the nation and its presumptions about the homogeneity of language, ethnicity and religion as the institutionalised category of analysis. Cyprus became a British protectorate and was eventually annexed by Britain at the outbreak of World War I. In the transition from the Ottoman to the British Empire, the change of power affected hierarchical relationships and the transition from an identity based on Moslems and Christians to ethnic Turks and ethnic Greeks sowed the seeds of ethnic nationalism as a force of colonial resistance. During the first decades of British rule the combination of colonialism and Cypriot diasporic consciousness led to a form of what can be termed colonial cosmopolitanism. It is noteworthy that literary modernity in Cyprus came belatedly, with the advent of British colonialism in the 1880s, the decade that brought the first printing press (a gift from Alexandrian Greeks) and the first newspaper to the island (published in Greek and English). The printing press was a catalyst for the production of local literature, translation and criticism. In his PhD dissertation, Lefteris Papaleontiou notes that in the period 1880–1930, which coincides approximately with the first half-century of British rule, more than 900 texts by about 400 writers were translated by 150 *literati* for local consumption (Papaleontiou 1997: 274). English education in Cyprus and Cypriots studying in British universities were important catalysts in this literary activity. In addition, there was a Cypriot diaspora in Egypt, Asia Minor and the Levant, which engaged with Eastern languages and cultures. The newly arrived English education and culture may have given further impetus to knowledge of the East through British Orientalism. It brought about its own kind of cross-fertilisation and intervention in the home culture, thus marking the island as a chiasmus of the East in the West and the West in the East.

These communities of the Eastern Mediterranean Cypriot diaspora dissolved in the course of the twentieth century for various reasons, most notably the Greco-Turkish war of 1919–22, which led to the Treaty of Lausanne recognising Turkish sovereignty over Asia Minor and agreement to an exchange of populations between Greece and Turkey deracinating two million people from heir homelands. Also the aftermath of World War I saw the rise of Egyptian nationalism and the beginning of the exodus of Egypt's community of Egyptianised foreigners known as the *Mutanassirun*. This culminated with the Suez crisis of 1956, which led to the expulsion and exodus of most of the remaining communities of Europeans and Jews. More recently civil war and strife in Lebanon from 1975 to 1990 caused an exodus of one million people from the country.

In Cyprus a unified sense of national identity has not held together in the post-colonial state as is testified by ethnic conflict in the 1960s and the *de facto* parti-tion of the island since 1974. Cyprus is an insular example and metonymy of the state of the region and the politics and economy of global modernity and a fault line for its tensions and conflicts. It began its post-colonial nationhood becoming a member of the Non-aligned Movement, and it became a member of the EU in 2004 while remaining a member of the Commonwealth. The island has links to multiple Easts: it had strong links with the Eastern bloc and links to Eastern Orthodoxy and the Islamic East of the territories close to its shores. Economic developments in the last two decades have attracted immigrants from Eastern Europe, South Asia, the Philippines, refugees from Lebanon and Syria, and, in the north of the island, Anatolian settlers have been brought in from Turkey.

The Mediterranean as a regional cultural formation appears to have received less attention from literary scholars than among historians. Yet for me, the writing of the Mediterranean's eminent historian Fernand Braudel opens up imaginative ways of thinking about literature and translation. In expounding his notion of the '*longue durée*' Braudel emphasises that 'It is not duration itself that is the product of our mind, but rather the fragmentation of duration' (Braudel 1972: 36). The memory of the *longue durée* emerges through fractures, which must also be conceived historically. Fractures give breathing space for the *conjuncture or 'court durée'* also referred to by historians as the 'event'. Applied to translation, we can consider that texts, like events, find time density when read within an economy of seeing in the *longue durée*. This involves an exploration of the imaginary in flight in deep time to open creative reappro-priation in a quest for fertile new beginnings in another time and space. Memory of the long duration makes available ways out of which cultures and societies may imagine a future. The short duration demands a rapid turnaround of information. Walter Benjamin calls for translators to go beyond information and pursue the anticipatory illumination of 'pure language' 'reine Sprache'. Pure language implies the impossibility of an unmediated memory, a paradisiacal pre- (and post-) Babelian language. Translatability implies an unforgettable life or moment, which can only be fulfilled in 'God's remembrance' (Benjamin 1973: 70), which is beyond the realm of memory of humans. For Benjamin therefore the *poesis* of the mode of translation has therefore a trace of cabbalistic mysti-cism. Translatability is in the promise of fulfilment, even when it is beyond the ability of men and women to translate.

Braudel implies something similar when he urges us to remember the sea, as if seeking a poet's experience of an originary vision. What does this scar in the earth's crust signify? In the opening lines of his posthumously published *Memory and the Mediterranean*, Braudel asks rhetorically if it matters that we remember the sea's ancient age, and then replies emphatically that it does. The long duration opens up economies of seeing, linked to remembrance and the art of memory and fractures. One may remember that the Mediterranean had dried up five million years ago when a geological shift closed the Straits of Gibraltar, leaving a huge subterranean wealth in salt. The Straits opened again and the sea was replenished. In Greek mythology, the Straits, known as the Pillars of Hercules, were said to carry the inscription *Non Plus Ultra* as a warning to sailors that there was Nothing More Beyond. This was the ostensible route of Odysseus, whom, not wanting to be contained eternally on his island of Ithaca, set out to go 'Beyond Hesperia', the route of the second Odyssey, or the way of untranslatable excess, alluded to by many poets. In Dante's *Divina Commedia* (Inferno, Canto XXVI), Ulysses recalls how he and his companions perished after they went beyond the Straits not heeding Hercules' warning. Tennyson's 'Ulysses' expresses his desire 'To sail beyond the sunset, and the baths/Of all the western stars, until I die ('Ulysses' lines 60–61)

Cafavy also speaks of the Second Odyssey in the 1894 poem of that name. In the poem, Odysseus after returning home 'finds all his Ithaca was small' and 'ghosts of Hesperia disturbed his sleep'. He then set off again toward the west, 'toward Iberia' and 'far from Achaean seas (my translation in Pieris 1996: 99–100). The inscription *Non Plus Ultra* was modified to *Plus Ultra* (More Beyond) as a motto by Charles V, the Holy Roman Emperor, to encourage Spanish explorers to go beyond and is today on the Spanish coat of arms. Derek Walcott alludes to Odysseus' Atlantic journey as he delves into transoceanic memory returning his gaze from the Caribbean to the Mediterranean reflecting on the supposed etymology of the name of Lisbon: 'swifts, launched from the nesting sills of Ulissibona, / their cries modulated to "Lisbon" as the Mediterranean / ages into the white Atlantic, their flight, in reverse' (Walcott 1990: 189).

At the eastern end of the Sea, we find other fractures. The straits of the Dardanelles and the Bosphorus join the Mediterranean to the Black Sea through the Sea of Marmara like a neural correlate of consciousness of the border of Europe and Asia. To the south-east, the man-made fracture, which is the Suez canal, was celebrated by Walt Whitman in his poem 'A Passage to India' as a feat of engineering that would open up our worldliness. More recently, the widening and deepening of the Canal has brought new fauna such as the lionfish from the Indian Ocean. While some ecologists are concerned with the pernicious effect of this marine invasion, others like Fred Pearce (2015) would argue that nature has a way of re-wilding itself – and we might add language and culture re-culturing itself.

The idea of the long duration might be understood in literary terms in relation to Bakhtin's notion of 'great time' (*bolshoye vremya*): 'Everything that belongs only to the present dies along with the present' (Bakhtin 1986: 4). While physical geography sets the framework of the long duration, for the artist, poet and seer, one would need to speak of the traces in deep memory of the very long duration or the invisible world beyond historical memory. Culture conceived as a layered imaginative geography often makes the afterlife of a text more intense than within the epoch in which it was written. Memory and economy of seeing are shaped by moments of fractures and ruptures, arrivals and departures, exits and entries that meaningfully coincide with texts and events that emerge in reading, writing and translation practices.

A Mediterranean classic that has entered the 'great time' is Ovid's *Metamorphoses*. Ted Hughes' *Tales of Ovid* begins with 'Now I am ready to tell how bodies are changed/Into different bodies' (Hughes 1997: 3), and then, like Ovid, evokes the world from darkness and chaos through the four ages – Golden, Silver, Bronze, and Iron – that resemble the four Hindu *'yugs'*. In his introduction, Hughes speaks of Ovid as writing in the psychological gulf of a time of great change, much like the sense of our culture at the end of the second millennium. Reading Hughes, we may find a connection between metamorphosis and translatability. The acts of metamorphoses, Hughes says, seem to arrive when unendurable intensity lifts stories onto a mythic or divine plane. If translatability is metamorphosis, it finds its articulation in the human victims who are transformed and remain in cultural memory in the forms they have attained. One could say that in Ovid's tales, bodies endure and exhibit translation as a memory, as in the final story of Hughes' translation. Pyramus and Thisbe are remembered by the colour of the mulberry fruit, which was transformed by their blood. These metamorphoses may be said to mark a passage to long duration from the short, a passage which could be compared to the performative enactment of translation.

In thinking about the passage of the imagination in translation, I have been intrigued by the work of Ibn Arabi, the Andalucian 13th century poet and philosopher who was concerned with the role of the imagination in the search for divine truth, and he approaches the experience of perplexity (in Arabic, *hayrah*) as a path to truth beyond the restrictions of reason. In the eye of reason, ideas may be either true or false, whereas imagination perceives notions as images, whose truth can be both true and false, and at the same time neither true nor false. It incites *hayrah,* a perplexity that disables our rational faculty and enables an opening of a visual economy. In *al-Futûhât*, he talks about imagination as one of the heart's two eyes. The one eye that is *qur'ân* unifies and brings together, whereas the other eye that is *furqân* differentiates (Stanford Encyclopedia of Philosophy 2015). The word *khayâl* (synonymous with the term *mithâl*) means image, shadows, dream and vision: for Ibn Arabi images bring together two sides and unite them as one. It is, the mirror as well as the object that it reflects, and neither the mirror nor the object. So any image of the Mediterranean I may have is both true and false, neither true nor false. There is a doubling in the economies of seeing, which seeks a moment of transformation in the doubling.

Orhan Pamuk frequently quotes Ibn Arabi (for example, in the opening epigraph of *The Black Book)* evoking the mystic and mysterious realm that is hidden from those who are confined to a world of what they believe to be empirical fact. In Pamuk's *My Name is Red* everything unfolds around the image, enacting an allegorical process where the real is somewhere between the ineffable source and its reflection. Ibn Arabi and his ontology of the imagination take on flesh in Pamuk's novel, creating what Bakhtin would call a chronotope in its 'intrinsic connectedness of temporal and spatial relationships that are artistically expressed' (Bakhtin, 1981, 258). Pamuk explores dominant discourses of

colonialism, orientalism, secularism, nationalism and modernity, giving particular attention to the mediating role of art and literature. The *kalem* (the pen)
of the writer and the illustrator is the potential of art to accommodate or give
agency to heterogenous desires where the constraints of ideology and politics
fail. I was first drawn to Ibn Arabi's poems not least by the title: *Tarjuman al-
Ashwaq*, (the *Translator of Desires*). *Tarjuman*, the Arabic word for translator
passes into Turkish *tercuman* and is the source of the word Dragoman, the
highest secular officer of the Christian minority (the *rayahs*) in the Ottoman
Empire. As translators, interpreters and diplomats, Dragomans had a powerful
mediating role between their communities and the Ottoman authorities, with
the concomitant dangers that come with such a role.

These two writers, from opposite ends of the Mediterranean, come together
in a *chronotope* placing in counterpoint events before the conquest/defeat of al-
Andalus with the world after the conquest/defeat of Constantinople in 1452. In
his discussion of Pamuk, Erdağ Göknar (2013, 127–162) translator of *My Name
is Red*, emphasises the importance of the concepts of *din* and *devlet*, the sacred
and the secular, religion and the state, and by extension the relationship
between poetics and politics in Pamuk's work. Pamuk introduces Ottoman
Islamic and Sufi forms into the Turkish Republican novel, often misread in
Turkey as being neo-Orientalist or simply not Turkish enough but written for
the West. However, from my island perspective, Pamuk's work opened up my
imagination to regional cosmopolitan or transcultural forms distinct from
Western literature. Pamuk engages both Western and regional literature and
opens up a post-secular and post-national imagination. His novel *My Name Is
Red*, set in Istanbul at the end of the sixteenth century, soon after Cyprus
became part of the Ottoman empire in 1571, reveals an occluded Ottoman past
within a present that has moved the island toward Western Europe and the
European Union. *My Name is Red* can be read as a project of re-imagining the
region and displacing the nation as the default category of analysis, so as to
explore the polyglot/cosmopolitan cities and empires with their ethnic and
religious diversity that comprise the pre- and early modern Mediterranean.
How might we see times before knowledge became nationalised, and what
possibilities does it have for our world-making capacities?

My Name is Red came into my hands soon after April 23, 2003, a week after the
Republic of Cyprus had signed the *acquis communitaire*. Turkey followed by
opening up a few check points across the border for the first time since the war of
1974 that brought about the island's partition. This unexpected political opening
unleashed a flood of memory and sudden movement of people now able to cross
the divide in search of lost homes and lost communities. The crossings made
possible after three decades aroused a feeling of the intensely familiar and the
strange, an uncomfortable plenitude where the possibility of return became
entangled with a sense of loss. This opened writers and translators to new
potentials or confrontations, new literary crossings in fresh voices across three
languages. For the first time I came into direct contact with a range of Turkish
Cypriot poetic voices. We exchanged thoughts through poetic dialogue and

mutual translation, usually with English as an intermediary language. I read a poem by Gür Genç, 'Not Poetry … Water' in which he tells poets that there has been 'too much poetry for such a small island, please don't write any more. Plant trees and water' (Genç 2011, 30). My poem 'Water for Poetry' was a response to the challenge of expanding the watery permeability of words and our languages and cultures (Stephanides 2005, 16–17).

I learned the word hüzün from reading Pamuk's *Istanbul*. He depicts the feeling as an ambiguous form of melancholy that veers between illness and a poetic state of grace. For the Sufis, hüzün is a divine desire that offers the possibility of recasting the self in a kind of negative capability when we know that we do not know. We face the possibility of the impossible when subjectivity is grounded in uncertainty and an absent centre of ontological life. It was a meaningful coincidence that I met Pamuk in India soon afterwards, when we were both invited to the *Katha* literary festival in Delhi in 2004. It was additionally meaningful that the Indian hosts immediately linked us together regionally and asked me to introduce his reading, where I spoke as a voice of our shared region at what felt at the like a historical moment for Cyprus. It did not matter that many in the Indian audience did not know about Cyprus, due to its smallness and remoteness, nor that they did not know that the Republic of Cyprus was not recognised by Turkey. I spoke with a sense of investment in the hope of a regional cosmopolitan future. I had encountered Pamuk in translation and I was speaking of Pamuk from my regional perspective, in turn translating what he meant for me to an Indian and cosmopolitan audience. In private, I told him about my own sense of 'hüzün' on returning to my lost village and finding the house where I was born. In contrast, his hüzün was experienced through how he remembered the past without having ever left the house where he was born.

I asked him about the translation of his work but it was not until a few years later when I met Maureen Freely, one of his translators, who said that what he told me understated his involvement in the process. She later wrote about her experience in translating Pamuk in 'Seeing Istanbul Again' (2015), noting that while at first she identified with his vision of the Istanbul of his childhood, she came to realise that her own vision and hüzün *involved* another dimension hidden in the gaps between the paragraphs of his work. While he evoked the greyness of the city, illustrated with black and white photos of his childhood, she recalled the deep blue of the Bosphorus in the blinding summer light. This doubling of vision that might be reflected in the style of writing made my reading Pamuk in translation all the more intriguing. Translation is a contest of re-presentation while making meaning across languages and fractures. This reflects the theme and plot of *My Name of Red*, which unfolds around the tensions of ways of seeing in artistic production. At one point, a tree in a miniature painting speaks to readers, reminding us that it wants to be seen as sign of Allah's vision not identical to the vision, and not to be seen as a real tree after the style of the Frankish painters. The tree says: 'And not because I fear that if I'd been thus depicted all the dogs in Istanbul would assume I was a real tree and piss on me. I don't want to be a tree. I want to be its meaning' (Pamuk 2001, 61).

An epiphanic moment in the novel is when Osman, the master miniaturist, expresses the idea that the art of miniature painting is not about melancholy and regret, but comes from a desire transformed into love of the world. An earlier chapter is narrated by Olive, an apprentice artist, who shares thoughts and stories about blindness and memory, echoing an epigraph from the Koran at the beginning of the novel stating 'the blind and the seeing are not equal'. Desire to see the world as God saw it motivates the art of illumination: 'to see is to remember that you've seen. To see is to know without remembering' (Pamuk 2001, 92). Thus painting is remembering the blackness of Allah, the longing for the divine is in the light and colour before and after his blackness. Before illumination there was blackness and afterwards there will also be blackness.

Maureen Freely's memory of the blinding brightness of the Bosphorus recalls Cavafy's poem 'Sea of the Morning'.[1] The title is has also been translated as 'Morning Sea', but the Greek of Cavafy often shifts the register of the language away from the everyday demotic Greek to what seems more akin to archaic 'katharevousa', marking both his style as a poet and perhaps his speech as an Alexandrian Greek. He employs the word 'morning' in the genitive form of the noun (*proiou*) rather than the more habitual adjective for morning. Cavafy's choice of syntax seems to imagine the sea of the long duration, not just any morning. The poem evokes a strangely revelatory moment in which he stands and watches the bright blue of the sea and the cloudless sky, experiencing the sensuality of nature within his own embodied memory. In a moment of originary vision, he tries to convince himself that what he sees is real: 'Let me stand here and delude myself, I saw it (truly for a moment when I first stopped)' (my unpublished translation). The glare of the blue stands in stark contrast to the closed world and feeling of *marasmo* (often translated as decay or wasteland) articulated in 'The City', a place with no exit. Andrew Aciman (2005) laments the inadequacy of the translation of the word '*marasmo*' in the many translations of that poem, but does not volunteer any alternative. The word evokes a sorrowful wilting, the meaning lying somewhere between '*ennui*' and 'hüzün', the French nineteenth-century decadent aesthetic of Baudelaire merging with an Eastern Mediterranean sensibility. '*Marasmo*' (deriving from the Turkish '*maraz*') has a high register but resonates with the more popular '*marazi*', which is frequently found in popular songs.

Pamuk writes about Cavafy whom he read in Turkish and English with the admiration and affection of a fellow Istanbulite. Pamuk seems to feel a sense of loss for the departure or expulsion of the city's religious minorities. I wonder how '*marasmo*' was translated in the Turkish version he read and the direction the Turkish translation of the word has taken, whether decadent/modernist or back along its Turkish route? Pamuk speaks of the root of Cavafy's name *kavaf*, an old Ottoman word meaning shoemaker, and imagines the poet's life in the city where he lived just three years, staying with relatives and perhaps having his first homoerotic experiences before returning to Alexandria. Cavafy, born in Alexandria, was a cosmopolitan Hellene whose family hailed from

Constantinople (officially re-named Istanbul in post-Ottoman Turkey in the 1920s), which distinctly shapes his sensibility and vision.

In his 1914 poem 'Returning Home from Greece' (1990, 110), Cavafy expresses post-orientalist resistance (*avant la lettre*) in longing for a homecoming in an Orient that the new territorialised nation excludes while still accepting orientalist essentialisation. Cavafy weaves transregional networks and affectivities, not in relation to territory but to open seas, and in terms of worldly estrangement. The poem unfolds new, strange centres of gravity in the erotics and entropy of the body's intelligibility. It was written the year the First World War began marking a turn in the demise of the Ottoman Empire and the shrinking of the Hellenic diaspora in the Eastern Mediterranean. Stavros Karayiannis and I have translated this posthumously published poem (Stephanides and Karayiannis 2015, xix–xxi) in which Cavafy employs the classical rhetorical trope of apostrophe and addresses Hermippus. We assume this is Hermippus of Smyrna, peripatetic philosopher and follower of Callimachus, and who (like Cavafy) was an Asia Minor Hellene who lived in Alexandria. Here Hermippus silently listens to the poet's voice:

> So we are close to arrival Hermippus
> The day after tomorrow, the captain said;
> But now we sail on our own sea,
> Waters of Cyprus, Syria, and Egypt,
> Waters of our beloved homelands,
> Why so silent? Ask your heart
> Didn't you rejoice?
> The further away we sailed from Greece
> Why fool ourselves?
> This certainly wouldn't be proper of Hellenes.
> Let's own up to the truth;
> We are also Hellenes – what else are we?
> But with Asian loves and emotions of Asia,
> But with loves and emotions
> sometimes estranged by Hellenism.
> The blood of Syria and Egypt
> That flows through our veins
> Let us honour and display.

There is a paradox in this homecoming: the boat is not taking them to Greece but away from Greece. This is a departure from national territory, and a process of artistic remembering that weaves its narrative of identification through the waters between Cyprus, Syria and Egypt. The poem thus embraces kinship with Asia and, in terms of worldly estrangement, unfolds new centres of gravity in one's spatial vision.

Four decades later, Giorgos Seferis, an Asia Minor Greek, whose family fled Izmir/Smyrne in 1922, felt a sense of *nostos* (homecoming) when he came to

Cyprus in 1953, and his sojourn on the island for several years as a diplomat inspired a series of poems. His presence on the island and his work had a re-territorialising effect on the anti-colonial Cypriot-Hellenistic nationalism that became fervent in the 1950s leading to armed struggle against British rule. In the poem 'Helen', he suggests an analogy between his poetic persona and Teucer, who settled in Cyprus after the Trojan War, citing Euripides's *Helen* in which Teucer states that Apollo has decreed that Cyprus should be his home. Yet reading the poem again recently in English translation, the sense of home-coming seems as ungraspable as it is ambiguous. Seferis's poem alludes (as H.D. did in her poem 'Helen in Egypt') to a version of the story of Helen recounted by some ancient authors, including Euripides, that Helen never went to Troy but stayed in Egypt throughout the Trojan war. Seferis laments the despair of war and the loss of life over the illusion of Helen, which was just a trick of the gods to destroy humanity. His poetics elude an easy sense of *nostos*. Seferis' poetics bring the sweetness of home, the homeliness of worldliness, and the strangeness of the world into critical collusion that challenges the construction of post-colo-nial Hellenistic nationalist identity politics, which fought for union with Greece.

Derek Walcott's Helen of the Antilles in his *Omeros* seems to want to resist, while perhaps also celebrating, the burden of representation as he seeks a sense of immediate presence. 'Why not see Helen / as the sun saw her with no Homeric shadow' (Walcott 1990: 271) he asks in the *aporia* of whether to metaphor or not to metaphor: 'When would it stop, / the echo in the throat, insisting, "Omeros"; when would I enter that light beyond metaphor?' (Walcott, 1990, 271). This is a question he could be asking Seferis, whom he addresses in a poem called 'From This Far'. Hearing the Greek poet' s lines across the ocean he says: 'Great lines, Seferis, heaved them this far' (Walcott, 1986, 314).

Ivi Meleagrou (b. 1928), the most eminent Cypriot writer of the first post-colonial generation, seems also to raise Seferis' questions 'Who is Helen? What is this island?' taking on a different resonance when read in a post-partition context. The image of Eleni/Helen in Meleagrou, as in Seferis, seems to bring out the fraught nature of the originary vision she has come to represent. Meleagrou corresponded with Seferis in his last years, during the rule of the Greek Junta that seized power in 1967. Seferis was critical of the Junta and was isolated from public life by the nationalists in Greece and their supporters in Cyprus during those years.

Meleagrou began to write her first and best-known novel, *Eastern Mediterra-nean* (1969) at the beginning of 1964, immediately after the inter-ethnic violence of December 1963, which marked the beginning of the partition. In conversation, she traced her experience of the fractures that mapped the equivocality of our socio-political life and explained how they shaped her writing. The diverse experiences that haunt both the author and her subject are articulated through the voice of her protagonist, Margarita, in a stream-of-consciousness style. Margarita, an urban housewife, gradually suffers a nervous breakdown as ten-sion and ethnic violence escalate in 1963. She drives around the labyrinthine, walled, medieval city of Nicosia feeling closed in and estranged. She names the voice of her subliminal consciousness Eleni, whose words were written in reddish-brown pencil, the colour of which is reproduced in the printed version. Eleni is the voice of the artist in a quest for an originary vision or memory: 'untrodden sands, like the first creation, each and every stone says something that should not be forgotten' (Meleagrou, 2015, 28).

In these shifting visions of Helen, we sense an attempt to unveil potentialities of the long duration in the fractures between past and present. It is in these moments that the performance of translation and writing intervenes like a moment of realisation of time lagging behind. Such a moment is succinctly expressed in the post-partition poem 'Thalassa' by Cypriot poet Andriana Ierodiaconou who longs to be remembered by the sea: 'Swallows fly to green days directly, without hesitation / we have been walking for years now and the sea has forgotten us and become a word' (Ierodiaconou, 2016, 88–89). Here as elsewhere, in the constraints and pressures of border and walls, the sea confronts border thinking. The fantastic liminalities of the seas serve the poet to remember or forget, confront, connect, and evaluate in an interplay of multiple constituencies and sensibilities and the permeability of territories of a world readership. Similarly, the perspective opened by the strategies and tactics of translation practice may serve as a powerful critique of omnipotent individual textual practices through deterritorialisation by probing the tension of divisions and partitions, the sea unfurling and echoing.

In the period after partition, perhaps in flight from a Mediterranean *marasmo* I drifted away from the Mediterranean on a journey beyond Hesperia, to work in the Caribbean nation of Guyana. As a young lecturer in the 1980s, in the province of Berbice I became involved with rural Hindu communities, descendants of Indian indentured labourers from the time the country was a British colony. My frequent journeys along the coastal road to visit temples did not go unnoticed. There were not many foreigners in the country, and people were intrigued. On a radio talk show with Guyanese poet and performer Marc Matthews, the interviewer asked me why I made so many journeys to Berbice. What I was seeking there? Before I had a chance to reply, Marc quickly quipped in Creole: 'he los' the oracle at Delphi, so he goin' to Berbice to find it'. There was truth in Marc's words, even though I had not thought of putting it in those terms. If I had replied for myself, I would have said that I went to receive the goddess' *'darshan'*. At the time I had not realised that the Sanskrit word *darsana* (*darshan*) shared an etymology with the ancient Greek word *theoria*. The original Greek meaning of the word *theoria* is contemplation or perception of beauty, especially as a moral faculty. In Eastern Orthodoxy, *theoria* takes on meanings related to the divine, and its meaning is related to the Sanskrit word. Both words are rooted in seeing, in the sense of an instance of vision or beholding, like an epiphany, to see with reverence or devotion. The consonant cluster *drs* is the root of 'to see'. One may receive *'darshan'* of the deity in the temple. In Greek *to theion* means the divine and *orao* means to see. Ian Rutherford relates the word *theoria* to pilgrimage-related phenomena in classical Greece, when people went to sanctuaries to consult oracles, attend festivals, make sacrifices or seek cures for illness (Rutherford 2000). *Theoria* is beyond rational knowledge and so is the way we move through time into an unforeseeable future. The word also shares a root with the word 'to see' in the Cypriot Greek vernacular '*thoro*', which is quite distinct from the modern standard Greek word. Although I had used that word all my life, its semantic potentiality was revealed to me as if finding a phantom limb in another cultural space. I could hear my grandmother saying to me: '*Thoreis?*' Do you see?

Returning to my native island after the Caribbean I brought back with me the returning gaze of another sea. The symbolic power of the Mediterranean resonates strongly in the Caribbean literary imagination. Alejo Carpentier designated the Caribbean as a New World Mediterranean. Edouard Glissant has famously compared the cultural geography of the Caribbean to the Mediterranean, claiming that it:

> is an inner sea surrounded by lands, a sea that concentrates (in Greek, Hebrew, and Latin antiquity and later with the emergence of Islam, imposing the thought of the One), the Caribbean is, in contrast, a sea that explodes the scattered lands into an arc. A sea that diffracts.
>
> (Glissant 1997: 33)

He compares this to a process of differentiation that takes place in translation as in Creole language practice. Glissant's gaze makes for productive reflection on the Mediterranean and its own 'poetics of relation'. I would perhaps challenge his notion that the Mediterranean contains, it has its fractures and points of entry and exit. However, I would argue that the Mediterranean compresses and sometimes explodes and scatters, bringing dissimilarities next to each other, and modes of noncomprehension, a charged speechlessness with osmotic moments in need of translations that re-imagine what has been denied or excluded or appeared to be obsolete.

The central mountain range on the island of Cyprus, known to geologists as the Troodos Ophiolite, rose from the sea due to the collision of African and European tectonic plates millions of years ago. It is of special interest as a rare phenomenon, because the oldest rocks with fragments of ocean crust are at the top, so the further up you travel the deeper you go into time. This seems also to suggest a situation of not knowing which time one is in, like Bloch's famous concept of *Ungleichzeitigkeit* (temporal incommensurability), shifting our horizon of expectations. The task of the poet/translator becomes a mediation and negotiation of *nostos* in the ruptures of dislocation in a layered cosmopolitanism, imagining a time and space that might have been and still might be. Wandering the old city of Nicosia, I sometimes visit the House of the Dragoman. I imagine my personal life, and my life as poet, translator and dragoman in the life of the *polis* and the layers of our past and possible futures. In a time of global societies in transition such as ours, acts of translation seem to circulate in ostensible moments often unexpectedly mediating human meaning in social time perpetually moving across multiple temporalities.

Note of thanks

This chapter developed from three keynote lectures I delivered: the first two at symposia on 'Mediterranean Fractures' at the kind invitation from Norbert Bugeja and Abdulrazak Gurnah, held at the Centre for Postcolonial Studies of the Department of English, University of Kent, May 2014, and the second at the Institute of Mediterranean Studies, University of Malta, November 2015; the third was at the kind invitation of Gabriel Koureas and Katia Pizzi to speak at a symposium on Transcultural Mediterranean Port Cities held at the Institute of Advanced Studies, University of London, May 2017.

Note

1 Original with translations available online in the *Cavafy Archive*: www.cavafy.com/ (accessed on August 14, 2017).

Bibliography

Aciman, A. 2005. 'The City, the Spirit, and the Letter: On Translating Cavafy'. *Words Without Borders* (e-journal) Aprilissue. http://www.wordswithoutborders.org/article/ the-city-the-spirit-and-the-letter-on-translating-cavafy Accessed 26 August 2017.

Apter, E. 2003. 'Global Translatio: The "Invention" of Comparative Literature, Istanbul, 1933', *Critical Inquiry* (Winter): 253–281.

Bakhtin, M. 1981. 'Forms of Time and of the Chronotope in the Novel'. In *The Dialogic Imagination*. Austin: University of Texas Press, pp. 84–258.

Bakhtin, M. 1986. *Speech Genres and Other Late Essays*. Ed. Caryl Emerson and Michael Holquist. Trans. Vern W. McGee. Austin: University of Texas Press.

Benjamin, W. 1973. 'The Task of the Translator'. In *Illuminations*. Trans. Harry Zohn, ed. and intro. Hannah Arendt. London: Collins/Fontana.

Bloch, E. 1991. *The Heritage of Our Time*. Berkeley: University of California Press.

Braudel, F. 1972. 'History and the Social Sciences'. In *Economy and Society in Early Modern Europe: Essays from Annales*, ed. Peter Burke. New York: Harper, pp. 11–42.

Braudel, F. 2001. *Memory and the Mediterranean*. Trans. Sian Reynold. New York: Knopf.

Casanova, P. 1999. *La république mondiale des lettres*. Paris, Seuil.

Cavafy, C. 1990. *Τα Ανέκδοτα Ποιήματα* (*Unpublished Poems*). Athens: Ypsilon. *The Cavafy Archive*www.cavafy.com/ Accessed 14 August 2017.

Damrosch, D. 2003. *What is World Literature?*Princeton: Princeton University Press.

Deleuze, G. and Guattari, F. 1986. *Kafka: Toward a Minor Literature*. Trans. Dana Polan (*Kafka: pour une littérature mineure, 1975*). Minneapolis: University of Minnesota Press.

Freely, M. 2015. 'Seeing Istanbul Again'. *New York Review of Books*, April 23. www. nybooks.com/daily/2015/04/23/translating-pamuk-seeing-istanbul-again/ Accessed 3 September 2017.

Glissant, E. 1997. *The Poetics of Relation*. Trans. Betsy Wing. Ann Arbor MI: University of Michigan Press.

Genç, G. 2011. 'Not Poetry... Water'. *Kunapipi, Journal of Postcolonial Writing and Culture* XXXIII, 1–2: 30.

Göknar, E. 2013. 'Reimagining_the_Ottoman_Legacy'. In *Orhan Pamuk, Secularism and Blasphemy: The Politics of the Modern Turkish Novel.* London and New York: Routledge, pp. 127–162.

Hughes, T.1997. *Tales from Ovid: Twenty-four Passages from the Metamorphoses.* London: Faber & Faber.

Ibn, Arabi. *The Tarjumán al-Ashwáq: A Collection of Mystical Odes by Muhyiddīn Ibn al-'Arabī.* Trans. Reynold Nicholson. London: Royal Asiatic Society, Oriental Translation Series (reprinted in 1981 by the Theosophical Publishing House, Wheaton, Illinois).

Ierodiaconou, A. 2016. *The Trawler: Poems 1977–2015.* Nicosia: Moufflon Publications (bilingual publication in Greek and English).

Kadir, D. 2010. 'To Compare, to World: Two Verbs, One Discipline', *Comparatist* 34: 4–11.

Meleagrou, I. 2015. *East Mediterranean.* Nicosia: Moufflon Publications. (Original title: Ανατολική Μεσόγειο)

Moretti, F. 2000. 'New Conjectures on World Literature'. *New Left Review* I (Jan/Feb): 54–68.

Pamuk, O. 2001. *My Name is Red.* Trans. Erdağ M. Göknar. New York: Alfred A. Knopf (original title: *Benim Adım Kırmızı*).

Pamuk, O. 2005. *Istanbul: Memories and the City.* Trans. Maureen Freely. New York: Alfred A. Knopf (original title: *İstanbul: Hatır.alar ve Şehir*).

Pamuk, O. 2013. 'Other Countries. Other Shores'. *The New York Times.* www.nytimes.com/2013/12/22/books/review/other-countries-other-shores.html. Accessed 15 August 2017.

Παπαλεοντίου, Λ. 1997. *Τα πρώτα βήματα της κυπριακής λογοτεχνικής κριτικής (1880–1930).* Λευκωσία: Πολιτιστικές: Υπηρεσίες Υπουργείου Παιδείας και Πολιτισμού. (Papaleontiou, L. 1997. *The First Steps of Cypriot Literary Criticism.* Nicosia: Cultural Services of the Ministry of Education and Culture; Greek only).

Pearce, F. 2015. *The New Wild: Why Invasive Species Will Be Nature's Salvations.* Boston: Beacon Press

Pieris, M. 1996. 'The theme of the second Odyssey in Cavafy and Sinopoulos'. In *Ancient Greek Myth in Modern Greek Poetry.* London and Portland, OR: Frank Cass & Co. Ltd.

Rutherford, I. 2000. 'Theoria and Darsan: Pilgrimage and Vision in Greece and India'. *Classical Quarterly* 50, 1: 133–146.

Said, E. 1977. *Orientalism.* London: Penguin.

Seferis, G. 1995. 'Helen'. In *Collected Poems*, trans. Edmund Keeley and Philip Sherrard. Princeton: Princeton University Press. www.poetryfoundation.org/poem/181856.

Stanford Encyclopedia of Philosophy. 2014. *Ibn Arabi.* https://plato.stanford.edu/entries/ibn-arabi/. Accessed 15 August 2017.

Stephanides, S. 2005. *Blue Moon in Rajasthan and Other Poems.* Nicosia: Kochlias.

Stephanides, S. and Karayianni, S. 2015. *Vernacular Worlds. Cosmopolitan Imagination.* Leiden: Brill.

Walcott, D. 1986. *Collected Poems. 1948–1984.* New York: Farrar, Strauss, & Giroux.

Walcott, D. 1990. *Omeros.* London: Faber & Faber.

Index